NeWest Plays by Women

NeWest Plays by Women

Edited by Diane Bessai and Don Kerr

Play Memory Joanna M. Glass

The Occupation of Heather Rose Wendy Lill

Inside Out Pamela Boyd

Whiskey Six Cadenza Sharon Pollock

NeWest Press / Edmonton

Copyright © 1987 NeWest Publishers Limited

First Edition (Second Printing 1990)

Canadian Cataloguing in Publication Data
Main entry under title:

NeWest plays by women

(Prairie play series; 7)
Contents: Play memory / Joanna M. Glass — Whiskey six cadenza / Sharon Pollock — The occupation of Heather Rose / Wendy Lill — Inside out / Pamela Boyd

ISBN 0-920897-16-9 (bound). — ISBN 0-920897-14-2 (pbk.)

1. Canadian drama (English) — 20th century. 2. Canadian drama (English) — Women authors.
I. Bessai, Diane. II. Kerr, Don. III. Series.
PS8315.5P73N48   1987   C812'.5408'09287   PR9196.3.N48 1987
C87-091163-5

Credits

Editorial Assistant: Donald Perkins
Department of English, University of Alberta
Cover Design: Susan Colberg
Typesetting: Mary Albert
Photos of Actors: Courtesy Canadian Actors' Equity Association
Cover Photo: B P Photo, Saskatoon, *Play Memory* by Joanna M. Glass, (Brenda Bazinet as Jean, Claude Bede as Cam)
Printing and Binding: Hignell Printing Limited, Winnipeg

Financial Assistance
Alberta Culture
The Alberta Foundation for the Literary Arts
The Canada Council

Printed and bound in Canada

NeWest Publishers Limited
Suite 310, 10359 - 82 Avenue
Edmonton, Alberta, Canada   T6E 1Z9

Contents

Introduction / *Diane Bessai*   *vii*

Play Memory / *Joanna M. Glass*   *1*

The Occupation of Heather Rose / *Wendy Lill*   *63*

Inside Out / *Pamela Boyd*   *95*

Whiskey Six Cadenza / *Sharon Pollock*   *137*

Further Reading   *249*

Introduction

The editorial decision to make the seventh volume of the NeWest Play Series an anthology of plays by women (the first regional collection of its kind) is a natural reflection of the increasing prominence of women playwrights in the Canadian theatre of the 1980s. Represented here are Sharon Pollock, Joanna M. Glass, Wendy Lill and Pamela Boyd, all with important links to prairie theatre, either past or present. The plays chosen, although not always prairie in subject, are in some manner the result of that association, and are in some manner regional.

Two of the playwrights are well-established dramatists. Sharon Pollock, of Calgary, whose work is widely performed in Canada and increasingly abroad, has premiered several of her major plays in Alberta theatres, either in Calgary or in Edmonton. Joanna M. Glass, now of Guilford, Connecticut, has won both American and Canadian attention for her plays depicting the Canadian prairie society of her youth in Saskatoon; her first training-ground in theatre was Betty Mitchell's noted Workshop 14 in Calgary. Wendy Lill, now living in New Brunswick, began to write for theatre five years ago while a journalist and broadcaster in Winnipeg. Her work with Leslee Silverman of Actors Showcase and Kim McCaw of Prairie Theatre Exchange resulted in two plays that are receiving increasing attention in Canadian theatres, with the promise of more plays to follow. Pamela Boyd is a new playwright. Growing up in Edmonton, she performed for some years in western Canadian theatres. Now living in Toronto, she has turned to playwriting, appropriating her acting experience to dramatic text.

In *Whiskey Six Cadenza* and *Play Memory*, the contrasting use of regional settings points to two different styles of drama. In some measure *Whiskey Six* resembles the characteristic Canadian regional play popularized in the 1970s: epic in scope, it gives dramatic identity to colourful stories and controversies of a particular regional past, in this play the southern Alberta of Prohibition days; it corrects the common assumption that Canadian history is dull, and by implication suggests that public issues of another era still have relevance in the present. The public and personal conflicts of *Whiskey Six*'s fictional characters are therefore largely informed by the representative social and moral tensions of its Crowsnest Pass mining community. By contrast *Play Memory* is entirely a domestic drama in which place and social milieu are background to personal family conflicts. The bleak representation of its Saskatoon setting of nearly forty years ago underlines the deterioration of a once happy and successful travelling salesman who still carries his city and territory in his head but shies from stepping outside his door. The characterization of the society around him is primarily the expression of his own jaded and sardonic point of view, but provides an amusing commentary on Canadian inter-regional cultural tensions.

For *The Occupation of Heather Rose*, Wendy Lill's Snake Lake is a fictional Northern community of the sort bordering every Canadian region west or east. As such the North, until very recently the mythical "last frontier" of Canadian society, is presented in its contemporary terms as a marginal region whose jurisdictional authority is South. Appropriately, therefore, the poverty and despair of its native population and the cynical demoralization of its white workers are seen through the eyes of an initially idealistic Southern nurse. Like Sharon Pollock, Wendy Lill makes her society and setting the foreground of personal conflict as well as the subject of political concern. In *Inside Out*, Pamela Boyd, like Joanna Glass, chooses an entirely domestic setting, the traditional 'region' of women's writing, here a realistically-rendered kitchen where the moment to moment crises of motherhood unfold on one particular day with all the comic determinism of Murphy's Law. In this play the kitchen is both centre and margin, a contradiction that vividly reflects the dilemmas of a modern young woman's need to fulfill all the roles available to her.

While neither Sharon Pollock nor Joanna Glass have deliberately set out to write women's plays, in their works the ironies and contradictions of paternalism are evident in both the male and female spheres they depict. The male characters are dominant, as appropriate to the times in which the plays are set, but in each the ultimate emphasis of the action is on its consequences to the women. In *Whiskey Six* the argument for free choice within the law takes a sardonic twist in the private life of its exponent Mr. Big, revealing his foster-daughter Leah impossibly caught between two male-defined versions of herself. In *Play Memory*, Cam MacMillan, the enemy and victim of impersonal company paternalism, in turn victimizes his wife and daughter through his self-righteous alcoholism; that he is the one who finally forces freedom on the women compares ironically with Mr. Big's ostensible magnanimity towards the women of his household.

The plays of Wendy Lill and Pamela Boyd are entirely feminine in point of view. Lill, like Pollock, reflects on paternalism in the public sector, in this case implicitly identifying it as the source of social demoralization in the people whose lives it purports to direct. Ironically the paternalistic representative is the well-meaning Heather Rose, who herself demonstrates the precarious hold that whites in the North have on their *own* value systems, let alone the native. While Ellen of *Inside Out* seems clear enough about her personal choices and priorities as mother, wife and would-be film writer, she suffers the normal difficulties in making them work out on a daily basis—with no help on this particular day from a husband preoccupied with his own affairs.

All four playwrights are inventive in their handling of dramatic structure and in their use of the theatre space. Both Glass and Lill employ retrospective narration in direct address to the audience. In *Play Memory* the daughter Jean both sets the scenes of her youthful memories and participates in their dramatic enactment. This mostly takes place on a two-level interior set that is gradually stripped of its furnishings as the family break-down unfolds. In the monodrama *The Occupation of Heather Rose*, Heather reconstructs the story of her past year in the North with a few simple properties to punctuate the stages of her personal disillusionment and deterioration. The high realism of Pamela Boyd's *Inside Out* set is wittily contradicted by the life-size puppet with a caricature face who represents the heroine's eighteen-month-old son (for whom a back-stage actress makes the appropriate sounds). Sharon Pollock's *Whiskey Six Cadenza* is the most elaborate in structure and stage design. Her multiple setting allows for overlapping action in two discrete interiors and occasionally the street; through impressionistic scenic projections she also suggests the physical environs of the town in a manner that reinforces the play's literal as well as metaphoric meaning.

One notable feature these playwrights have in common is their sense of humour. *Whiskey Six* is rich in folk humour, particularly in its exuberant group scenes of tavern camaraderie. The less the unrepentant patriarch of *Play Memory* can manage himself and his affairs, the more outrageously articulate and funny he becomes. Even Wendy Lill's Heather Rose is aware of the comic absurdities of food guides and fitness classes, while Pamela Boyd's Ellen consciously and unconsciously projects the inanities of domestic confusion.

Since all four playwrights are writing for a general audience, it would be inappropriate, perhaps, to insist too much on the particularities of women's theatre in their work. It is sufficient by these examples to note how well a woman may break the barriers that traditionally have allowed her access to the footlights, but less often the satisfaction (to paraphrase James Joyce) of 'indifferently paring her fingernails' behind the scenes.

Sharon Pollock

Sharon Pollock began her career in the theatre as an actor, first at the New Brunswick Playhouse (to become Theatre New Brunswick) and later in Calgary where, in 1966, she won a Dominion Drama Festival Best Actress Award for her performance in *The Knack*. Her first stage play, a black comedy entitled *A Compulsory Option*, won an Alberta Culture award in 1971 and was produced the same year under the direction of Pamela Hawthorne at the Vancouver New Play Centre. Her work to follow, however, primarily expressed the combination of historical and political interests that was to be most characteristic of her early plays. *Walsh*, 1973, re-examines the flight to the Canadian North West of Sitting Bull and the Sioux (after their defeat of Custer at Little Bighorn in 1876) from the point of view of the troubled NWMP officer in charge; *The Komagata Maru Incident*, 1976, exposes official racism against Asians in 1914 when a boat-load of Sikh immigrants were refused landing in Vancouver Harbour; *One Tiger to a Hill*, 1980, indicts the modern prison system through its dramatization of a hostage-taking incident, roughly based on events at New Westminster Penitentiary in 1975.

With *Blood Relations*, 1980, she begins to focus more on the issues of private lives, particularly as they relate to the repressive power structures within the family. For this play Sharon Pollock draws on the famous Lizzie Borden axe-murder case of 1892, but less to provide a playwright's solution to the officially unsolved Fall River, Massachusetts murder of the Borden parents, than to explore their possible cause in the restrictive family life for a spinster daughter of the period. The playwright acknowledges her theme to be of contemporary feminist concern through her innovative structuring of the material in a double time frame: ten years after the event, Miss Lizzie and her friend the Actress together enact a "dream-thesis" version of past events that may or may not reveal the historical truth. In their performance (for the audience a depiction of the interpretive process itself) the Actress as

Lizzie interprets the situation as an identity crisis that left her 'character' with no choices beyond suicide or violence. The audience is nudged into the unsettling recognition that, in like circumstances, anyone might be caught in the same desperate situation. Thus Pollock uses her historical material metaphorically, to explore in feminine terms the theme of threatened or repressed selfhood, in this, as in those plays to follow, a pervasive factor in family life. *Blood Relations* won the first Governor General's award for drama in 1981.

In the contemporary naturalistic farm play, *Generations*, 1980, in *Whiskey Six Cadenza*, 1983, as well as in the partly autobiographical *Doc*, 1984, Sharon Pollock has continued to examine the politics of the family both in its traditional and unconventional guises. In *Doc* she devised an intricate structure that combines the double perceptions of memory and hindsight simultaneously on stage. Catherine and her estranged father Ev, together and separately, remember and confront their troubled family past in the light of present discontents. In *Whiskey Six Cadenza*, she returned to an historical setting in order to reflect once again on the public issues of the day and their effect on the course of individual lives. Here, as in the earlier plays, the law is critically scrutinized for its intrusion upon personal responsibility. Paradoxically, the apostle of free choice in this and most other matters is the local bootlegger, an expansive character popularly known as Mr. Big who uses a six-cylinder McLaughlin car for getaways. He is a man whose charismatic rhetoric and generous nature wield a special power over those he draws into his orbit, in the community as well as in his own family. The legal and moral issues of Prohibition and Temperance, as well as the working conditions of the miners of Blairmore, are an integral part of the play's personal and family-related conflicts and their sadly destructive consequences. The contradictory "multiple realities of the universe" that Mr. Big so grandly claims to have mastered are exemplified in the two contrasting families of *Whiskey Six Cadenza*: his own, consisting of the deceptively quiescent Mama George and his "chosen daughter" Leah; and the Farleys, the mother a temperance zealot and the men, with the exception of the youngest, Johnny, labourers in the mines. In the tragic conjunction of these lives, inescapable questions about the power of parents over the lives of their children, and about the ironies and attendant responsibilities of free choice are personally rather than polemically focused in the play's tragic outcome.

Sharon Pollock is much in demand both as playwright and director: in the past two seasons she has directed two major productions of

Doc (winner of the Governor General's Award for 1986), at Theatre New Brunswick in 1985 (under the title of *Family Trappings*) and Neptune Theatre, Halifax, Nova Scotia, in 1987. She has two new plays in progress, *Egg*, for Theatre Calgary's Arts Festival showcase at the 1988 Winter Olympics and an historical work for Theatre New Brunswick on Loyalist society in the aftermath of the American Revolution.

Joanna M. Glass

As a high school student Joanna McClelland Glass developed an early interest in theatre, and after graduation performed with the Saskatoon Community Plays while employed as an advertising writer and broadcaster at a local radio station. Within a year she moved to Calgary (1956), intent on joining Betty Mitchell's Workshop 14, while supporting herself as a television continuity writer. Her lead role in Maxwell Anderson's *Anne of the Thousand Days*, the Calgary entry in the 1957 Dominion Drama Festival, won her a scholarship from Alberta Culture to study acting for a summer at the Pasadena Playhouse. She stayed a year in California, but after the "horrific experience" of Warner Brothers Drama School, she left for New York, met and married her physicist graduate student husband and moved to New Haven. Here she acted with the Yale Dramat, but relinquished the avocation of acting when her three children were born.

Joanna Glass discovered herself as a writer while at home caring for her young offspring; she began to write in this period, although more "seriously", she has noted, after the children started school. The 1960s were her apprentice period, in which she completed an early version of what later became her comedy *Artichoke* and the unpublished *Santacqua*, workshopped at the Herbert Berghof Studio, New York, in 1969. Continuing to work on *Artichoke* in the early 1970s, she also wrote several one-act plays, two of which were premiered as companion pieces at the off-Broadway Manhattan Theatre Club in 1972. These, *Canadian Gothic* and *American Modern*, were to become familiar fare on Canadian stages later in the decade.

At the time, however, Joanna Glass was discouraged enough about the problem of getting Canadian material on the stage that she began to write fiction, publishing her first novel, *Reflections on a Mountain Summer*, in 1974. The situation improved in 1975 when Long Wharf Theatre, New Haven, gave a full production of *Artichoke*, starring Colleen Dewhurst in the role of Margaret Morley. Meanwhile, well before Tarragon Theatre's Canadian premiere of this witty prairie comedy (in Oct. 1976), Manitoba Theatre Centre, then under the artistic directorship of Len Cariou, commissioned a new work, planned for that theatre's twentieth anniversary season. This became *The Last Chalice*, premiered Oct. 7, 1977, to a decidedly mixed critical response that was to result in the playwright's withdrawal of the work until she could devote time to major revisions. She eventually, in 1983, transformed the play into *Play Memory*. By this time, Joanna Glass had completed another play, entirely American in setting, entitled *To Grandmother's House We Go*. It opened in Houston in late 1980, starring Eva Le Gallienne as Grandie, and was transferred in the new year to the Biltmore Theatre on Broadway.

Play Memory, under the direction of Harold Prince, enjoyed a successful pre-New York run in October, 1983, jointly sponsored by the McCarter Theatre, Princeton, and the Annenberg Centre Theatre, University of Pennsylvania, Philadelphia. Its transfer to Longacre Theatre, New York, the following April, however, was brief despite the generally positive critical response that led to a Tony nomination for the playwright. It was produced at the Ensemble Theatre, Sydney, Australia in 1985 and given its Canadian premiere in Jan., 1986, at Twenty-Fifth Street Theatre, Saskatoon. Joanna Glass published her second novel, *Women Wanted*, in 1985, for which she is commissioned to write a film script by Zanuck/Brown and MGM for shooting in late 1987. Her most recent work-in-progress for the stage is a farce entitled *Towering Babble*; in 1985 she was awarded a Rockefeller Grant for its development at the Yale Repertory Theatre, New Haven.

In *Play Memory*, Joanna Glass brings together several themes already broached, sometimes tentatively, in her earlier work: the destructive father (Jack in *Canadian Gothic*; Jimmy Rutherford in *Reflections on a Mountain Summer*, not to speak of the cameo portrait of Jimmy's own father, a swindling stock-broker lapsed into alcoholism); the theme of betrayal, and with it the abiding sense of injury that the author attributes to certain Scots-Canadian "qualities of pride and self-importance" (Margaret Morley in *Artichoke*); the need for children to forgive their parents (Jay Rutherford in *Reflections*). All these themes relate to the characterization of Campbell MacMillan in this play, in some measure an autobiographical reconstruction of the playwright's own memories, and father, and a characterization already sketched in the short story "At the King Edward Hotel" (1976).

In the MTC version of the play, *The Last Chalice*, the character of

the extravagantly resentful, and comically élitist, alcoholic father dom-
inated the play. In *Play Memory* Joanna Glass reshapes the material
into the daughter Jean's memory play, thereby providing clearer
dramatic focus on the family history. Also, Cam's obsessive preoccupation with past betrayal by his business friends is more incisively
counter-balanced by his own daily acts of betrayal against a vulnerable
young daughter and a doting wife. But Jean's recollections of her
father's destructive power in their lives are also tempered by the
recognition that the bonds of family relations are not all bondage; that
love may still pertain despite the enormity of its violation. In after
years she is able to view his ultimate act of rejection as his gift of freedom, the liberation of both wife and daughter to take up elsewhere the
"normal" life he has come to despise.

Wendy Lill

Wendy Lill differs from the other contributors to this volume by coming to the theatre as a writer rather than as a performer. For several
years she was a freelance journalist and broadcaster in Winnipeg,
developing her craft through the writing of radio documentaries on
contemporary themes. She first expressed her interest in native issues
with a series for Information Radio entitled *The Native Urban Migra-
tion* (1980), followed by *Métis Anoutch* (1983), on the Manitoba Métis
Federation, for CBC. Her work in radio, film and video for Manitoba
School Broadcasts included the ACTRA Award winning radio docu-
mentary *Who is Georges Forest?* (1981), about the St. Boniface
insurance salesman who raised the matter of French language rights in
Manitoba by challenging a unilingual traffic ticket in the Supreme
Court of Canada.

   Although she had written two one act plays in the middle 1970s,
Wendy Lill's first performed stage work was *On the Line*, produced by
the semi-professional Agassiz Theatre of Winnipeg, under the direction of Nancy Drake. This was a political play about current work
problems among Winnipeg women garment workers, particularly the
exploitation of new immigrants with low wages, long a black mark in
Winnipeg labour history. She began this work with the *Paper Wheat*
model in mind, a combination of writer research and actor improvisation. While the production had a strong impact on its immediate audience (it was sponsored by the Women Garment Worker's Union),
retrospectively the playwright feels that it "lost the original spark of

the women's struggle" in its rather "plodding" plot; although workshopped later, it never developed into a finished text. However, *On the Line* did serve as the apprenticeship piece for the striking success of the play to follow.

This was *The Fighting Days*, premiered in 1984 at Prairie Theatre Exchange, Winnipeg, under the direction of Kim McCaw, remounted the following season and toured both provincially and nationally. A frankly feminist and pacifist play, *The Fighting Days* looks back to the famous Manitoban struggle for women's suffrage during the era preceding and continuing through World War I. While Nellie McClung was the leader of the movement emerging from the notable membership of the Winnipeg branch of the Canadian Women's Press Club of that day, the lesser known Francis Marion Beynon is the heroine of Wendy Lill's play. The issue is votes for foreign-born women; Francis, who is uncompromising both as a suffragist and a pacifist, comes into conflict with Nellie McClung on both matters. For the playwright the ultimate question is what women do with power and influence once they have acquired them through the feminist struggle. *The Fighting Days* also makes its contemporary points. In a 1985 interview, the playwright noted the connection she sees between present-day women's concerns and those of Francis Beynon's time:

> ... I could have been listening to my friends talk. There really was a similarity between the kinds of things I am interested in and what those women were interested in: the discussions about war and pacifism, the discussions about women's rights. We're not talking about the vote now, but we're talking about wife-abuse and things like that. Basically they're different variations on the same theme.

Since *The Fighting Days*, Wendy Lill has participated in a four-part National Film Board project on the Métis with the general title *Daughters of the Country*, produced by Norma Bailey; Lill's *Ikwe* won the Sheaf Award at the Yorkton Film Festival in 1986 for the best dramatic script of the year. She has also written a CBC television version of *The Fighting Days* for filming in 1987, and, since her removal to New Brunswick, has served as dramaturge at the Mulgrave Road Co-Op of Guysborough, Nova Scotia, for a collective play on unemployment with the title, *Occupational Hazards* (1985). She is currently working on a new play based on the life of Elizabeth Smart which has been already workshopped at Theatre New Brunswick.

Her monodrama *The Occupation of Heather Rose* was premiered at Prairie Theatre Exchange in February, 1986, with Laurel Paetz in the title role. In this play Wendy Lill draws not only on the native concerns reflected in her radio documentaries, but in some measure on her personal observations while living in Northwestern Ontario between 1977 and 1978. These interests, in combination with her experience of writing for the theatre, have resulted in a play of rare frankness and power on the complex subject of Indian-white encounter in contemporary Canada. That this subject is explored through the callow idealism of an inexperienced young nurse of Northern Medical Services, makes its own ironic comment on officialdom's handling of Northern needs. But also of interest are Wendy Lill's further views on the use women make of whatever power and privilege they have. In this play the absurd, even comic, complacency of Southern cultural assumptions backfire and Heather Rose, denied the reassurances of her normal support systems, becomes hideously 'occupied', her flimsy citadel of selfhood invaded by her own worst fears of degradation.

Pamela Boyd

Pamela Boyd, the newest playwright of this collection, has been an actress since the age of seventeen, performing variously in theatres from Montreal to Calgary, and training in mid-career at the Drama Studio, London, England. After working in England and Scotland for some time, she returned, in the mid 1970s, to Edmonton (where she grew up) to perform with many theatres, and also in radio, television and film, throughout western Canada and eventually in Toronto. She was living in Toronto when her son Finlay was born in 1980, and out of the recognition from her own experience of the modern woman's need to maintain the difficult balance between motherhood and career, her first play, *Inside Out*, was born.

The play was workshopped at the Blyth Festival in 1984, under the direction of Katherin Kaszas, with another actress playing the role that Pamela Boyd herself was to assume in the premiere stage production. At the 1985 Edmonton Fringe Festival she presented the play as a reading, with actress Margaret Carmichael as the voice of Arran, the toddler who is both the joy and the bane of his mother's particularly trying day. Under the direction of Jackie Maxwell, *Inside Out* opened in February, 1986, at the Extra Space, Tarragon Theater, Toronto, to popular critical acclaim as a timely examination of "What every mother knows and what Dr. Spock forgot to mention." This, according to *The Globe and Mail* reviewer, Liam Lacey,

> is that mothers' bonds with their children are often the result of the negative things they have in common: new mothers, like children, feel powerless and are struggling for independence, and because they spend so much time together, the child can take on almost every possible role, from confidant to dictator within the confines of the two-person society.

To realize this theme on stage, the playwright needed to draw on her combined experience as an actor and a young mother. She needed to know how to make the toddler as much a theatrical reality as its parent and so devised a life-size puppet (with caricature face) whose expressive movement requires the skill of the performer to make him walk, wiggle and bash objects about, as the mood demands, his activity co-ordinated with the off-stage sounds of a second actor. Theatrical experience also taught the playwright about the dangers of monotony in a one-person play. In *Inside Out*, Ellen's dramatic relation to the world outside the confines of her kitchen is established through the telephone and the voices of the radio and telephone answering machine. These devices also function to underline the comic frustrations of her inevitably divided attention during the course of the day.

While Ellen is dedicated to the careful training of her child, she is also committed to a small but insistent hope that her work as a film writer (executed over the course of some "five hundred naps") might be of some importance as well. Pamela Boyd herself has said that her time spent at home with a young son also allowed her the opportunity to discover herself as a writer. No sooner was her first play completed than she began a second, commissioned by Alberta Theatre Projects, of Calgary, where she and her stage designer husband Terry Gunvordahl were living at the time. Tentatively entitled *The Bare Wood*, this is a play about female violence and the heroine's psychological journey to discover its roots; it was workshopped by Jackie Maxwell and Allen MacInnis at Alberta Theatre Projects, Calgary, in 1987. Pamela Boyd is also extending her writing interests to broadcasting with a project about immigrant women from behind the Iron Curtain.

Diane Bessai
University of Alberta, Edmonton
May 1987

Play Memory

by Joanna M. Glass

In Memory of
Morrill MacKenzie McClelland
and Kate

First Performance

Play Memory premiered in October, 1983, at the McCarter Theatre, Princeton, N.J., followed by an engagement at the Annenberg Centre Theatre, University of Pennsylvania, Philadelphia. It opened at Longacre Theatre, New York, April 26, 1984. Directed by Harold Prince and designed by Clarke Dunham, the cast was as follows:

Cam MacMillan — *Donald Moffat*
Ruth MacMillan — *Jo Henderson*
Jean MacMillan — *Valerie Mahaffey*
Billy — *Jerry Mayer*
Ken — *Edwin J. McDonough*
Roy — *James Greene*
Miss Halverson — *Marilyn Rockafellow*
Mike Melzewski — *Tom Brennan*
Duncan — *Rex Robbins*
Ross — *Curt Williams*
Ernest — *Steven Moses*

The Canadian premiere was at 25th Street Theatre, Saskatoon, Jan. 31, 1986. Directed by Tom Bentley-Fisher and designed by Michael Bantjes, the cast was as follows:

Cam MacMillan — *Claude Bede*
Ruth MacMillan — *Jane Roth-Casson*
Jean MacMillan — *Brenda Bazinet*
Mike Melzewski, Roy — *Wendell Smith*
Miss Halverson — *Patricia Lenyre*
Ken, Duncan — *Dwayne Brenna*
Ross — *Max Hansen*
Billy, Ernest — *Richard Wolfe*

B. P. Photo

Jane Roth-Casson as Ruth, Brenda Bazinet as Jean
25th Street Theatre, Saskatoon, 1986

Characters

Cam MacMillan: approximately fifty, fifty-five years old
Ruth MacMillan: Cam's wife, forty-five to fifty years old
Jean MacMillan: Cam's daughter. This character ranges from four,
   to puberty, to adulthood, at twenty-eight in the play.
Billy/Ken/Roy: the salesmen who worked for Cam
Duncan and **Ross**: Cam's sponsors from Alcoholics Anonymous,
   middle-aged
Mike Melzewski: a middle-aged, Ukrainian bootlegger
Miss Halverson: a high-school counsellor, approximately thirty
Ernest: Melzewski's nephew, a twenty-year-old delivery boy

Setting

Time: 1939—1968

Place: the MacMillan home

The set contains a living room area with a front door, a telephone desk area which can become Miss Halverson's office, a dining room area, and a hint of a kitchen. Cam has an antique rocking chair. On a second level are stairs, a landing with acting area, and Jean's bedroom. The set should be abstract enough to allow an aura of memories conjured. An easy fluidity and melding of scenes is essential.

Act One

*A spotlight comes up on a table phone, which is ringing. Cam shuffles
to the phone. He wears a baggy old sweater, with the elbows gone.*

Cam: Hello? No, Jean's not here. Wait a minute . . . wait a *min-ute*! I
have a sinking feeling that this call is settin' a precedent. I have a
distinctly sinking feeling that I am speaking with a young person
of the masculine gender. Am I? *He frowns.* Oh, dear. What's your
name? MacLeod. God, I've always hated that tartan. Plaid, man,
tartan! The MacLeods have sported a putrid sort of tartan for
several hundred years now. It's a kind of bilious yellow with great
blobs of black. It is, in my considered opinion, the most undis-
tinguished of Scottish tartans. If you don't mind my asking,
MacLeod, what do you want with my Jeannie, as if I didn't know?
He listens. Uh huh. Uh huh. Uh huh. Jean's fourteen, how old are
you? Ah. Sixteen's a bad age. Horny all the time at sixteen.
Listen, lad, I think what you really want is one of those floozies
from the west side. Y'see, Jean's a member of the noble clan
MacMillan. Yes. If there is any such thing as a Canadian aristocracy, we are it. *Becoming irritated.* Look, fish and chips and a
hockey game is a lot of crap. What you're lookin' to do,
MacLeod, is slip it to my Jeannie. And I won't have it. I'm old
and battered. I've suffered more losses than you'll ever know
gains. I'm dirt poor and I drink too much and my brain cells have
run amok. *He almost whispers, feigning begging.* Please, lad,
spare me. Don't saddle me with a bastard MacLeod in a putrid
yellow tartan. *He hangs up, smiles at the audience, and exits.*

*An adult Jean enters, smiling at this memory. She walks onto the stage
slowly, somewhat preoccupied. She wears a fine woollen suit, silk
blouse, high heels. She is dignified and assured. She is not lofty or
preachy or grudge-bearing. One feels that she has achieved a healthy
perspective on her past.*

Jean: I am Jean. The boy, Ian MacLeod, reported that conversation
to me several days later. At the time, we were ending our term as
a family. *She slips her hands into her pockets, and ambles a bit
across the stage.* I like to think that I remember that conversation,
but of course, I don't. As is the case with so much of memory, it's

an amalgam of what actually happened, and what was reported. I've discovered that what actually happened is often the most suspect—only half of the story. We were too entangled then, too mired in the dailiness of living to ever see ourselves as others saw us. Some memories are startlingly accurate, right down to the shoelaces. Some are sporadic; they don't happen in sequence. Images crop up, helter-skelter, at unpredictable times. There was a bar of soap in a hotel room recently. When I unwrapped it and smelled the scent, I was suddenly with my mother in our yard on the Saskatchewan prairie. She was snipping sweet peas from a vine. *She moves again.* I began, of course, with my mother.

Ruth enters wearing a pretty housedress. She goes to the phone and sits.

Jean: In the time that *preceded* me, her hours were often idle. My father was gone all week, out on the road, selling. She had not even a rudimentary education. She couldn't read. I think she spent much time during the week living through the technological wonder of the Thirties—the telephone. *Jean exits.*

Ruth: *Picks up the phone and begins to chat. Her gossip is more wonderous and incredulous than sarcastic. There should now be evidence of middle-class comfort in this room: china, books, a Persian rug.* Well, Myra, what can I say? It was dinner at the mayor's and it was exciting! I *am*, Myra! I'm tellin' you in my own way. I know I talk all over the barnyard, but I do, eventually, tell it all. Well, they were an awful quiet bunch. Politicians, y'know, not like Cammy and his salesmen. The liquor flowed, y'know, but it had no effect on the mayor and the aldermen . . . no . . . they had a look of permanent worry. And y'know, Myra, there's some kind of new fashion in the upper classes. They eat their food raw. We had to chew forever on the green beans, and there was blood runnin' out of the roast. She called it "Oh Jews," but *I* think she just didn't time it right. Well, the *nicest* thing was the biffy, downstairs. She called *it* a powder room, and you know what? She had four bottles of French perfume standing out on the counter. As the evening went on, all the ladies had to pee, as ladies always do, and we all sampled the perfumes. Well, you can imagine. The living room began to smell like a west side hoorhouse. And it wasn't till the end, when we were saying our goodbyes, that Cam finally broke the ice. He took her hand, and bowed, and he said, "Mrs. MacEwan, thank you for a very aromatic evening." Oh, Myra, I hear him janglin' his keys. I have to go. I'll tell you the rest tomorrow.

Cam enters. He wears a suit, tie, and fedora hat. He carries a box containing silk mufflers.

Cam: Hello!

Ruth: *She goes to him, and they embrace.* I was so proud of you last night! The way you held your own with those people.

Cam: Thank you! And you were the best woman at the table. Maybe not the richest, or the smartest, or the prettiest, but the very best! *Pause.* You look happy, Ruth.

Ruth: I am!

Cam: Well, it was an event, wasn't it? Dinner at the mayor's. But what a lot of poor, sad buggers. Not an ounce of juice left in any of 'em.

Ruth: *She has been bursting. She can no longer hold her tongue.* Cam, I have a piece of news.

Cam: And so have I.

Ruth: Oh? Well, mine can wait.

Cam: *Gravely.* I heard something this morning, down at Dixwell's.

Ruth: Ah . . . did you order the new suit?

Cam: I did. And . . . four silk mufflers. Monogrammed.

Ruth: Campbell! Four?

Cam: I have to, Ruthie. When I stroll into these little prairie towns, I have to make an impression. They expect a little "sartorial splendour." *He puts on a muffler.*

Ruth: Well, that's nifty. Whatja hear?

Cam: It's not nice. I was standing there, looking at a bolt of wonderful British stuff, and I asked if I could see Ludwig. Ludwig, y'know . . . the tall, skinny one, built like a pencil . . .

Ruth: Oh, yes . . .

Cam: Well, he's gone home to Germany.

Ruth: What for?

Cam: To join the army. To fight for his country.

Ruth: *Frowning.* Ah.

Cam: There's a mood creepin' in. I felt it last week, too, on the road. There's a little town of German settlers ... Neudorf. All the towns around are suspicious of 'em, Ruth.

Ruth: But I was born there! My mum and dad homesteaded—lived in a sod hut—tilled this prairie with hand-hewn ploughs! And besides all that, they weren't German, anyway. They were Austrian.

Cam: Sweetie, it's a moot point.

Ruth: It's that damn, ugly house painter! He ought to be taken out and hung up by the ...

Cam: *Going to her.* I don't want you to worry about it. I just want to warn you that you may hear things you won't like. And with me gone all week, and you being alone ... you've got a terrible temper, Ruth. Promise me. If you hear things, let 'em pass. Okay? *She does not reply.* Okay, Ruth? Let 'em pass. *Ruth, finally, nods "yes". They sit.* Now, what's your news?

Ruth: *She proceeds, happily.* Cam, I haven't come unwell.

Cam: *He registers shock. His question is disbelieving.* How long?

Ruth: Well, I don't keep track, y'know, I mean, all these years and nothin'. No reason to keep track ...

Cam: You have to see a doctor.

Ruth: I have, Cam. *Brief pause.* I am.

Cam: *His thoughts race in all directions. He is momentarily dumbfounded.* Well, I ... I'm speechless. Well, for God's sake! *He begins to smile.* Congratulations!

Ruth: Thank you. *Holding out her arms.* Doesn't the old hen deserve a hug?

Cam: Indeed she does! From the aging rooster.

Ruth: Isn't it grand, Cam?

Cam: It is. A miracle.

Ruth: That's exactly what I thought. God's giving us a child for our old age. It's an Act of God. *Seeing Cam's preoccupation.* Campbell? Aren't you happy?

Cam: I am. It's cause for celebration. *He ponders the news.* But it isn't *simple*, is it, at middle-age? It's major. I mean, it'll take major adjustments. Think of it, Ruth! A child. Responsibility for a life.

Ruth: Thousands less responsible than us have done it.

Cam: It's just . . . if I'm going to be a father, I'd want to be the very best father. I'd want to be on top of all the little situations, y'know, all the time. Jesus, Ruth, I see fifty looming on the horizon. I give all my energy, every waking hour to . . .

Ruth: To the damn company!

Cam: Don't damn the company! Look around you, Ruth. Look at your china and your silver and your two Persian rugs. Go upstairs and look at your amethysts. If we want the rewards, we have to pay the price.

Ruth: Cam, when you were young you were getting together your team. You were staking out your territory. Now it's done! Why can't you sit back and be fat and sassy? Why can't you relax a bit?

Cam: I'm not fat and sassy, and the day I am is the day I go under. Yes, I've done it—bloody arduously, I've done it. Now it has to be maintained, *tended.* It won't just lie fallow, you know, like some field out in the east forty. And God knows, the men seem to get more and more dependent, the older they get. I feel drained, Ruth. I give myself to the men and the company and the ad campaigns, and the town and the clubs and the fund raisers. I go to bed at night spent. There's not an ounce of me left over, and that won't *do* with this news. That'll have to change. *He glances at his watch.* Christ, even now, you know what I'm thinking?

Ruth: Yes, I do know what you're thinking. You're late for your appointment with Kenneth. You have time for *his* daughter, haven't you?

Cam: She's got diabetes, Ruth. I said I'd go with him to buy the insulin kit.

Ruth: Well then, go. Go ahead and tend to Kenneth's daughter.

Cam: I promised, Ruth. It really is a matter of life and death.

Ruth: *Relenting.* I know. I know. And heaven help me, I love you for it.

Cam: *Touching her stomach.* Dear me. It's in there, isn't it? And it's ours. What in hell are we arguing about? Surely, it's a blessing. And blessings will be accommodated! I must go!

Ruth: You'll be the very best father. You've always been the very best at everything you've turned your hand to. And, Campbell, think of this. If it's a boy, it'll carry the name.

Cam: *Genuinely happy at this thought.* That's something, isn't it? I'll think of that. *As he goes.* Let's celebrate at dinner. I'll be calmer then, when I've got this damned injection out of the way. *He exits.*

The lights dim. Ruth moves into a spotlight.

Ruth: Names don't mean much to me. They mean a lot to him, though. It's his only flaw. If he hears "Powanski," "Ostafichuck," "Garfein" . . . he gets all of a sudden superior. Maybe because he's Scottish, and that's the safest thing to be. Or maybe because these people are staking out their own territories, and it scares him. It's amazing that he married me. A farm girl, no education, my folks were pioneers. But we clicked, y'know. The question always comes up in the eyes of people. It did last night, at the mayor's. "What's a man like that doing with *her?*" I always want to say: "We clicked, folks. That's all there is to it. We clicked." *She exits, with the box of mufflers.*

Cam enters, having removed his jacket, loosened his tie, opened his collar. He is in high spirits.

Cam: Somewhere in there . . . that year . . . I got a letter from headquarters. All about "consistency." *He sighs.* It had come to the attention of some sallow little man at Havilland Tobacco, that all the venetian blinds, in all the regional offices, were different colours. Well, he had his knickers in a twist over that. It wasn't consistent, you see, it was *erratic.* There followed an edict that all the window blinds in all the Havilland offices, in every city in the country, had to be the same colour. Well, what the hell. I'd laboured in the Havilland vineyard some twenty years, successfully, profitably. And I was feeling pretty frisky that day. So I thought I could afford to have a little fun. *He quickly whips a letter out of a pocket and flips it open.* Here's what I replied:

The Havilland office in Charlottetown
Has window blinds that are chocolate brown
And miles away at Hudson's Bay
The Havilland man prefers his blinds gray.

While we on the prairie in Saskatoon
Refuse to use anything but maroon
That curious fellow down east at Broad Cove
Dresses his windows in lavender-mauve.

We Havilland men will defend this variety
And so I must say, with a certain impiety:
He who would dictate one hue of the spectrum
May shove all his window blinds far up his rectum.

He smiles, broadly.

Blackout. Cam exits.

Lights up on Ruth, carrying a casserole to the dining table, where there are plates, glasses and cutlery. There is a time lapse between this and the previous scene.

Ruth: *She begins to sing and then strut, moving into the living room area. The song is an old favourite that Cam and Ruth frequently perform at parties.*

Tiptoe to the window
By the window
That is where I'll be
Come tiptoe through the tulips, with me.

Cam joins Ruth. Arm in arm, they sing and strut.

Tiptoe from your pillow
To the shadow
Of a willow tree
And tiptoe through the tulips, with me.

Billy, Ken and Roy enter and join them.

Knee deep, in flowers we'll stray
We'll keep the showers away . . .

They form a "chorus line," with Ruth in the middle.

And if I kiss you
In the garden
In the moonlight
Will you pardon me?
Come tiptoe through the tulips, with me.

Ruth: *At the end of the song, she stands back, plants her hands on her hips, and feigns annoyance with Billy, Ken and Roy.* Don't you ever go home? You've got houses, you've got addresses, you've got wives.

Roy: *His face drops. He pouts.* All but me.

Ruth: Oh, for God's sake, get on with your life, man! *Angry again.* And how come we're blessed with your presence right around dinnertime?

Billy: We're celebrating, Ruth! Cam's come up with a solution.

Ruth: He always does, doesn't he? You ought to be ashamed. Three grown men, can't tie your shoelaces without Cam. He's got a life of his own, y'know. We've got a birthday party here tomorrow. Jean's turning three and six kids are coming. *To Cam.* And I thought you were going to string balloons.

Cam: I will, Ruth, I will. But this is important. We've found a way around it.

Ruth: What?

Cam: The gas rationing, Ruth, the gas rationing!

Roy: We can't continue this three-day work week, Ruth. Draggin' in here Wednesday nights, sittin' on our asses Thursday and Friday. We can't cover this prairie with the coupons we're gettin'.

Ken: What are we supposed to do, Ruth? Piss in our engines?

Cam: *A reprimand for the language.* Kenny ...

Ken: *To Ruth.* I'm sorry.

Ruth: *To Cam.* I thought you wrote headquarters. I thought you explained you needed special dispensation for your men.

Cam: I did. And they replied. No. Not in the national interest. Firemen, yes, ambulances, yes, but not salesmen.

Ruth: They don't like you at headquarters, Cam. Oh, they like your *earnings*, but they think you're uppity. You shouldn't have wrote that poem about the window blinds.

Cam: Oh, for chrissake, Ruth, this has got nothing to do with window blinds! This is national policy! Those farts sit down there in the east, the towns are twenty miles apart—they've got no *conception* of the vast distances out here. Now, look, here's what we're gonna do. *Billy, Ken, and Roy become excited.* These little prairie towns, they've got a cafe, a hotel, a general store—and all those people are getting the same amount of rations we are! And they don't have to *go* anywhere. So they've got coupons *left over* at the end of the week ...

Ruth: They're supposed to turn 'em back to the government.

Roy: They don't, Ruth! Nobody turns 'em back. They sell 'em. Oh, sweet lady, gas is gold! There's a regular black market going on with gas rations.

Cam: So: we're going to start taking part of our commissions in coupons. Everybody benefits that way. The merchants get the product for less, and we get to drive four, maybe even five days a week. Swappin', see? Commissions for coupons.

Ruth: *After a moment.* It's illegal.

Cam: *Becoming irritated.* Oh, Ruth, I wish you had a head for the larger world! *He continues, as if talking to a child.* Sweetie, I get the office, the expense account, the car. I get salary plus commission. The boys don't. They're on straight commission. Billy can't meet his mortgage payments, Roy can't make his alimony,

Kenny's old mother's in the sanatorium. I've built a team here, Ruth. We're the best damn hustlers in the province and we have been for twenty years. The *team* is my responsibility!

Ruth: Cam, it's a very patriotic time. I've been glued to the radio. They're rationed one egg a week in London ... they're hiding their children down in the Tube at night. They've got bombers sittin' in hangars for want of gas. And you know what? Even the little princesses are wearing gas masks!

Cam: Oh, screw the little princesses!

Ruth: But that's the larger world, Cam! That's what you want me to know about.

Cam: *Gravely.* Billy went to Eaton's last week, applied for a job. Selling shoes in Eaton's basement. It's the Black Hole of Calcutta down there, Ruth, it'll kill him. I won't have it. I can't in a million years put a team like this together again. I won't bust up my boys on account of frigging coupons! *A moment passes as Cam's anger reverberates through the room.*

Ruth: And what if you get caught?

Billy: Ruth, do you remember when the Watson Club invited Cam to join? He said, "Thank you very much, but there are four of us."

Roy: And they said they only wanted Cam, and Campbell said no dice. He gave 'em his motto: "Cam's boys *come* of a piece, and Cam's boys *go* of a piece."

Ken: And we all joined the Watson! That's what'll happen if we get caught.

Ruth: *After absorbing it, slowly.* You mean you'll go of a piece. They'd have to fire the lot of you.

Ken: And that, they can't do. We'll take a united stand. Don't you see? We *are* Havilland Tobacco. We've got this province tied up tighter than a virgin's ...

Cam: Kenneth!

Ken: I'm sorry. The point is, if push comes to shove, we'd go of a piece.

Ruth: *A moment passes. She is dubious.* Is that a deal?

Roy: What do you mean?

Ruth: I'd like to see you shake on it.

Cam: Oh, Ruth, after twenty years we're practically blood brothers!

Ruth: Shake on it! Let me see it.

Cam: *He sighs, then reluctantly reaches out. They ad lib, "It's a deal, Cam." "We're with you, man," "Word of a gentleman," etc.* Billy, m'boy. Roy? Kenny? Get the rye, Ruth! We'll drink to health, and prosperity, and five days o'gas in the tanks! *Ruth leaves. Cam begins the song again. The four men move to the dining table, repeating their little "number."*

Cam, Billy, Roy, Ken:

> And if I kiss you
> In the garden
> In the moonlight
> Will you pardon me?
> Come tiptoe through the tulips, with me.

The stage darkens. Lights up on Jean in her bedroom. She wears slippers and a flannel nightie and her hair is tied back in a ribbon.

Jean: I am four years old now. I have a friend named Beth. We run down the sidewalk singing, "If you step/on a crack/you will break/Hitler's back." We have three new kids on our street this year. They're from England. They've been sent to aunts and uncles and cousins, so they'll be safe. And at Hallowe'en we don't ask for apples. We ask for money, so we can ship milk to the old country. We go from house to house, knocking on doors shouting, "Bottles for Britain! Please! Open up! Bottles for Britain!"

The salesmen and Ruth enter the living room with plates and glasses.

Jean: Our house is always full of people! *She leaves her room, moving out to the stair landing, above the party.*

Radio music is heard. Vera Lynn, "The White Cliffs of Dover".

Jean: Everybody likes my Dad! He sings, and makes them laugh, he reads Bobby Burns, and makes them cry. Sometimes he has too much to drink. I don't like that. His eyes get peculiar. Mum says salesmen are hard drinkers, and always have been. *Pointing.* We have a big mahogany dining table. When guests are coming, my Mum sends me under it, to dust the pedestal. We have three whole sets of fine, bone china. My Dad gets it, as a bonus, every Christmas. Head office gives him gifts, because he makes a lot of money. *Moving onto the stairs.* Nearly every Saturday night there's a party. My Dad comes and gets me and carries me into the living room where everyone thinks I am very *cute.*

Suddenly, she slumps and closes her eyes. Cam lifts her from the stairs and carries her away. She is like a rag-doll, falling over his shoulder.

Cam: *As he lifts Jean.* Come along now, wee bairn. Oh, my wee bairn is so sleepy! They're askin' for you lass. They all want to see Bonnie Jean. *Cam now enters the living room area, where Ruth, Ken, Billy and Roy are assembled. All have drinks and the air is smoky. Ruth wears a party dress, silk or tafetta. Billy, Roy and Ken have loosened their ties and are slightly drunk. The four ad lib conversation. They discuss the wheat crop, the bushels per acre, in the towns of Melville, Weyburn, Kerrobert. There are plates, stacks of sandwiches, dirty napkins, strewn about. Setting Jean down.* Da-Dah! And here she is!

Ruth: Oh, Cam, I wish you wouldn't do this!

Ken: Will you look at this, boys! Look at her! My God, she's *cute!*

Billy: A beauty, Cam! A beauty!

Roy: Oh, it won't be long now, Campbell! You'll soon have the tomcats, howlin' on your fence.

Cam: *Proudly.* All right now, Jeannie. Say your prayers, lass, for the boys. *Cam takes her onto his lap.*

Jean: *She dutifully closes her eyes and holds her hands in prayer.* Now I lay me down to sleep / I pray the Lord my soul to keep / If I should die before I wake / I pray the Lord my soul to take. *Pause.* God bless Mum, and Dad, and my friend Beth, and her Mum and Dad and all the boys fighting overseas.

Cam: *And,* Jeannie?

Jean: And Dad's boys, too. Roy and Ken and Billy. God bless you all.

Roy, Billy & Ken: *Ad libs.* Beautiful, Jean, lovely, very nice, thank you.

Jean: You're welcome.

Roy: *Going to her.* And what's all this I hear about alterations in your bedroom?

Jean: Oh, it didn't have a closet, so Dad's put in a great big new one.

Cam: For all the frocks, you know. A space for all the frocks.

Jean: And it's got a beautiful walnut door, all hand-carved. Dad bought it out of a mansion.

Billy: The old Drummond place, Cam?

Cam: Yes, a bit of a *coup*, if I do say so myself.

Jean: It's even nicer than the doors at the Bessborough Hotel. I think it's the most beautiful door in all of Saskatoon.

Ruth: It is, Jeannie. Come along now. Back to bed.

Cam: Oh, Ruth, let her stay . . .

Ruth: No, no, no . . .

Roy: Got a kiss for Uncle Roy?

Billy & Ken: Sweet dreams, Jeannie. Nightie-night.

Ruth and Jean race up to Jean's bedroom.

Blackout. Radio music up, "String of Pearls" or "Frenesi".

We move in time to after the party. Lights up on Cam in living room. Ruth is seen tucking Jean in. Cam swirls a bit to the music, finds a tray and begins to gather dirty glasses and plates. Ruth leaves Jean's room and Cam addresses her as she comes down the stairs. There is sexual tension between them as they proceed, together, to clean up.

Cam: *Turning the radio down.* Jeannie asleep?

Ruth: Yes.

Cam: "While visions of sugar plums dance through her head."

Ruth: Visions of frocks, Cam, frocks to fill the closet.

Cam: Nice party, Ruth. Fun.

Ruth: They do make a mess.

Cam: They do. But that's the way you gauge the success of a party. At the mayor's, for instance, on Dominion Day? Not one good laugh the whole damned night, and not a crumb was dropped.

Ruth: Look at this. White circles on the wood. I'll have to get out the Old English and give that a polish. *They stop activity for a moment.*

Cam: *He reaches for Ruth.* Now?

Ruth: No. Tomorrow. *Cam makes an advance. Quickly, Ruth moves away and begins shaking a finger at him.* Campbell, we really do have a bone to pick. You do everything in your power for those men all week long. Why do we have to be entertaining them all the time? They take us for granted. They eat our food and drink our whiskey and stain our tables. . . . I'm tired of having no other friends. You're so well-known in town, Cam, why can't we widen our circle?

Cam: I don't see them all week! We're all off, covering our various territories. We have a lot of news to exchange on the weekends.

Ruth: I don't think that's it at all. I think being with them gives you a feeling of power.

Cam: That's just nonsense! They happen to be my favourite company, that's all. They're like my own sons.

Ruth: Sons? Roy's a year older than you.

Cam: I have a great affection for them! They move me, Ruth. They touch me. Sometimes, in the winter, we'll all be out on the road and the whole province is under a blizzard. And I always know exactly where they are. I can see them, in my mind's eye, alone in the storm, scared, shovelling their cars into Kamsack or Weyburn. We're hundreds of miles apart but I feel connected to them. *Pause.* Maybe only a man could understand it. It's a connection of men and their work. *Another pause, a smile.* Maybe you're a wee bit jealous?

Ruth: *She sighs and smiles.* Well, I guess there's no use ruining the rest of the evening. *They kiss. She separates herself and says, quietly.* I'll call you in a minute. *She exits, up the stairs.*

Cam: *Cheerful and smiling, he places a few more glasses on the tray. He chuckles, then breaks out into laughter.* We were invited one evening, oh, ten years ago, to a great celebration. The second richest man in town, Humboldt was his name, opened his house for a wedding reception. There were two mounties present, dressed in scarlet, and one of them couldn't keep his eyes off my Ruthie. Well. That mountie got himself a snortful, and finally he couldn't keep his *hands* off my Ruthie. I was ready to kill the bastard, but it's intimidating, y'know, all that scarlet. By midnight, it was pretty disgusting. People were draped over bannisters, people were vomiting in the rubber plants, the hired piper stopped pipin' ceremonials and started playing laments. And that mountie was chasing Ruth around with a shameless bulge in his pants. She ran upstairs into a bathroom and I ran after her. And I knew lust like I'd never known it before. I locked the bathroom door and I grabbed her, and I sat her up on the sink and I unzipped my fly . . . and you know what?

Ruth appears on the landing, wearing a pretty peignoir.

Ruth: We were never invited to the Humboldt's again, because the sink broke off the wall! *She lets out a hoot of laughter. Cam dashes up the stairs, chasing her, laughing.*

Mood change. The adult Jean enters, smiling. When Cam and Ruth are out of sight, she addresses the audience.

Jean: Havilland Tobacco had always considered my Dad too independent, too much of a western maverick. In the spring of 1944, it was discovered that Havilland allowed the swapping of gas coupons. The practice was denounced, and the company was censured in Parliament. At that time Havilland supplied tobacco to the entire armed forces—land, sea and air. The government threatened to cancel their contract unless Havilland took a strong, well-publicized stand against black marketeering. They needed a scapegoat, and they chose my Dad.

During the following, the dining room table is removed and replaced with Cam's desk, from his office. Most of the china is removed, and all of the books. Two painted kitchen chairs are placed at the desk. A few Christmas decorations are set. This action occurs behind a scrim. Jean remains onstage.

Cam enters, wearing a bathrobe over his trousers. He carries a telephone. He is ostensibly on the road, in a hotel room. Simultaneously, the three salesmen are seen, each carrying a phone.

Cam: Hello? Can you hear me? We've got a bad connection. Listen, I'm in Prince Albert. I've just got word from head office. The shit's hit the fan.

Roy: *After a moment.* Whaddya mean?

Cam: Ruthie was right. We're going to have to pay the piper. They're sending a hatchet man to my office Friday night at seven. I want you to move heaven and earth . . . burn rubber if you have to, and meet me there at six-thirty.

Billy: Cam? What do you want us to do?

Cam: Absolutely nothing. Stand there and listen. He won't mince words, he'll be quick and brutal. And when he's done, I'll tell him.

Ken: Tell him what?

Cam: Oh, for chrissake, Kenny! "Cam's boys come of a piece and Cam's boys go of a piece."

Roy: Jesus, Cam, what the hell are they looking for?

Cam: A scapegoat, Roy! Everybody's swapping coupons and they need to save face in Ottawa.

Roy: I see. And you're the sacrificial lamb.

Cam: So they think.

Ken: Cam, listen. If that's what they want, I mean if that's what they're really *intent* on, they just might take the whole damned flock.

Cam: They *won't*, Kenny! They'd have to close the province down. Christ, man, if one thing is certain, that is! Look, it's going to take less time to resolve this guy's little excursion than this phone call is taking. All I need is your bodies, and I'll guarantee your future. So be there, at six-thirty, Okay? *Pause.* Fellas? Can you hear me?

Pause.

Billy: Cam? This is really a lousy connection. There's magpies or something on the goddamn line. We'll have to get back to you.

All three salesmen hang up, simultaneously. After a moment, Cam hangs up, leaving the stage slowly as the men exit hastily.

Jean: It was quick and brutal. He didn't come home that Friday night. The following day the contents of his office were sent, in a van, to the house. The day after that, Sunday, he was brought home in an ambulance. He had pneumonia. The police had found him in a hotel in Yorkton. He had taken two forty-ounce bottles to his room; he drank them; he got into a bathtub. The water turned to ice around him as he lay there, unconscious, for forty-eight hours. Billy lived on Twenty-Eighth Street, Roy on Bedford Road, Ken on Avenue H. My mother and I were never allowed to walk on those streets again. And, gradually, things began to disappear from our house. *She exits.*

In darkness, we hear the noise of high winds: a blizzard. Cam shuffles down the hall, wearing the sweater he wore at the opening. He carries an empty bottle of Canadian Club.

Cam: Dead soldier. *He drops the bottle into a wastebasket.* Only one reliable man in this town. *He goes to the phone and dials.* Keeps his promises, delivers his goods. You have to keep in touch with a man like that. *Into phone.* Hello? I say, is this Melzewski the bootlegger? Ah, good. This is MacMillan, the town clown. *Brief pause.* I'm callin' to give you a weather report. I want you to know it's forty below. *He laughs.* Oh, no, Michael. All the witches' tits dropped off long ago. The Saskatchewan prairie is known, Mike, world renowned, as the home of the titless witch. Tell me now, what are you chargin' tonight for a forty? Oh, that's steep. You're talkin' to a Scotsman, you know. I'm canny. I'm thrrrrifty! Fifteen bucks you say. No wonder you're driving a Cadillac. Did I ever tell you, Michael, I don't like Cadillacs. Nope, ostentatious. Well, I've got a rifle I could let you have. A Winchester. Oh, top of the line, Mike. Bagged an awful lot of deer in its day. Thank you, Mike. That's a good boy. Make it snappy now. *He hangs up.*

Ruth and Jean enter from the kitchen area. Ruth wears a faded housedress. She carries three Christmas cards and a sheaf of stapled papers. Jean, now ten years old, wears saddle shoes, a skirt and sweater. She carries books and sits at the desk to study. Cam is "dry", physically miserable, mentally scattered. But he is mercurial, always within an inch of violence.

Ruth: Would you believe it? Only three Christmas cards this year. From the milkman . . . the mailman . . . and of course we know what *they* want. And this great garish thing from the bootlegger. The bannister used to be so full of cards. So full we used to string 'em in the hall. I was just lookin' at the old Christmas list. What do they think we are? Lepers?

Cam: Church mice, Ruth. As in "poor as." Did I ever tell you my theory? A man's life is most accurately documented in his chequebook. Is he eatin' steak or sausage, is he dining out? Is he sendin' bouquets, is he buying season's tickets? Does he winter in the Bahamas? . . . Does he donate to charity? *He cups his hands and calls into the distance.* Archeologists of the world, do you hear me? *Mumbling.* Misguided fools, digging around for shards and splinters. *Calling again.* Find a chequebook, lads, and you've found it all!!

Ruth: Cam, I think you need a meal. I think you think you need something else, but *I* think you need a meal. You know what they say at A.A. Regular meals are part of the cure. "The *cure* begins at the stove."

Cam: Baloney.

Ruth: I'll fix some eggs.

Cam: The very idea nauseates me. Eating some animal's *ova.*

Ruth: *As she goes.* Nice scrambled eggs with ketchup, and a little muffin . . . don't worry. We'll get it down. *She exits.*

Cam: *Aroused by his battle cry to the archeologists, he is suddenly hyper-alert. He paces and stares at Jean, who is studying. She feels his stare, and meets his eyes.* That desk is too big for this room.

Jean: *She knows, immediately, where he is leading. From this moment on she senses danger and tries to avoid it.* Dad, I have to memorize the multiplication tables. Will you help me?

Cam: I might get back on my feet, y'know, might have a *chance* if I didn't have to look at the bloody desk every day.

Jean: Would you like me to move?

Cam: For twelve years in a row my office led the national profits. For twelve years in a row *I* led the Travellers' Day Parade. Elected, by four hundred salesmen, to lead their parade! Jesus, I didn't have enough ass to *kiss* in those days.

Jean: Mum's got the toast in. I can smell it.

Cam: When he came, y'know, the hatchet man, he stood behind that desk, my desk, as if it was his. Stripped me bare. Took away my title, my car, my pension—took my name off the door. Within twenty-four hours my name was mud in this town. And a moving van delivered the desk here, home. *Pause.* It's too big for this room.

Jean: Maybe we should put it in the garage.

Cam: Why are you cowering like that? Makin' yourself so small?

Jean: I'm not cowering.

Cam: You are. And you're sulking. I hate it when you make that face. I am bone dry, Jean, and the craving is on me. Try and understand. *Jean nods a conciliatory "yes", which infuriates Cam.* Leave it to Ruth to have a girl! You can't imagine how I wanted a boy to carry the name. I sat in that delivery room, I was in a cold sweat, and then he came. Dr. Kincaid. Do you know what he said?

Jean: Dad, please . . .

Cam: He said, "Sad tidings, MacMillan, sad tidings. It's got a cloven crotch." *He waits for a reaction. There is none. He sits opposite her.* That's what the man said. So, what's on your mind?

Jean: I think we should go into the kitchen.

Cam: You want something, don't you? Don't sit there like a ninny. Speak up! Ask! What *is* it you want?

Jean: *She has tried to delay the combat he is looking for, but he is too persistent. She jumps up.* All right! A Christmas tree! Why can't we afford a Christmas tree? You get rye whiskey when you want it. You've given Melzewski our dining room furniture, your golf clubs and all of our bone china! Give him something and get us a tree!

Cam: I'd like to give him *you*, you little bitch! *He runs for her. She runs.* I wonder how much you'd fetch on the open market! *Cam catches her. He hits her hard, in the face. Immediately we see blood, running from her nose. Jean screams. The following dialogue overlaps and crosscuts.*

Jean: Daddy, please . . . no! Oh, God. Oh, damn you!

Cam: Four hundred men marched behind me in the parade! I had clout in this town. I took no sass from anyone!

Ruth runs in, alarmed. She carries a tea towel.

Ruth: Oh, Lord, Cam! Oh, Jeannie, what now? *She runs to Jean, with the towel.* What is it? A nose bleed? What did you say?

Cam: *He doubles over, with debilitating remorse.* Oh, sweet Jesus, sweet Jesus . . .

Ruth: Put your head back! . . . Get your head back! . . . Is your face okay?

Jean: Just . . . my nose . . .

Ruth: *Gravely, in a whisper. She feels Jean's skirt.* Did you wet?

Jean: No.

Cam: Oh, for chrissake . . .

Ruth: She does, you know! She wets when you hit her. If you had to pay the cleaning bill, you'd know what I mean. *To Jean.* I think it's clotting. Hold it, there. I'll get the coats.

Cam: The coats? What the hell for?

Ruth: We have to see the doctor.

Cam: There's a raging blizzard out there!

Ruth: *Getting coats, hats, boots.* I want to be sure nothing's broken.

Jean: The doctor'll call the school! He always does. He'll call the school counsellor.

Ruth: Campbell, when are you going to stop this? You're a grown-up adult . . .

Cam: Grown-up adult is redundant! And you always say "rich millionaire". Millionaires are *always* rich! Adults are *always* grown-up!

Jean: *Boldly.* Not in *your* case, Sir! You are the exception!

Cam: Oh, you're a smart-assed brat! What are you lookin' for? A fracture? *Jean takes her coat. She holds the tea towel to her face.*

Ruth: *She stands, in her coat, holding a small bowl. She glares at Cam.* There was five dollars bus money in this bowl this morning. Have you got it? *Cam reluctantly nods "yes".* Get it! *Cam sits down, removes his shoe, and hands Ruth the bill.* Thief!

Cam: Now, Ruthie, what little we have we must regard as *ours.* Community property.

Ruth: You're going to need your sponsors tonight. Call them.

Cam: *Groaning.* Ruth, I've got no *conviction* in A.A.

Ruth: Call them! *She takes a waiting stance.*

Cam: *Goes to the phone and dials, feebly.* Hello, Duncan? Cam. Listen. *Pause.* Yeah, I need company. It's forty below, Duncan, what about your car? *Pause, anger.* Oh, for chrissake, you've lived on this prairie all your life, you ought to know anti-freeze doesn't do sweet bugger all in forty below!

Ruth: Tell him Ross can bring him.

Cam: Maybe Ross could pick you up.

Ruth: Tell him you'll put the coffee on. You'll have it waiting.

Cam: I'll put the coffee on, Duncan. I'll have it waiting. Pardon? *He pauses and looks at Ruth, incredulously.* Sanka? *To Ruth.* Jesus. *To Duncan.* Well, lad, I'll see if we've got any. Hurry along, now. 'Bye.

Ruth: *Tying her headscarf.* With all the junk that's gone through that man's system, does he really have to worry about caffeine? *She hands Cam some pieces of A.A. literature.* Here's some pamphlets. Read these till they come.

Cam: Jean? *He does not look at her. The question is a strain.* How is your face?

Jean: It's still on the front of my head, thank you. *Ruth and Jean exit. Jean takes the bloodstained towel with her.*

Cam: *He opens a pamphlet and makes a desperate effort to concentrate on the print.* "We admitted we were powerless over alcohol. That our lives had become unmanageable. We came to believe that a power greater than ourselves could restore us to sanity. We made a searching and fearless moral inventory of ourselves. Made a list of all persons we had harmed."

Melzewski appears. He is a man of fifty. He wears a coat, scarf and hat, and carries a paper bag containing Cam's forty-ounce bottle.

Mike: Goddammit MacMillan! MacMillan, the least you could do is shovel your bloody walk.

Cam: Oh, Michael, come in! It's nice of you, Mike, to come over so quick.

Mike: Nice has got nothing to do with it. It's Christmas, Cam, and bootleg rye is flowing like the Ganges. *Pause.* Ruth and Jean are out?

Cam: Yep.

Mike: *Handing Cam the bag.* Here it is, man. Your lifeline.

Cam: Thank you. Take your coat off. Stay awhile.

Mike: *Sighing.* I've got a lot of calls ...

Cam: Oh, for chrissake, Michael, what's ten minutes here or there? I'm turning into a babbling idiot, living with these two females.

Mike: Well, okay.

Cam: Good! *He fetches two glasses and pours a shot in each one.* There's no *chat*, y'know, in families. There's nagging and scolding, and God knows there's recrimination, but there's never any plain *chat*. *He gives Mike a drink, and lifts his own glass.* You're my saviour, Michael. My bohunk St. Bernard.

Mike: Hey, wait a minute! No toast?

Cam: *Accommodating him.* Here's to the girl in the little red shoes / She'll spend your money, and drink your booze / She's lost her cherry, but that's no sin / She's still got the box the cherry came in. *They both laugh; Cam drinks.* I see you've got a new coat.

Mike: Yep, last Saturday, down at Dixwell's. *He pauses, sensing the room.* And you've got heat. How did you manage that?

Cam: There was one insurance policy left. Ruth cashed it in and shut 'em up for a couple of months. What are you staring at?

Mike: That sweater. It looks like the moths had an eight course meal on the elbows. Y'know, my mother used to say, "There's shame in a hole, but there's none in a patch." I'm surprised Ruth allows it.

Cam: I won't let her near it.

Mike: Why the hell not?

Cam: *Strutting a bit.* Oh, there's a certain aristocratic seediness to it, don'tcha think? A kind of fatalistic nonchalance. A patch, Michael, is a pretentious thing.

Mike: Tell me about it. I've never heard your theory about patches.

Cam: A patch announces to the world that you still care. That at some precarious level in your miserable little existence, appearance still matters. A patch puts on airs. It's a bourgeois label I don't care to wear.

Mike: *Shaking his head.* You're one helluva specimen, Cam. You know what they ought to do? They ought to put you in a big glass jar out at the university, and leave you there for observation.

Cam: Oh, I'd like that. I'd be pickled, in a big glass jar.

Mike: *Patting his pocket.* Hey, I gotta little something special. *He takes out two cigars.* Havanas!

Cam: Bless your soul. My God, Mike, these ain't cheap!

Mike: Hang the expense.

Cam: And you're buying your threads down at Dixwell's now, too?

Mike: Uh huh. The amazing thing is, they like bohunk money just as well as they liked yours. Your old Watson Club is the only exception. I've applied twice, and they've refused me twice.

Cam: It's your name, Mike. Melzewski. They can't spell it and they can't pronounce it. Why do you bother? You've done very well.

Mike: You're damn right I have! I've got a five-bedroom house with three bathrooms. I've got a new Cadillac every two years. I own three apartment buildings on the west side and I just bought half a hockey team. I've even got a library. Well ... your library. I've got only one trace of the immigrant left.

Cam: Oh. What's that?

Mike: In church, on Sunday morning. I still, when I put a paper dollar down on that collection plate, I still take fifty cents back. I hate it when I do it, but, shit, I still do it! Gimme the frigging gun.

Cam: Ah, yes. *Takes one, of two, off a rack.* Here it is. Top of the line. Nice bit of engraving there, on the stock.

Mike: Not bad, not bad.

Cam: You bastard, you'll sell it for thirty.

Mike: You could sell it for thirty yourself, if you'd bother to place an ad. Or if you got *real* adventuresome and went out. You know damn well you can buy that bottle for seven bucks at the liquor store.

Cam: The liquor store's got the drinking population by the balls! They're open eleven to twelve on Tuesdays, four to five-thirty Wednesdays, one to two-fifteen Thursdays, and I've got no car, man! It's a plot, y'see, a conspiracy, to drive the drinking man berserk. They know our brains don't function anymore. They know I could climb Everest sooner than I can get the trolley schedule to coincide with the liquor store schedule.

Mike: Bullshit, Cam, bullshit!

Cam: Michael, listen, I've got a problem.

Mike: *Incredulously.* Really?

Cam: Seriously. Christmas. It's weighing on me something awful. God, it's a pain in the ass, the way it exaggerates everything. *Pause.* I want to get a tree for Jeannie, and a bird for Ruth.

Mike: *Looks around the room.* Well ... what about the other rifle?

Cam: Let me hang onto that for a while. Look, these Constable prints have been in the family for years. They're quite valuable.

Mike: Constable? Constable don't mean dick in my market, Cam. My people buy pictures to cover holes in walls. I'll give you ten bucks for the frames.

Cam: Lord, you're a weasel! Fifteen.

Mike: Twelve-fifty, final.

Cam: Okay, okay, but look at this, now. This rocking chair's got a wonderful history. A great-great uncle of mine married a woman who fled the American Revolution. She came up to Canada on the Hudson River, with a group of Loyalists . . .

Mike: Loyalists?

Cam: Loyal to the crown, Mike. They preferred majesty, y'see, to representation. This chair was made in 1770 in New York.

Mike: Campbell, for me, this is just a piece-a used furniture. *Brief pause.* On this you should write to an antique dealer in Toronto. You should send a photograph. You should get top dollar on this. Twelve-fifty on the frames, and that's it.

Cam: What'll you give me on the chair?

Mike: *Slightly upset.* I won't take this chair, Cam.

Cam: Fifty . . . sixty . . .

Mike: I will not have this chair on my conscience! Now, look. *Seventeen-fifty* on the picture frames, and that's final. You'll get a tree and a bird and enough left over for Ruth to make a little fruitcake. Deal?

Cam: Deal.

Mike: *Peels bills off a wad from his pocket, and digs in again for the fifty cents change.* Listen, Cam, it's getting worse. I mean, it ain't healthy. You're holing up here like a goddamn mole. And I've heard on the street that you aren't even trying to go to A.A. meetings anymore.

Cam: Don't have to. They come here. Make house calls, y'know.

Mike: It was good for you, going to the meetings. Why'ja stop?

Cam: Had to ride the public transportation.

Mike: What's the matter with that?

Cam: The public transportation rather consistently carries the public. Perilous lot, the public. They believe what they read in the newspapers. And if you remember, I was all over the headlines.

Mike: Cam, it's long forgotten!

Cam: Nope. It was a very patriotic time. *He smokes and drinks.* Seen 'em lately?

Mike: *He shrugs, makes an impatient gesture.* Saturday, at Dixwell's.

Cam: Ah ha. Buying up bolts of British tweed, no doubt. How'd they look?

Mike: Prosperous. Is that what you want to hear? They looked prosperous.

Cam: Didja give them my regards?

Mike: They don't act like guilty men, Cam! They're never going to apologize.

Cam: They'll have to. Sooner or later, conscience will bring them around. They owe me, Mike.

Mike: *Patiently, quietly.* It was illegal. And it was your idea.

Cam: *Flaring.* Of course it was my idea! I was the manager ... the brains of the operation. They were two-bit salesmen. They worked for me for twenty years and *never* had an idea!

Mike: They weren't two-bit salesmen. They were your friends. Cam, *accept* it. It's over.

Cam: Easy to say, Mike, easy to say. Not so easy to practice.

Mike: Listen, Swift Meat's is looking for a salesman. National Cash Register's lookin' for a salesman. Everyone knows you were the best. Why the hell won't you make a call?

Cam: Michael, I went down in disgrace! *Pause.* They want freshmen. Green young guys in their twenties, guys who'll take the worst territory. I'm getting old, and I'd be low man on the totem pole. They'd send me into the muskeg, the goddamned tundra, on straight commission! *He is irritated. He wants to get rid of Mike, but he is careful not to alienate him.* Oh, we've been over this a hundred times. Go home, Mike. Go home and count your blessings, and have a nice big rowdy Ukrainian Christmas. *Mike gets his coat and hat. Cam hands him the rifle and the frames.* How many kids you got now?

Mike: Eight.

Cam: Eight! Heavens! *Whispering.* Coitus interruptus, Mike. Coitus interruptus!

Mike: Easy to say, Campbell, easy to say. . . .

Cam & Mike: *Together, laughing.* Not so easy to practice!

Cam: Take care now, that sidewalk's really treacherous. *Melzewski leaves. Cam guzzles from the bottle and sways slightly. His feelings are pent-up, explosive. He begins to mumble.* Smarmy goddamn foreigner. Comin' in here, tellin' me those two-bit salesmen were my friends. Tellin' me to call Swift Meat Company. *Moving about, in frustration. Pause.* Tellin' me what his *mother* used to say! *My* mother used to read Shakespeare! My mother was fourth-generation Canadian! But when he's here, I make the appropriate noises. Because I need the bottle more than he needs the visit. Look into any man's survival kit and you'll find nothing there but appropriate noises.

Suddenly, great noise and banging are heard. Cam immediately drops to the floor, lying on his belly. Cam stays in this position for the duration of the calling. Duncan and Ross are outside. They are seen, bundled up, hovering in silhouette behind a frosted front door.

Duncan: Campbell, we're here! Open up, lad!

Ross: There's a blizzard out here, Cam, it's forty below. . . .

Duncan: We know you're in there, Campbell, and we didn't come 'cross town to play hide and seek. . . .

Cam: *On the floor.* My God, what an arrival! D-Day in Normandy!

Ross: Now, Campbell, I'm countin' to five, and then we're leaving. One . . . two . . . three . . . four . . . five.

Cam: May all your extremities freeze and fall off!

Duncan: Bastard! I've a mind to take this shovel and bust in a window.

Ross: Now, Campbell, I'm counting to ten, and then we're leaving. I mean it, man. Six . . . seven . . . eight . . . nine . . . ten. That's it! We're goin' home, Cam. Don't call your sponsors unless you intend to let them in. *They shuffle away, mumbling.*

Cam: Sponsor, sponsor, go away. I'll be saved another day. *He pounces on a pile of pamphlets from A.A.* And take your pamphlets with you! *Realizing they have gone, he examines the pamphlets.* Here we have the vast and somewhat repetitive literature of Alcoholics Anonymous. Alcoholics Anonymous. *Pause.* Bad enough to be an alcoholic. Worse, to be anonymous. It's against human nature.

Ruth and Jean enter and see the bottle.

Ruth: Oh, God.

Jean: Oh, Dad.

Ruth: Well, we'd best take inventory. . . . The Constables.

Jean: And a Winchester.

Ruth: That's one helluva load for just one bottle.

Cam: Ruthie, I wheedled some cash out of him, so you could fetch in a turkey for the Yule.

Ruth: I'll believe that, Campbell, when I put it in my mouth and chew it. *I* think you got in a grand supply and stashed it away somewhere.

Cam: Oh ladies, please. I need a little affection. Ruthie? I need a friend.

Ruth: You've got your friend there, in your hand.

Cam: Oh, you're a hard, hard woman.

Ruth: And you're a great big infant! You send us to the doctor, you call the bootlegger, and then you pout when you don't get a hug. And you've been diddling with the thermometer again. My God, it's like the tropics in here.

Cam: It's just comfortable, Ruth.

Ruth: *Turning down the thermostat.* Comfort *costs*! Did your sponsors come?

Cam: Their cars wouldn't start.

Ruth: Will you look at the man? He wants hugs and cuddles.

Cam: *To Jean.* Insane, isn't it? Insane to expect affection from this woman who is the bane of my existence . . .

Jean: Oh, Dad, please . . .

Cam: . . . this woman who thinks there is salvation in a *meal.* I live in this house with a peasant mentality that wears me down like sandpaper. Get this straight, ladies. This disintegration of mine didn't start with the firing. . . . No! . . . earlier! At the altar. When I took a kraut peasant for a wife.

Jean: *Moving to leave.* I cannot listen to this . . .

Cam: *Stopping her, vocally or physically.* Yes, you can! Listen and learn how to do combat! Your mother hasn't got the mental resources. Your mother's got nothin' to recommend her but goodness. Charmin' the world with her rural simplicity. Simplicity is fine when your man has lots of money, but it doesn't mean *dick* in hard times!

Ruth: It means I stay, dammit! I've kept you off relief. I've gone to work!

Cam: Oh, yes, you relate to work!

Jean: I will not stay here . . .

Ruth: *Grabbing Jean.* Yes, you will! Stay and learn how to handle a man like this! God forbid, you might marry one someday. *She pushes Jean into a chair.* Sit down! And listen! And get some steel in that spine of yours. And it doesn't take *mental resources* to have a good fight; all it takes is sticking power. *She whirls on Cam, doing the mental equivalent of rolling up her sleeves.* You're damned right I relate to work! I'm proud of that. I *relate* to a minimum wage. *The two of them now prowl around Jean, who is penned in a chair. There is a great deal of humour underlying each of their arguments.*

Cam: That's what these prairie farm girls relate to! The minimum. That's what they aspire to: the minimum. When you have no history, no culture, you're thankful when they give you a dollar and a quarter an hour for back-breaking, mind-boggling, monotonous work. And then she comes *home* and delivers herself of her small, diffuse, minimal thoughts!

Ruth: You were offered a job last week, you bastard. *To Jean.* Driving the elevator at the Connaught apartments. *Back to Cam.* At a minimum wage, yes, and you sitting here without two cents to rub together, and you turned it down. *Explain to me* why you can't drive an elevator!

Cam: I *can* drive an elevator! I *won't* drive an elevator!

Ruth: You drove a car for thirty years!

Cam: A car goes horizontal, Ruth, natural, like the land. Oh, you'd be happy, wouldn't you, having me stand in a claustrophobic cubicle with my hand on a clutch all day—me, with my gift of gab; reduced to ... *He uses a falsetto.* "Going Up," "Going Down," spending the next twenty years driving *vertical* at a minimum wage! *To Jean.* Do you know what your mother did on her eighteenth birthday? She was let off the farm for the first time, and she caught a bus into the city, and she went directly to the ladies room at Eaton's. And she stood there the entire day, watching the toilet flush at Eaton's department store. *Mesmerized* at the miracle of modern plumbing because, you see, she'd peed in a hole in an outdoor biffy all her life. On *my* eighteenth birthday, I went with my grandfather to my great-grandfather's grave. Major David MacMillan of the Third Dragoon Guards. Major David fought with Wellington, at Waterloo, and saved his life, and was decorated afterward. And the Duke of Wellington *gave* Major David a tract of land in Canada. And *that* is how the MacMillans came to these shores!

Ruth: *To Jean, but for Cam's benefit.* You're a fool if you're impressed with all that hogwash. It's all dead stuff, a lot of old bones in graveyards. I never heard of it till he lost the job, then all of a sudden the MacMillans were bloody nobility! *My* history I seen with my own eyes! Now listen to this. I was ten and there were six kids younger, and I was drug out of school in second grade. Kept home, to mind all those kids. And one day Mum and Dad were out with the plough, and who comes roaring across the land but Indians! Wild Indians! We seen 'em on the horizon, comin' bareback on horses. If you left two sacks of milled white flour, they didn't burn your house. So I left the flour and I ran all the kids up to the attic, and I bolted the trap door. *Pause.* Now, *that* is impressive. I *remember* that. Nobody *told* me that. I'm a daughter of pioneers, strongest stock on this prairie, and no man anywheres'll make mincemeat of me! *Cam and Ruth now revert from Jean to each other.*

Cam: You're an illiterate, peasant, German-descended country bumpkin!

Ruth: And you're a wordy, Scots-descended, whiskey-sodden son-of-a-bitch!

Cam: I am Canadian *aristocracy!*

Ruth: *Petering out, without Cam's resources.* You're a brute, and a bully, and besides all that, Campbell, you know what you are? *Pause.* You're no damned good!

Cam: *Slowly, he begins to chuckle at the lameness of this remark.* And besides all that, I'm hungry. *A moment passes.* You win, Ruth. The cure begins at the stove. Feed me, lady. Feed me.

Ruth: *Feeling exorcised, as does Cam, she calms down. She is genuinely pleased that he will eat.* Good, Cam, I'm glad. I'll go fix it. *As she goes.* Stay here, will you, Jeannie? Tend to your old dad. *Ruth exits.*

Cam: *Looks at Jean, sheepishly.* Know what I need?

Jean: What?

Cam: A hug and a cuddle. *Gesturing.* Come, sit down with me. *Jean sits beside him, on a couch. He puts his arm around her.* Let's do something pretty. We haven't done something pretty in a long, long time.

Jean: What'll we do?

Cam: You start, I'll follow.

Jean: *She thinks briefly, then recites.* My heart's in the Highlands, my heart is not here . . .

Cam: My heart's in the Highlands, a-chasing the deer . . .

Jean: A-chasing the wild deer, and following the roe . . .

Cam: My heart's in the Highlands, wherever I go . . .

Jean: Farewell to the Highlands, farewell to the North . . .

Cam: The birthplace of valour, the country of worth . . .

Jean: Wherever I wander, wherever I rove . . .

Cam: The hills of the Highlands forever I love. *They are relaxed and calm. Cam is drowsy.*

Jean: Daddy? What does it do?

Cam: What, lass?

Jean: The rye whiskey. What does it do?

Cam: Oh, my. Well, it's like a . . . great mother. Old mother rye. A great, vast blimp of a woman. She reaches out and puts her arms around you, and envelops you. And she whispers in your ear. She says "Cam, you're a good lad. You tried. You trusted. Your heart is kind, and your mind is first-rate, and additionally, Cammy, you're awful easy on the eyes." Of course, she's a bit of a whore, old mother rye. She costs. But, oh, the comfort! The way she takes the hard edge off the day. And the whisper in the ear is like a warm zephyr. She puts her mouth right here, *he points to his ear* . . . and she says, "Cammy, life is possible."

Ruth bustles in, wearing an apron.

Ruth: Cam, I want you to wash up. Come along now.

Cam: Oh, Ruthie, I'm in my nice hazy-dazy. Bring it in here.

Ruth: I will not! You need to walk, and circulate your blood . . .

Cam: *Rising, with Jean.* My *blue* blood . . .

Ruth: Your blue blood, yes. You need to sit up straight in a chair and eat proper.

Jean: *Helping him up, and out.* Come on now, Dad, into the kitchen.

Ruth: *On the other side of him.* Up, now, baggage, up and away. That's it. That's good.

Cam: Feeding time.

Ruth: Yes, indeed.

Cam: In the company of my two ladies.

Jean: That's right.

Cam: A maiden and a . . . matron!

Ruth: Come on, baggage, come on.

Cam: Jeannie, I am truly in the bosom of the family!

Jean: Yes, Daddy, you truly are.

Cam: May I always be. May I always be. *The three exit to the kitchen.*

Blackout

B. P. Photo
Brenda Bazinet as Jean
25th Street Theatre, Saskatoon, 1986

Act Two

A spotlight comes up on Cam. He is slumped in a rocking chair. He shakes his head violently. He groans. He stares at invisible creatures.

Cam: Some son-of-a-bitch opened the cage. *Pause.* Some s.o.b. opened the goddamn cage! *He whirls around, in the chair.* Some feather-brained, key-happy, son of a whelping bitch opened the bloody cage! *He recoils from the creatures he sees.* Vermin. Parasites. On parade. *He lights a cigarette, addresses the audience, and takes a lighter tone.* Ordinarily, I'd grab the yellow pages. Call a fumigator. Little man with a spray gun, arrivin' in an unmarked car. Ordinarily the wee beasties gather at the baseboards. My misfortune is, they gather in my head.

In the half-light, we see Cam sitting in his rocker at one side of the stage. Jean enters, opposite, stage right, into full light.

Jean: I am fifteen now. On Saturdays I work for Mrs. Sampson, who has two little children. I take them with me, to the cellar, where I do the laundry. They like it when the clothes have to be put through the wringer. I let them do that while I take the wet pieces outside, and hang them on the line to dry. Mrs. Sampson got very mad at me last Saturday. It was thirty-eight degrees below zero, and the sheets froze on the line. One of them cracked, broke in two right in the middle, as I brought it through the door. Mrs. Sampson hollered at me and said I was irresponsible. On Sundays I work down at O'Malley's fish and chips. I weigh the chips on a scale and then I put them into little plastic bags. There's an electric machine, a hot iron clamp that seals the bags closed. It's a long walk home afterwards, but I don't take the trolley. My clothing smells of fish and oil and I'm afraid there'll be someone I know on the trolley. My mother cooks in the kitchen at the old folks' home. She makes fifteen pies every day of the week, all by herself, with no machines to help. In the evenings she sits and mends things, and she remembers what it was like, in the old days, when I was little. Last fall I was called into the counsellor's office at school. *Pause.* I have ... bladder trouble. She asked me if I could tell her something about the changes that had occurred at our house. I remembered a poem, by John Dryden, from an old book that belonged to my Grandfather MacMillan. It described a time that was: "A very merry, dancing, drinking / laughing, quaffing and unthinking time." I told her it must have been like that, in the old days, when I was little. *Jean exits.*

The lights come up on Cam.

Cam: *He leaves his chair and ambles to center stage, rolling a cigarette. He is wry, bemused, very much the raconteur.* A minister from the United Church of Canada had the audacity to come around yesterday and *imply* that I'm losing my mind. The Reverend Angus Gordon. Lives down the street, therefore gets the most salient facts hot off the press. *He sips his drink.* I made the appropriate noises, all of them eminently sane, and then he, satisfied, began to tell me *his* troubles. Seems he's taken on a new preacher, twenty-four, fresh out of theology school. A young man to run the boy's choir, the boy's Sunday school, and the boy's summer camp. In short, a young man to play with the boys of the congregation. And that's what's transpired. He's playin' with the boys o' the congregation. *He laughs, lightly.* So there, in the men's room, in the basement, of the United Church of Canada, paradise got lost once again. Still the man was hurting. The sadness in his face made his collar less . . . threatening. He looked, for a moment, ordinary. Like one of us. I avoided the crucial question, which is: "When God gives us only this one, brief life, why does he make it such a raw deal?" I was afraid he'd direct me, rather predictably, to the Book of Job. Now, I've been to the Book of Job many times, voluntarily, to no avail. God took from Job all of his possessions, then his family, and then saw fit to inflict him with boils, from head to toe. Job withstood all these tribulations, kept his faith, and was rewarded in the end. But the resolution, if I may say so, has always seemed deplorably materialistic. Did God restore Job's most lamentable loss? Did God return Job's innocence? No. He gave him *things.* Fourteen thousand sheep, six thousand camels, a thousand yoke of oxen and a thousand she-asses. Which, no matter how you stack it, amounts to one helluva load of shit. At any rate we avoided all Biblical chat, for which I was grateful. I gave the Reverend Gordon my two-bits' worth of advice, offered him a drink, which he accepted with some alacrity, and sent him off, back to his God, and his scandal.

Blackout. The voice of a clerk in the office at Jean's high school is heard over an intercom system, or a loudspeaker.

Clerk: *Voice-over.* Would Jean MacMillan please report to the counsellor's office? *Short beat.* Jean MacMillan to Miss Halverson, please.

The lights come up on Miss Halverson's office. She is a woman of thirty, humane and caring. There may be two photographs on a wall and also one large print. The photos are of King George VI, and Winston Churchill. The print is a reproduction of a painting by Tom Thomson. Miss Halverson rises from her desk as Jean enters.

Halverson: Good morning, Jean.

Jean: *She is distraught. She tries, heroically, to control herself.* Good morning.

Halverson: *Gesturing.* Please, sit down.

Jean: No. *Pause.* Thank you.

Halverson: *Embarrassed, hesitating.* You're . . . wet.

Jean: Yes. I've had an accident. I really must go home.

Halverson: This is the second accident in class, Jean. And your elementary school records show it was a problem there, too. I think we have to talk about some medical attention.

Jean: No! *She tries to maintain her calm.* The doctor knows my troubles. I . . . only wet when I'm hit.

Halverson: But you were in home-ec last period, Jean. No one hits you in home-ec.

Jean: I got . . . confused, for a moment.

Halverson: Can you explain that?

Jean: There was a lot of noise in the class. A lot of girls, arguing, and lots of machines running. And I . . . mistook it, you see. I got scared.

Halverson: Yes?

Jean: And then Miss Pendleton lifted a yardstick over my head. I'm sorry. I know it doesn't make sense. I thought she was going to hit

me, and I wet. *Pause.* I don't understand it. Usually, see, it's here
... *She gestures* ... in the lower back.

Halverson: Where you're hit.

Jean: Yes.

Halverson: But last year, when I called you in, you had a large crescent on your cheek. I think you weren't truthful then, Jean. You
said you fell on an opened tobacco can. You said the rim caused
the mark.

Jean: Yes. He has to roll his own nowadays. So the can was open.
She sees Halverson's disbelief. It was thrown.

Halverson: It would have to be thrown with some force, to leave
such a contusion.

Jean: *Relenting.* It was shoved. Against my face. *Pause. A new note
of hope.* But he doesn't do that anymore. My mum says a
woman's face is her calling card.

Halverson: Why does he hit you, Jean?

Jean: He's very unhappy. He was fired, you see, and disgraced.

Halverson: That was 1944, Jean. Ten years ago.

Jean: He says he hates my smell. I sometimes smell of fish from ...
Catching herself. ... A place I go on the weekend.

Halverson: I won't ask about that. You're under age.

Jean: Yes. Thank you.

Halverson: Does he hit your mother?

Jean: No. Well ...

Halverson: Yes?

Jean: *Tears begin. She tries not to break down.* He ... last week ...
burned her arm.

Halverson: How?

Jean: *Her temper flares, but at her plight, rather than at Halverson.*
You don't *know*, you see. You don't know when you're safe, so
you're always walking on eggs. You just can't gauge his moods.
She put a fresh teapot down in front of him and he jumped up and

threw it at her. It was scalding hot, and she had a thick sweater on, so it stuck. Till we unbuttoned it and pulled it off.

Halverson: *Goes to her with a couple of tissues. She touches Jean's shoulder, gently, and gestures to the chair.* Please sit down. Really, it's all right. *Jean sits; Halverson moves behind the desk.* Had she angered him?

Jean: No. She has an odour, too, you see, from lard. She makes pies where she works. He can't stand our working smells. He says we smell *menial. She pauses, and inhales deeply.* What you have to understand, Miss Halverson, is that my mother loves him. They go at each other something terrible, but she loves him.

Halverson: I understand that.

Jean: *Quizzically, rather daringly.* Do you?

Halverson: *Smiling.* I think your disbelief comes from my "Miss."

Jean: Well . . .

Halverson: I was engaged to a man once. He was killed at Dieppe. August 19, 1942.

Jean: I'm very sorry.

Halverson: Three thousand Canadians, you know, lost at Dieppe. *There is a brief silence between them.* Well. Your father refuses to work?

Jean: Oh, I don't think he could, now. He talks to himself. And he imagines things. Vermin. Parasites. He's lost all of his books, so he goes to the library sometimes. Sneaks over there, just before closing time. He hardly ever goes out during the day.

Halverson: Why?

Jean: Well, he'd been powerful in town, you know, and he was disgraced.

Halverson: Yes?

Jean: He's embarrassed about his clothing. He's ashamed of his appearance.

Halverson: *Settling back, examining Jean's face.* Jean, do you know the main difference between humans and animals?

Jean: *Thinking.* Well, we . . . walk . . . upright . . .

Halverson: We think. We have choices. We're very lucky that we live in a free society. Our boys died for that. No matter how bad things may get, we are human, and we do have alternatives. Remember that, will you?

Jean: Yes, Miss Halverson, I will.

Blackout. The lights come up on Cam, sitting with a bottle, a glass, and a book. The book is the play, Macbeth. *It is approximately four in the afternoon. Jean enters, carrying school books. She is in a mood of frustration and anger.*

Cam: Hello. *Jean does not answer. She undresses, hurriedly, perhaps drops things. Then, in irritation, she throws her books on Cam's old desk.* May I deduce that things did not go well at school today?

Jean: Perceptive deduction.

Cam: Ah! Perceptive deduction. Nice. Slightly insolent, but . . . rhythmic. *Per cep tive de duc tion.*

Jean: *Starting for the stairs.* I have to change my clothes.

Cam: What happened?

Jean: Nothing. I can handle it.

Cam: Oh, I'm sure you can. Whatever you inherited from your mother will handle it. *Jean starts to move up.* Jean? Stay awhile. One misses, you know, the human voice.

Jean: Mum'll be home in an hour.

Cam: But you're the one with all the opinions. Brimming with opinions and biting your tongue to hold them in. Let's talk.

Jean: Do you really want talk, or do you want combat?

Cam: The former. I promise. *Jean comes back into the room.* Tell me, what are they saying out there, in the larger world?

Jean: About what?

Cam: About me.

Jean: *After a moment, proceeding carefully.* Well, they say you used to be so good you could sell refrigerators to the Eskimos.

Cam: *Bitterly.* Or coal in Newcastle. Or steel in Sheffield. Stupid thing to say.

Jean: You asked.

Cam: I'd hoped we could talk ... candidly. I guess not. *Pause.* Are you afraid?

Jean: Yes.

Cam: But I promised.

Jean: *Impatiently.* What does *that* mean, nowadays?

Cam: It means a lot! Three men made a promise once. They had a statement prepared in my defence. There was going to be a pitched battle in my behalf. They were too cowardly to test it. They forgot.

Jean: *Sympathetically.* I know, Dad. I know.

Cam: So. Candidly, what are they saying?

Jean: That you were betrayed. That you were a victim.

Cam: *Bitterly, again, with anger.* Victims are a dime a goddamn dozen!

Jean: Dad, you promised ...

Cam: And I'll keep it! But you must permit me a little, private rage. For chrissake, the world's been torn apart in this decade. They bombed Coventry, they bombed Dresden, they killed six million Jews, they burned Hiroshima: victims are a dime a frigging dozen. *Daring her.* I'm lookin' for *talk*, lass, not condolences!

Jean: They are *saying* that after all the bombing, after all the carnage, the whole world rebuilt. Half the men that came home didn't have arms or legs, but they started again. And you were in your prime, with all your limbs. And you were knocked down, and you *stayed* down!

Cam: Took to the bottle and the rocking chair ...

Jean: Yes, that's what they're saying! *Long pause and transition. They both calm down.* Why, Dad? What happened?

Cam: I don't know. Something ... cracked.

Jean: It's the waste that kills me.

Cam: Is it? If I went out at nine, and grubbed for money, and dragged in here at five, you'd feel better?

Jean: Yes, I would! I'd feel that we were normal.

Cam: That's your mother's word.

Jean: No, it's mine.

Cam: Well, I'm sorry to hear that. *With a sudden spurt of energy.* You know what normal is? Normal is where nothing happens. Normal is some neutral zone where everything is mean and average. You know why I could've sold fridges to Eskies? Because I knew who I was. I set goals and I pursued them, singlemindedly. I didn't bend, I didn't conform, I didn't compromise. They praise you for those qualities in success, and they damn you for them in failure. Jean, I can't begin to understand the world, let alone the decade. The Coventrys, the Dresdens, the petty human betrayals. I don't understand how that two-bit triumvirate lives with their indebtedness. I don't understand how the company I worked for dismissed me so summarily and forgot me so completely. I don't understand how I could have done anything *but* swap coupons when my boys were driving three days a week. *Pause.* But sometimes, rare, infrequent times, I do understand me. It isn't the waste that kills *me*, Jean. It's the bloody disease.

Jean: What disease?

Cam: The one that victims carry. Victims are contagious animals. They badger their wives and batter their daughters. And when they go to bed at night they say, "God, when will you stop me? When will you send someone in to stop me?"

Jean: I feel so helpless, Dad. Isn't there something I can do?

Cam: No. No, I'm afraid it's a job for the grown-up adults.

Jean: Is there anything . . . *anything* that gives you peace of mind?

Cam: Sometimes, the pleasure of the written word. *He picks up his book.* Sometimes I am still amazed. What would you say if you looked at the sky on a starless night?

Jean: Well, I guess I'd say there weren't any stars.

Cam: Yeah. So would I. Mr. Shakespeare said: "There's husbandry in heaven. Their candles are all out."

Jean: That's lovely.

Cam: Isn't it? What are you reading at school?

Jean: Alfred, Lord Tennyson.

Cam: *Heaving a great sigh.* Minor. There's so little time in this life. And the world's collective mind is all caught up in the minor. And, the minimal. And, the normal. Run along now. I can see you need to . . . change your clothes.

Blackout, as Jean goes up the stairs.

Lights up on Cam, Duncan, and Ross. The sponsors from A.A. are casually dressed, and there is much wear and tear on their faces. But they have been "converted," and Ross, especially, is well-meaning. They all smoke. Cam has arranged a coffee pot, cups, cream and sugar. The sponsors have been at the house a short while.

Duncan: *To Cam.* I see you're smokin' roll-yer-owns. *Offering a package.* Wouldja like a tailor-made?

Cam: No, thank you. I've gotten used to these ratty old things. *Lifting the pot.* Another cup, Duncan?

Duncan: Oh, no, thank you. When it isn't Sanka, one has to be my limit. This real stuff gets me all churned up.

Ross: Have you eaten lately, Cam?

Cam: *Thinking.* Yesterday, I think.

Duncan: Well, that's bad. You know where the cure starts, Cam. At the stove.

Cam: I do know that, Duncan. You could conclude, I suppose, that I haven't much interest in the cure.

Ross: It's this hopelessness, Cam. It finishes you off every time. Can you analyze it?

Cam: Ross, the best I can do is this: nothing matters.

Ross: *Nothing?*

Cam: *Losing patience.* Oh, for God's sake! Send me down to Dixwell's and dress me up in the best of British tweeds. It would still all be *gone*. My youth, my job, my friends, my trust. Unrecoverable.

Ross: What you're describing, Cam, is a total lack of will. You've got to tackle the hopelessness. You're a stronger man than the two of us . . . God knows, a smarter man. If we had the will, you must have it too.

Cam: Ross, it's good of you to come by. There must be a million things you'd rather do. *He sighs.* I can't relate to your words. *Will. Faith.* Anymore than you can relate to abject hopelessness.

Ross: Campbell, there were no drunks anywhere worse than us. I flooded my own basement one time, to get insurance money for whiskey. I stole everything that wasn't tied down, lived two whole years in freight cars. And Duncan, well, Duncan even did time in jail.

Cam: *Trying to control sarcasm.* Did you confess that, Duncan? The way you're supposed to? Publicly, at the lectern, at A.A.?

Duncan: Many times.

Cam: I never heard it.

Duncan: You never come to meetings. The hardest ones to convert, Cam, are the solitary drinkers. And that's what you've become.

Ross: Now, now. . . . Easy does it.

Duncan: *Beginning, reluctantly, to tell his story.* It's a state of being I don't much like to recall. I was human scum, Cam. My wife wouldn't let me touch her. I was slobbering drunk all the time. Disgusting, with my personal habits, and my food, and . . . in the bathroom. She found me ugly, and I was. This particular New Year's Eve, my son Clark was only ten. We were goin' to a big party, so he needed a sitter. I really tied one on that night. Afterwards, I had to drive the sitter home. She was a pretty girl, sixteen. I . . . stopped the car and . . . attacked her.

Cam: Oh, Christ.

Duncan: I didn't . . . succeed. But she got hysterical, y'know, and the ashtray was open. I banged her head against the ashtray and cut her face. Eight stitches then, at City Hospital. *Pause.* So they left, my wife and Clark. Went to the States. He'd be a young man now. *He is suddenly incredulous.* Isn't it *amazing*? The craving's on me now, talkin' about it. Oh, God help me, I want a drink! It's this damn house.

Cam: Don't blame your craving on my house.

Duncan: When I tell my story at the meetings, I know there's none to be had. *To Ross.* But this man dares to have it on the premises.

Ross: No, he doesn't!

Cam: I *do*. Christ, this is a waste of time. . . .

Duncan: You do! And if I asked you for a shot I'll bet you'd give me one.

Ross: Jesus, Cam, be careful . . .

Cam: If you asked, I probably would. So you'd better hie your way out of here!

Duncan: You see? This man is dangerous! He has no interest in sobriety. He'd send me back to hell. *Whirling on Cam.* You're awful near it Cam. Your wife's out punching a clock, you beat the shit out of your daughter, and still you'd offer me poison. I'm getting the hell out of here and I'm never coming back. *He goes for the coats.*

Cam: *Don't* come back! Whadya think you are, Duncan, my Saviour? You're a *clerk*. That's all you ever were, a clerk in a hardware store, selling nuts and screws and molly bolts!

Ross: Now, watch it, Cam! That's your biggest problem . . .

Duncan: It is, Cam, you're arrogant . . .

Cam: And you're so self-righteous it makes me vomit!

Ross: Campbell, you've developed one hell of a superiority complex.

Cam: *A moment passes. It is for Cam a moment of contrition.* It's because I've lost so much, and I'm trying like hell to hold onto something. And I've realized that all I've got to hold onto is what I carry around in my head. My judgements, my opinions . . . my standards, if you will. *He turns to Duncan, furiously.* Damn it, Duncan, you admit, don't you, that a Chevy ain't a Rolls? That cotton isn't silk, that copper isn't gold? But when it comes to human beings you get very *Marxist*. You want to level me off, so

I fit your own scheme of mediocrity. I can't, and I won't accept it! *He continues, losing all logic and finally, ranting.* Hardware clerks don't run the province! I ran the province for Havilland Tobacco! For twelve years in a row my office led the national profits. Christ, I didn't have enough ass to *kiss* in those days!

Ross: Campbell, it's the past! Turn the page, man, it's all negative!

Cam: I didn't rape, I didn't flood, I didn't steal! All I did was *trust.* Three men gave me their word and I trusted it. There was a promise of a pitched battle in my behalf, and do you know what there was? Silence. The turncoats made their appropriate noises. That's all you could hear in the hushed silence. The sound of their coats, turning. And I will never recover from that!

Ross: Cam, Gordie Robertson, the pharmacist, he lost . . .

Cam: *Calmly now, as if by rote.* Gordie Robertson lost two sons in the war. Bill McAskill's missus crashed the car, and you can see him any day, wheeling his paralyzed wife around the grocery store. Andrew Forbes got cancer and they cut off his testicles. The town is *full* of recovery stories. Those were acts of fate, Ross. The worst crimes are the crimes of men. And I can't find recovery in your volumes of sanctimonious, therapeutic, A.A. platitudes.

Ross: The recovery's not in the literature, Cam. It's in yourself.

Duncan: You're weak, Cam! You're a gutless wonder. All you ever had was ass to kiss. In here, *he gestures,* where the innards are supposed to be, you're an empty vessel.

Cam: Get the hell out! I won't be called names by the likes of you! G'wan! Get out!

Duncan: Child beater!

Cam: *Rapist!*

Ross: Duncan!

Cam: Get out!

Duncan: Gutless bastard!

Cam: Get out and don't ever come back!

The lights dim slowly to black. Very gradually, a faint light is seen, moonlight, in Jean's bedroom. Jean is in bed. In this almost total darkness, we see Cam. He moves stealthily past the bed to the beautifully carved walnut closet door. Simultaneously, at the moment Cam enters, a dim light comes up on the living room area. Both scenes are taking place at approximately three a.m. Melzewski lingers in the living room, wearing his coat, waiting. He removes two bottles of whiskey from a paper bag and sets them on a table. Cam must remove the two pins from the hinges on the door. There is no anger, and there is no haste in this activity. There is only quiet resignation. In deep shadow, Cam takes a pair of pliers from the tool case, and loosens the top hinge. At the first noise, Jean sits up in bed, startled. She reaches back and pulls the chain on the small silk-shaded reading lamp that is clamped to the top of her bed. Cam stops his activity and the two look at each other. It is a look of ineffable sadness, and it is broken only when Jean glances in Melzewski's direction. She knows he is there, waiting in the living room, for her closet door. Cam removes both pins and lays them in the tool box. Jean watches him complete the task, wordlessly. He lifts the door out of its hinges and then, as he prepares to carry it out, he pauses. He is unable to look at Jean. He steadies the door and looks at the floor.

Cam: The sad thing is, we'll forget the dozen years we had the door. Time will pass and it'll all blur, and we may even forget each other. All we'll remember is this long night.

He takes the door out of the bedroom and carries it into the living room. Melzewski takes the door, turns and exits. Jean turns off the light.

Lights up on Cam in the rocker, two weeks later. Ruth enters the living room area. She drags in, bone-tired, emotionally-spent. Cam does not acknowledge her. She looks at him, realizes she will get no notice, and then begins to remove her coat and boots. Jean remains, sitting in the bed.

Ruth: Any change in Jean?

Cam: None.

Ruth: I haven't been at work. I lost four hours today. Five dollars. Two meals. *Pause.* Do you want to know where I was? *No reply.* You don't care.

Cam: Halverson didn't check on Jean today. First time in two weeks she didn't call.

Ruth: She didn't call because she sent for me. That's where I was. *Suddenly flaring.* I can't handle all this, all alone, Cam! How much energy do you think I've got? I feel like a sponge that can't absorb another drop. I can't *deny* we've got big trouble. I can't *explain* why Jean won't talk. *Pause.* I tried to. She was a nice lady.

Cam: Was she? Decent?

Ruth: Very.

Cam: Good.

Ruth: I told her the silence started two weeks ago, when Melzewski took the door. I told her Sarah, at work, offered me twenty dollars so I could go to Melzewski and buy back the door. You know what she said? She said it wouldn't do any good.

Cam: It wouldn't. The door isn't the problem.

Ruth: But that's when it started! Two weeks now . . . not a word out of her . . . force-feeding the child . . . she gets up twice a day for the bathroom and that's it! If the door isn't the problem, what is?

Cam: All of it. Her life. Me. *He gestures to himself and to Ruth.* Us. What did Halverson want?

Ruth: *She is on the verge of tears.* I can't tell you.

Cam: Of course you can!

Ruth: It's horrible!

Cam: It can't be more horrible than this. You have a daughter who lies in bed in a depression so deep it resembles a coma. You have a husband who sits in a chair like a massive, festering wound. You have a house that's been gradually emptied by the bootlegger: what did she say that's more horrible than that?

Ruth: She has a place for us. Me and Jean. There's a family across the river, Baldwin. They're looking for a cook and a girl for child care. It's room and board and a hundred a month. They have a nice apartment, for the help. I went to see it. *Pause.* It's horrible!

Cam: It sounds very good.

Ruth: *Desperately.* Oh, Campbell!

Cam: It does, Ruth. A chance, for you and Jean.

Ruth: *She waits a moment, examining his face.* It's gone, isn't it? You don't love me anymore.

Cam: Oh, I have great love for you, Ruthie. I have great sympathy for you, standing there in your five-dollar dress from Eaton's basement. And when I hold your hands, I feel your minimum wage. The kitchen, the dishpan, the scouring pads. You wear a halo, Ruthie. That's what makes you beautiful.

Ruth: But, the *Baldwins!* You want that for us? You want us to go there?

Cam: I talked with Halverson at length, on the phone. She says I'm jeopardizing the lives of both of you. She says it's up to me alone, whether I sink or swim. *Pause.* The fact is, Ruth, I don't want to swim. I don't want to drive an elevator, I won't work as a short-order cook, I won't sell Swift's sausage in the muskeg on straight commission. I will not do those things to preserve your paltry minimum. So, yes. I think you must go to the Baldwins'.

Ruth: I can't! I can't leave my house. You don't understand, Cam! You think this poverty is harder on you than on me. You think because you grew up with fine things, you think losing it all makes your loss something special. You think since I never had it in the first place, I don't miss it so much. *My* loss is special, Cam! I never had it in the first place, I had a little taste of it, I miss it all the more. You get drunk, you sit and wail, you say, "Oh God, my loaf of bread is gone!" I can't do that. I want to stay and fight for the crumbs.

Cam: What *are* they, Ruth? The crumbs?

Ruth: It is *still* good to be Mrs. MacMillan! Oh, not like the old days, when the name got me credit at the butcher. But it's still good to belong in this neighbourhood, to have this address. Selkirk's name came up the other day. They said, "He's the manager of the Bank of Montreal." I said, "Yes, he lives on my street." ... "The Reverend Gordon? ..." "Yes! ... He lives on my street." *Brief pause.* Even now, Cam, it's good to wake up with you, in the morning. And it's good for Jean, believe me, to have a private room, and a mother and a father under one roof, at one address.

Cam: You're talking about appearances! You're talking about standards and values brought in from the outside world. We have to find a truth of our own. *He pauses, and gestures in frustration.* Sometimes I don't know who's done Jean more harm, you or me.

Ruth: I have never laid a hand on that child!

Cam: No, you haven't. I send her to the doctor. I've scarred her, damn near maimed her. But we share something, Jean and I, awful as it is. We share the most excruciating remorse at what I've become. You have no concept of remorse, Ruth. You seem to think that life is some kind of mindless endurance test. You teach her *acceptance*. You teach her, by your example, that there is some kind of *honour* in getting up in the morning. Getting up and going through the motions, and never questioning the circumstances. For God's sake, Ruth, even *pigs* respond to the dawn! *Pause.* This house is an unacceptable place to live. Halverson's offered you a life-line. Take it, Ruth. Go. Leave me with my demons.

Ruth: How will you live?

Cam: It doesn't matter. It can't be your concern.

Ruth: What will you eat? I can bring you a little money. I could maybe cook a little extra, sneak it over in the evenings . . .

Cam: Yes! On the trolley. I can see you on the trolley with your proper little hat, and your galoshes held together at the back with electrical tape, and a Tupperware container in your lap with a piece of stolen chicken! I despise your goodness, Ruth. Your every gesture, your every word diminishes me all the more. And if I have to sit another week with my wee bairn in that room in that bed that's become her asylum, I swear to God I'll lock the lot of us in here and burn the place down! *He is crying. Ruth moves to go to him. He holds up a hand to stop her.* Do me a kindness, Ruth! Rid me of this pain. Grab hold of Halverson's life-line, and go. *Ruth moves slowly into the bedroom. Very gently, she helps Jean leave the bed. Supporting her, Ruth exits, with Jean.* I think I sat with Baldwin once, at a curling bonspiel. Fred? Frank? Gave him a cup of coffee from my thermos. Can't recall his face. Should have paid more attention since he's now to be the . . . steward of my family.

Lights fade. Cam exits. Knocking is heard at the door.

Halverson: *From outside.* Hello? Hello? *Cam returns and goes to the door. Lights up. Jean's closet is empty.* Good evening.

Cam: Hello.

Halverson: I'm Martha Halverson.

Cam: Yes, may I take your coat?

Halverson: No, thank you. Are they ready?

Cam: They'll be down in a minute. Nasty weather out there.

Halverson: Yes! Isn't it?

Cam: Have they ploughed the streets?

Halverson: Only Avenue A. Luckily, I have chains.

Cam: Please, sit down.

Halverson: *She seats herself. There is an awkward moment of silence.* This can't be easy for you. Would you like to talk?

Cam: Oh, no, thank you. All talk has become reproach these days.

Halverson: I didn't mean to do that. I mean if you had any questions.

Cam: This man, Baldwin. Is he part of the lumber concern?

Halverson: Yes. He and his two brothers run it. Mrs. Baldwin was a nurse at City Hospital, before her marriage.

Cam: I see.

Halverson: She's originally from Winnipeg. They're very active in the Presbyterian church, and Mr. Baldwin belongs . . .

Cam: Miss Halverson, there's no need to present their credentials. I'm sure everything is in order. *He turns away, not wanting to make small talk.*

Halverson: *She understands, and detours the conversation.* I saw you and Mrs. MacMillan on the stage once.

Cam: Really?

Halverson: Yes, it was a talent show, at the Roxy Theatre. Some years ago.

Cam: Oh, yes. That was a benefit for the Watson Club.

Halverson: You sang "Tiptoe Through the Tulips."

Cam: Yes. I think we got third prize. We weren't very good because we were very nervous. We'd only done it at parties, y'know. Never before strangers.

Ruth and Jean are seen on the landing, carrying suitcases and a canvas carry-all.

Ruth: Hello, Miss Halverson.

Halverson: Hello. Well, you seem to be all set. I'm parked right out front.

Ruth: Have you got chains?

Halverson: Yes.

Ruth: *She pauses, not knowing how to proceed. She then goes for her coat.* I think it's best that we get on with it.

Halverson: Jean? Is it clear to you? Do you understand about the Baldwins? *Jean nods "yes".*

Ruth: She's not scared. She's willing.

Cam: Excuse me, may I—would you mind? I'd like to speak to Jean, before she goes. *To Ruth.* Alone, Ruthie.

Ruth: Oh?

Cam: I won't hurt her.

Halverson: *To Ruth.* Perhaps we could wait in the car.

Ruth: Yes. *She goes to Cam and embraces him. She does not kiss him, nor does she meet his eyes.* I'll call you in a few days, when we're settled in. *She moves away, quickly.*

Halverson: Please, take your time. *She guides Ruth out. Ruth pauses for a last look at her house. They exit.*

Cam: Would you like to sit down? *There is no reaction.* You'd like to stand, I guess, after so much time in bed. I'd like you to know, Jeannie, that nothing escapes me. I see the threadbare couch. I see the mends in the fingers of your gloves. I see your mother's faded dresses hanging on the line. She wears them, I suffer for them. I know your loneliness. You have no social life. You're not invited because you can't return the favour. I'm an embarrassment. *He treads carefully. He is desperate to break her silence, but he is afraid that his effort will alienate her totally.* How do you feel? *No reaction.* You must feel . . . abandoned. Betrayed. Jesus, those feelings are as personal to me as my signature. And what I've dreaded all these years is that I'd hand them down to you. And I have. People tell me . . . used to tell me . . . that you were a pretty girl. I look at you, and try to see it. You know what I see? Me. The results of my brutality. You're like a little sapling, forced to grow sideways, around an impediment. It's so painful to see, sometimes I want to block you out entirely. Snuff you out. *Another pause. Cam feels it is hopeless to touch her.* Well, you'd best go. They're waiting.

Jean: Do you hate me?

Cam: Sometimes I do. I hate you because I can't love you. And I can't love you because I've failed you.

Jean: I remember the first time I knew I loved you.

Cam: I think you should go now, Jean.

Jean: You took me with you one time, out on the road. It was before school, I think I was five. We went south through the Qu'Appelle Valley. We drove through the rolling hills, and there were herds of wild horses, running.

Cam: They're not there anymore, Jeannie. They captured 'em and sold 'em for dog food.

Jean: I know. That's why this memory is very clear. Because the horses are gone, forever. We were alone in the car, and you were quoting poetry, and singing, and your sample case was banging around in the back seat. And your left arm—your window arm, was tanned almost black. And your inside arm was white. I thought you were nice to be with. Then we got to a town, I think it was Lumsden, and you started to sell. An old woman came out of the general store, so happy to see you. Her name was Mrs. Dennison. You told me she was eighty. She put me up on her glass counter, and gave me candy, and told me I was very lucky because my dad brought happiness to little towns where they never saw a new face. And you sang for her—Mrs. Dennison, and of course she bought everything you had. Last year you stole ten dollars out of my wallet. I'd done ironing for it, and I was very angry. Then I saw your newspaper lying open to the obituaries. Mrs. Dennison had died. I knew you'd spent the ten for flowers. I loved you for that, but I couldn't tell you because I'd done all that ironing and I thought it right to be mad. I haven't been able to love you since then, because you're making me sick.

Cam: These people, the Baldwins. They'll make you work, but I don't think they'll make you sick.

Jean: *Begins to put on her coat.* You should eat something.

Cam: Yes.

Jean: Mum's got egg salad in the refrigerator. You could make yourself a sandwich. *Cam nods "yes". He does not look at Jean.* Goodbye. *Jean exits.*

Cam goes to the telephone, and rips it out of the wall.

Melzewski enters with Ernest, a lean, attractive boy of twenty. Ernest wheels a dolly. There is a cardboard case on the dolly, containing six bottles of whiskey.

Mike: Have they gone?

Cam: Yes.

Mike: This is my nephew, Ernest.

Cam: Ernest?

Ernest: Hello.

Cam: How do you do? Tell me, lad, didja ever hear the one about the worm that was crawling in dead earnest?

Ernest: No, sir, I never heard that one. Where do you want the carton?

Cam: *Pointing.* Right there is fine. Well, look at this. Six amber beauties. Enough to take the hard edge off many, many days. *To Ernest, referring to the dolly.* You can take that right around to the kitchen. Will you want a hand with it?

Ernest: No, sir. I can manage it. *He goes.*

Mike: Cam, with this piece of goods you're cutting your throat. Are you crazy? What's happened?

Cam: Jean's been walking around here like a goddamned mental case since you took her door.

Mike: Uh huh. Jean's a mental case, Ruth's a kraut peasant. I'm your bohunk St. Bernard. We're all assholes but you. Cam, this is no ordinary piece of goods! A kitchen stove's the hub of the home. Even on the west side the bums, the winos, the guys drinking vanilla extract, they hang onto their stoves.

Cam: Michael, spare me. All I want from you, man, is consistency. So that, a month from now, if you find me on my ass in a snowbank, you'll give me a pint and take my cufflinks.

Ernest enters, rolling the dolly with the stove strapped onto it.

Mike: Well, now let's see. *He opens the oven and peers in.* Oh, that's nice. Spotless. My mother used to say, "A good woman keeps a clean oven." Come on, Ernie, let's roll it on the truck. *Mike and Ernest move to the door.*

Ernest: Goodnight, Mr. MacMillan.

Cam: Goodnight, Ernest. *To Mike.* What's his last name?

Mike: Staychuck.

Cam: When the hell are you people going to learn to make proper introductions?

Mike: *Pausing at the door.* Cam, I've got all your cufflinks.

Cam: I know. It's a bitch. Goodnight. *Mike exits. Cam goes to the thermostat and turns it down. He goes to the door and shoves the bolt across. He pulls the cord from the wall and throws it over the radio. His eyes fall on some A.A. pamphlets, which he picks up.* "We admitted we were powerless over alcohol, that our lives had become unmanageable." *The pamphlets fall.* I admit, I admit. But what do you do after that? How do you *live*, after you admit? *He has had a bottle tucked under his arm. Quickly, he opens it and peers into it.* Are you there, demons? Vermin? Parasites? Any suggestions you might offer would be deeply appreciated. *He exits as:*

Jean enters. She is dressed as she was at the beginning of the play.

Jean: He gave us, as Miss Halverson said, choices. At first, there was terror in our freedom, but we quickly learned the appropriate noises of survival. We worked, and we saved, and we prospered. He'd isolated himself to such an extent, it was hard to find pallbearers for his funeral. The Reverend Angus Gordon presided at the ceremony, and concentrated on the early, rosy days. When Dad had maroon window blinds and led the Travellers' Day Parade. As we sat and listened to the tribute, we squirmed a bit in the pew. We had both come to realize that the most admirable thing he'd done in his life was let us go. And that, of course, wasn't mentioned in the pulpit.

Ruth comes part-way down the hall, in dim light. She is smiling. She is dressed as she would have been for a dinner at the Bessborough Hotel.

Jean: Shortly afterwards, I was given a scholarship. We celebrated by putting on our best finery and going down to the Bessborough Hotel for dinner. The maitre d' greeted us and said, "And don't you two ladies look very well tonight!" Mum turned and said, "That man's judging us by the way we look now." She settled back into her chair and said, "The truth of people isn't where they are now. It's in the space between that, and where they came from."

Cam is seen, up left of Jean. He is smiling. He is dressed in the suit, tie and fedora from the early forties. The house lights dim as Jean stands center stage, flanked by each parent.

Curtain

The Occupation of Heather Rose

by Wendy Lill

First Performance

The Occupation of Heather Rose was premiered February 27, 1986, at
Prairie Theatre Exchange, Winnipeg, under the direction of Kim
McCaw, with original music by John McCulloch and lighting design
by Larry Isacoff. Heather Rose was performed by Laurel Paetz.

"What sort of people live about here?"

"In that direction," the cat said, "lives a Hatter and in that direction, lives a March Hare. Visit either one you like. They're both mad."

Alice in Wonderland

"I went a little farther . . . then still a little farther—til I had gone so far that I don't know how I'll ever get back."

Heart of Darkness

Hubert Pantel
Laurel Paetz as Heather Rose
Prairie Theatre Exchange, Winnipeg, 1986

Act One

*Heather Rose enters room wearing a light jacket over a nurse's uni-
form, carrying a brown paper bag. There is a table and chair in the
room, a blackboard, promotional posters for Northern Medical Services, Indian Affairs, Ministry of Natural Resources, Northern Affairs
etc. on the walls. Heather looks around at the posters, puts down her
paper bag, and looks at her watch.*

Heather Rose: *To herself.* I wonder if I still look the same.
I asked her to meet me at nine o'clock.
But I'm always early.

Oh, I'm not ready for this.

Turns towards audience.

I have always been an optimistic cheery type of person. I take
after . . . both my parents on this score. On Saturday mornings, the
three of us competed to see who could be the most bubbly, the
most cheerful at the breakfast table.
That's probably why my sister left home so young. She just
couldn't stand the pressure.

It began nine months ago. No, of course it didn't. It began long
before that.

My mother had been a nurse in the slums of London. And my dad
was a high school principal, the kind everyone visits years later
with things like plastic ice cubes with bugs inside.

Every Christmas, we had refugees from the International Centre
sent over for turkey dinner.
So when I told my parents I was going to work on an Indian
reserve, they were positively bubbly. I guess they thought I was
. . . following in their footsteps.

I remember that first day barrelling through space in that hollow
hairspray can of a plane, the sound of a thousand mosquitoes
approaching my pillow in the dark, the hard cold metal wing
vibrating against my thigh, long pink and purple tubes of land
forming then breaking off into water, then land, more water, more
wing . . . and in front of me, Ray, the pilot, lighting one Player's

after another, blowing lazy circles of smoke back towards my waiting nostrils.

Did he know how sexy I thought he was?

"What's it like being king of the skies, Ray?" Carrying the Royal Mail and life-giving medicines, on the lookout for red handkerchiefs and downed planes and forest fires and horny . . . living out one's dreams?

"You must really love your work, Ray. No speed limits, no parking tickets, no Sunday drivers." What a flirt.

"Who me? What brings me here? Oh, I've always been attracted to the north . . . like a firefly to light. No . . . never this far before. Mainly the Barrie area, but it's a lot like this. One-sided trees, fiery sunsets, loons. . . . You've heard of Camp Cocano?"

The bugger didn't answer me. Just laughed. And turned the nose of the plane down. Suddenly I was on the Salt And Pepper Shaker at the CNE, giggling and holding onto my pockets so my money wouldn't fall out!

I was going down, down, downward into another place, another time, falling through a rabbit hole into a green and silver world below. I was Alice in Wonderland. Shall I fall right through the earth? Splashing into a shower of diamonds and purple morning mist and water . . . bobbing up and down in a plane which had miraculously become a boat.

"No Ray, I didn't mind. Rough? Was that rough? Hey! I love *rough*. Excitement, danger. Makes me feel like I've really arrived! Really alive!"

And I had.

Arrived.

Nurse Rose had arrived. The metal door swung open and the sun blasted in. And there below me, on the dock, was a sea of brown faces all looking up at me, in my slingback pumps and my seersucker dress. What made me suddenly feel that my heart would fall out, that I would die on the spot? And also, that I was . . . the Queen?

Heather gives a regal smile, even a wave.

But not for long.

"Holy Jesus Mary . . . what the hell have we got here?"

He stood there inspecting me like a catfish just hauled in off the bottom. Then he laughed . . . no, he snorted at me.

"Name's Ramsay, Miss Rose. The local freetrader, skirtchaser, swindler, philosopher and long-term survivor. Welcome to Snake Lake."

Suddenly back in the present, Heather looks at her watch, then towards the door. Seems agitated, uncomfortable, then retreats back into her recollections.

The nursing station. It had such a nice ring to it, I thought. The nursing station. Where the nurse was stationed. Where she was present and waiting for people in distress. In need of help. The first thing I did was unpack Mother and Grandmother. I mean their pictures! I set them up on the arborite desk with their nursing caps and serene smiles to guide me in my work at Snake Lake. Then I began to plow through Nurse Bunny's eight months of medical records. I've brought back a couple of entries back to show Miss Jackson.

Takes some rumpled papers from bag and reads.

"March 10. Jobit Loon died of a shaking fit. Out on his trapline with a beaver in his mitt. And no toque on. The day was dark when they brought him in, his skin grey, his wife watching. Her eyes a long way away."

That's quite poetic I think.

Holds up paper. Then a sketch of a broken snowshoe.

Bunny did a lot of things like that. Sketches, cartoons. And cigarette burns. Bunny was a chain smoker. And this. *Reads another.*

"March 15. Moonias Turtle died of exposure. Frozen stiff like a chicken you take out of the freezer." Imagine someone even thinking a thing like that? But Bunny did. Then this one.

"May 15. Entire bottom end of reserve has diarrhea. Toilet backed up. Closed early." *Laughs.* That one always killed me! Entire bottom end . . . toilet backed up. . . .

Then a series of "closed earlys". Translation: "Hung over." But I only learned that later. Once Miss Jackson gets a better picture of the place. . . .

Heather turns, sticks the pages up on the bulletin board. Turns back to the audience, looks nervous.

I don't really drink. *Not completely convincing.* But Nurse Bunny did.

Lorraine McCain, one of the Snake Lake teachers, came by ten minutes after I arrived at my trailer with a bottle of scotch and a bag of chocolate chip cookies, . . . " just to welcome the latest lamb to the slaughter." Immediately started telling tales out of school about Bunny—about what a *good head* she was, and about how they'd had to take two cartons of Jack Daniels empties out of our trailer after she left. I'd been told that Snake Lake was a *dry* reserve and I thought that meant *dry*. No alcohol. When I mentioned that to Lorraine, she just gave me sort of a fishy look, said I could be as dry as I wanted, or as wet.

Friendly. "Would you like some herbal tea? I've got Spicy Apple, Morning Thunder, and Sleepy Time somewhere in my suitcases, if I can find it. . . ." I really said that. Yeah, I did.

"Never touch the stuff," she said. Tugged down her bra, hauled herself up off the chesterfield. Said she'd better let me get some sleepy time myself. And then was out the door . . . with the bottle of scotch.

Rough and tough Lorraine. What a character. But I felt sort of rough and tough myself. Gutsy. Ready for anything. I unpacked, got my posters up on the wall, toothbrush in the little holder in the bathroom, shoes lined up in the closet. Uniform pressed and ready for the morning. I remember I wandered from room to room, touching everything, and when I caught sight of myself in the bedroom mirror, I couldn't help smiling. No. . . . Grinning! It was like "Hey, look at me. I've really done it! I'm *here*! In the middle of an adventure."

And then it was night. Black night. There were no street lights. No big blue neon "H" from the hospital bathing my room with light 'til I closed it out with sleep. No strains of Lionel Richie coming through the flimsy residence walls. A gentle autumn breeze stirring the pines outside ... sh-h-h-h ... the drip drop drip drop of the nylons I'd hung to dry in the shower stall. Were there animals out there in the darkness? Bears, wolves, moose? Were there Indians out there? My patients? Was there a world outside in the shadows waiting for me? Of course there was. But what was more important right then was what was going on *inside* me! I've heard women describe a feeling that comes over them right after giving birth. Sort of a humming. That's how I felt that first night lying in the dark. Kind of a humming.

Big sigh. Looks at watch, paces. Clearly agitated.

I think it's really shitty to keep people waiting. I flew eight hundred miles to be here this morning and I'm ten minutes early. Miss Jackson just lives a couple of blocks away. And she's already ten minutes late. I guess she wants to keep me waiting. Well, I'm used to it. I probably won't be able to really talk to her anyway. I tried on the phone one time but she wasn't 'amused'. Might as well have been talking to a brick wall ... to a wooden one.

Heather goes over to the blackboard, writes the word: INDIAN.

Indians.

One night in the middle of winter I wrote that word four hundred times on my dining room table cloth.

My first patient was Camilla Loon. She arrived with Mary Kwandibens, the nurse's aide. Mary and her beautiful daughter Naomi. Camilla and Naomi. My first patient and my last.

Camilla's face was like a worn old leather purse without the coins. And when she opened her mouth, soft little noises came out, like coos from a dove. Her wooden leg was hurting her.

"Well no wonder Mrs. Loon. I've never *seen* such an old prosthesis! We'll have to get you fitted for a new one, and while we're at it, how about a new set of false teeth."

Heather looks pleased with herself, competent. Then looks behind her.

"What is she looking at Mary? Does she understand what I'm saying?"

At orientation, Miss Jackson told us Indians don't look you in the eye. And it's true. She was at least right about that. Camilla Loon looked at the top button of my uniform as if it had some mysterious power over her. And Mary K. looked at my feet when I tried to shake hands with her. But that didn't bother me 'cause it gave me a chance to study them.

Mary and Naomi Kwandibens for God's sake. Loon. Moonias. Atlookan. Quill. Makoop. Names that hold laughter one bubble below the surface. Names out of the blue, out of the any old where . . . soft, velvety names like their eyes. Which don't look into yours.

Indians.

Mary Kwandibens is very fat. Her skin is very brown and there is so much of it. And when she laughs, her whole body jiggles and she was laughing a lot that day. So was Naomi. So was Camilla. She probably felt great about ordering up a new set of legs and teeth. They were eating their lunch at the diagnostic table while I kept on with old Bun's medical records. But really I was studying them.

There is something to the theory that opposites attract. All my life I'd wanted to have hair like Naomi's. Black and silky like a raven's. Not this dirty old mop. And other things too. I'd wanted to be dark, not fair. Straight, not curly. Enigmatic, mysterious, not an open book. It wasn't that I wanted to be an Indian, but I sure wouldn't have minded being a bit more complex.

As I watched Mary and Naomi and Camilla sitting there, I had this overwhelming urge to hug each one of them. To engulf them. As if some of the good things might rub off them onto me. And vice versa. I'd learn their customs and they'd learn mine. About my Scottish grandmother, my highland dancing lessons and Robbie Burns' poetry. And we'd all get on like a house afire. And when I caught Naomi's eye and she smiled, I remember thinking she was going to be just like my little sister.

"Move over, Naomi. How 'bout letting me try some of that

bannock!"

I went to see the chief.

"This is a real honour, sir. Chief Red Sky. I've never met an Indian chief before. I guess I was expecting you to be ... older. Kind of like Dan George.

"Where did you get those topaz rings? God, they're *so* beautiful! I love it here. It's ... beautiful! The air smells so fresh, and the birds, and the wildflowers. ..."

To audience. He'd already heard about my order for artificial limbs and false teeth.

"Oh heavens, they'll show up. I ordered them through Northern Medical Services. They promised them within four to six weeks!"

Unlike most Indians, the chief had eyes that looked into yours, sort of drew you in then pushed you away again. Maybe that's why he got to be chief. Told me it was getting harder and harder to eat well and stay healthy at Snake Lake. That the fish were full of chemicals from the paper plant up the river, that the wild rice didn't grow since the government put in the hydro dam. And that it was hard to keep your kids clean when there wasn't enough money for proper sewage. And that. ...

Heather holds up her hand to interrupt.

"Hey! Excuse me, Chief! But I *know* all about the problems. (I learned it all at my orientation week.) I want to talk about *solutions*. I've been thinking about an exercise club for women to improve their self image ... women always need to improve their self image. And a good food club to work on our eating habits now that fish and wild rice have been kind of blown out of the water. Ha ha. We'll draw up a list and get Mr. Ramsay to start stocking more nutritional foods. ... I mean I've taken a look at his store and. ... *Gesture of dismissal.* Cling peaches and red hots are all right, but a little goes a long way. ...

And at orientation, I heard your alcohol and drug abuse commit- tee has kind of lost direction. So I want to join that and add some life to it. *Big confident smile.*

And as for the teenagers, well, they just don't have anything to *do*! When I was that age, I'd have gone *crazy* without camp. If we could get a drop-in centre happening at the high school—do some arts and crafts, show movies. . . . *Listens.*

I'm twenty-one, sir. I guess you're thinking that I'm kind of young and inexperienced. But I like to think I've got a fresh new outlook.

Mr. Chief Red Sky, I know there are some really terrible problems here but . . . look at me! I managed to scrape through nursing school and I'm no Einstein! And I've been dieting for ten years so I wouldn't look like an elephant leaping about in my kilt at dancing competitions.

Things can get better, can't they? Well, can't they?"

Heather walks around the room, musing over the experience in her mind. Goes to blackboard. Writes the word: WHITES.

Whites.

That's a funny expression, isn't it?

Whites. 'Cause we're not really white, are we? We're sort of pink and beige. The whites at Snake Lake dress in Saturday-at-the-laundromat clothes seven days a week, and they march purposefully about, from store to community hall, to church, to canteen, to dock, to teacherage. . . ." Hiya Janie, how's by you!"

"How's she goin' Ray?"

"Takin' her easy are ya?"

Pushing the Indians off the roads as they barrel from place to place. And always visiting . . . no . . . checking on one another.

Lorraine lived in the teacherage, a pink townhouse complex built, she said, to lure teachers to the North. Wall-to-wall carpets, central heating, glass doors on the shower, wrought iron bannisters, cathedral ceilings, but according to Lorraine, the units were cold in the winter and not bright enough. They needed skylights and more cupboard space, more this, more that. . . .
I would have sold my soul to the devil to live in one of those units. I'd hang spider plants and wandering Jews from the ceiling, swish up and down the broadloomed staircase in my velour robe . . . who needs skylights?

"You're gonna kill yourself and then what'll they do for a nurse?"

Lorraine was visiting with her cannister of gin gimlets, watching me puff my way through my Raquel Welch dancercises. Filling me in on the Snake Lake gossip. About the legendary teacher Annadora.

Apparently Annadora "did it" with anything that wore pants. Every Friday night, she'd make a batch of butter tarts, then bellow over to Ramsay to come help her eat them. By ten o'clock, they'd be riproaring drunk, full of tarts and chasing the cat up and down the redwood staircase.

Annadora laughed backwards like a donkey. And as the evening wore on, the sound of her laughter rose higher and higher so that it kept the whole reserve awake. You'd think that would have been enough of a reason to fire old Annadora, but in fact, what finally did her in was something else.

Annadora began inviting Indian boys over after school. That's when Joe Red Sky told Education Services that they didn't want Annadora teaching their children anymore. In fact, the Indians actually carried her down to the dock and shoved her on the plane. Goodbye Annadora.

Lorraine said she got "hooked" on brown meat, that Indian men were different than white men. That they smelled different, and they they had warm skin and that they were better in bed. I could tell she was trying to shock me, so I just kept doing my exercises all the harder, my face to the wall.

"Got a boyfriend, honey?" She actually called me honey!

"No, but I'm keeping myself in shape in the event that someone might come along."

As Lorraine. "You have to take what you can get here. I have a little thing going with a Mountie stationed at Sioux Falls. 'Bout Thursday I start praying for hunting accidents or drownings, so he'll fly in for the weekend to investigate. Rest of the time, I make do with Ray, the bootlegger. Keeps me in gin."

As Heather. "Do you mean Ray, the pilot Ray?" None other. He was probably carrying booze that day I arrived, not antiseptic and the Royal Mail. So much for living out one's dreams.

Lorraine, and her Mountie, Annadora, Ray and then Ramsay. Ramsay! When I went to see Ramsay about stocking brown rice and fresh vegetables. . . .

As Ramsay. "It's hard living on an Indian reserve," he said. "Your friends in the South forget you, your magazines never come. People hear every word you're saying on the radio telephone so you can't be intimate with someone a long way away. Everyone will talk about you, even laugh at you. It'll get to the point that you even think the ravens are laughing at you, and when that happens, come and see me. Old Ramse will give you a shot of stamina."

Thanks but no thanks. What were all those people doing at Snake Lake? Not exactly the type you'd invite home for Sunday dinner. Not exactly sparkling representatives of our culture. They were there because they didn't fit anywhere else. But they'd be the last to admit it.

Lorraine told me she didn't much like Indians 'cause they were a "broken people" but not to worry 'cause they didn't like us much either.

Well what's to like, I wanted to say. If all you're getting is leftovers, how do you know whether you'd enjoy the meal. I was determined not to be like them.

Heather writes the word: CULTURE *on the blackboard.*

Culture.

At orientation, we spent a whole afternoon on culture. Miss Jackson told us that going from white to Indian culture was like going from your rumpus room into your fruit cellar.

She said that cultures were all about imagining. For example, she told us when Indians looked out on a lake, they imagined shaking tents and spirit visions and powwows and canoes filled with braves moving silently across the water, thunderbirds circling overhead. . . .

Whereas when we look out on a lake, we see something different. When I looked out on Snake Lake, I imagined hundreds of bodies lying elbow to elbow on little sandy towels, sailboats and air mattresses bobbing, tiny voices emerging from sandy radios. . . .

Culture.

Norma Redbird lived with her parents, her brother, her wrinkled grandmother, and five assorted others in a white frame shack no bigger than my kitchen nook and living room combined.

Part of my culture was to feel uncomfortable about barging into other peoples' homes uninvited, but that was my job, so I swallowed hard and. . . .

Cheery. "Hi, Norma! How's the new mom! I'm here to check you and the baby! What are you doing inside on a beautiful day like this? This is Indian summer. *Laughs.* I've heard about your winters that last from October to May. You and little Dolores should be outside getting some fresh air, some exercise while you still can!"

Watching *Let's Make A Deal* reruns is what they were doing, all of them, including the five-day-old infant.

Heather looks uncomfortable, smiles, shifts about.

"The baby looks good. Good colour. Alert. Curious. That's a cute top she's wearing. I think she could use some eyedrops. Why don't you bring her in this week and I'll give her a thorough checkup."

A huge piece of frozen meat thawing out in front of the TV; Monty Hall making jokes with two women from South Dakota dressed up as chickens; me in my nurse's uniform yacking away about cute tops and eye drops.

How did I feel? Like a spaceship which had landed in the middle of their living room, sending out little beeps.

"Spaceship Rose to earth. . . . I've located the Indians. . . . What am I supposed to do now?"

Focus on food. Highlight hygiene. Win them over. Make connections.

"Oh-h-h-h . . . it's so *dark* in here. I saw some calico at the store for two-fifty a yard. . . . It would make nice curtains for those windows, and if you had some leftovers, you could make a tablecloth to cover up that oilcloth. Really brighten up the place. *Smiles nervously, fidgets.*

Pulls out some filecards from her brown bag.

"What are you having for dinner tonight? Oh ... I'm not inviting myself. I just saw that piece of meat thawing on the floor. I've never *seen* such a large roast. It looks so *fresh*! Wild! But I'm trying to cut down on meat. Have you ever heard of cholesterol? It's very bad for us. Very. These are some suggestions to help us all be a little less meat-dependent. I'll just leave them here to help you with your meal planning."

... to ... to help you with your meal planning. ...

Heather shudders, rips up her meal plans, tacks up the pieces on the bulletin board.

That day, at Norma Redbird's, was the first time I really began wondering about ... a lot of things.

Someone was lying and I wasn't sure who.

Miss Jackson told us that part of Indian culture was close family ties, and that was why they lived in such cramped quarters. Bullshit. They were poor. They had no jobs. And nothing to do all day but watch reruns. And nothing to do tomorrow either. No prospects. I had never seen or tasted or smelled poverty before, and it scared me.

At orientation, we called her Ironpants. She always smelled like baby powder, and she was no baby. She's old and wrinkled and warty and never had any babies at all ... probably no sex at all. No babies, no sex, no bad odours ... what did she know about Indians or family ties, or poverty or culture? All that shit about rumpus rooms and fruit cellars. And imagining. What were the Redbirds imagining—me standing there with my *Canada Food Guide* and sunburned nose, trying to out shout two women dressed in chicken suits, telling them their house was dirty and their food disgusting. Who the hell did I think I was?

Saying someone has a different culture is just a polite way of saying they're *weird*. Not special, not privileged. Not exotic. Not mysterious at all. They're inferior. And therefore need to be helped. Translation. Altered. So much for culture! *Rips up* Canada Food Guides.

Distraught, pacing.

An Indian reserve is not a nine-to-five place. Nor a September-to-June place. It's a hanging-around place. I watched Naomi the Raven and her silent stalking friends in their bright satin jackets that said TRIUMPH and BLACK SABBATH, sauntering around the reserve in their Puma sneakers and blue jeans, quiet; making long-legged circular treks along the dusty roads that went nowhere. They went in and out of school like casual visitors. They never carried books or pencil cases. Even though Naomi was in Grade 10, she could hardly read. Mary said she was getting into trouble. That she was a bad girl. "Oh Mary, who isn't *bad* at that age? Everyone wants to be bad!"

So bad! I did. But I wasn't. In fact, I was still trying to be bad six years later, but without success! Instead, I settled for gourmet dinners on Friday nights with Nancy Anderson, the gym teacher. My only *real* friend at Snake Lake. The first time I met her, she was jogging along the beach in sweatpants and a t-shirt that said HAVE AN INDIAN AFFAIR!

Nancy and I were kindred spirits. She was helping me with the women's fitness program, which after eight weeks of promotion still just brought out two women—Nancy and me. We were both on the alcohol and drug committee. Trying to get some action on the reserve's bootlegging problem. Apparently Ray flew the booze in and Ramsay sold it at any hour, and at any price. Both of us had written off the "white trash" at Snake Lake; and both of us were saving for trips to Europe. We talked for hours about Eurailpasses and adapters for hairdryers, and the Orient Express and running into Jean Paul Belmondo on the Champs Elysée. It passed the time. Summer was gone and the nights were getting longer and longer. . . .

There was a cold mist on the lake in the mornings when I opened the station.

I felt kind of lonely, adrift. . . .

Mimes picking up phone.

"Hi Mom! Hi. I sound far away? Well I guess that's because I am! Ha ha. I sound *funny*? It must be the line. No. There is nothing wrong. No, I just called . . . to talk. To talk! *Talk.* You know . . . *talk.* I'm fine. Great. Oh yeah . . . lots of fun. Lots of buddies. Lots of fun. Tons. I said *tons*! No, it's just the line. It's a radio phone. That's why it's so fuzzy. Gloomy? No, I'm *not* gloomy! Great. Put him on. Hi Dad! No . . . it's just the line. Oh yeah. Cold . . . brrr. . . . Frost in the air! How's Skippy?"

Hangs up phone, begins pacing.

There was more than frost in the air.

Naomi the Raven and her friends stopped frequenting school altogether. There was a rash of vandalism on the reserve. Nancy Anderson had her tumbling mats slashed. She cried one whole evening in my trailer. Lorraine was happy. Her Mountie flew in two weekends in a row.

One night, there were gunshots outside my trailer, I lay in the dark waiting for the end. Hoping that it was a nightmare and I was going to wake up. But it wasn't a nightmare. It was the real thing. Someone shot out the windows of the Catholic church. It sat there like a scared, hapless, toothless face against the cold autumn sky. What kind of people shoot the windows out of churches? I was getting discouraged about our Indians. Things weren't working out. They still seemed so far away . . . yet their problems were so *close*! The drinking, the fights. I dreaded the weekends. The nights. The nightmares. I dreaded what I was going to see in the morning. I dreaded it all. . . .

Except when the plane arrived. That little silver sliver of wing cutting through the clouds and it was magic every time. It became a day blessed with . . . possibility.

November 2. I remember because it was my birthday and I was at the dock waiting to get a present from my parents, waiting for my medical supplies, my order of teeth and legs . . . my winter parka, my *Chatelaine* magazine, maybe for the results from the water samples.

And there was a man framed in the doorway of Ray's plane. A white man. But he was really brown. I mean *tanned.* And he had the clearest robin's-egg blue eyes in the northern hemisphere.

Stares enchanted.

I closed the nursing station an hour early so I could rush home and have a leisurely bubble bath. Wash my hair. The works. Put on my tweed slacks, my most clingy sweater. Then fashionably late, wandered over to the community hall where Mr. Blue Eyes was giving a talk about land claims. Why not? I was a member of the community. Sort of. Wasn't I? I was trying to make connections.

Flirtatious. "Hi! I'm Heather Rose. The resident Florence Nightingale! I had no idea that aboriginal rights and treaties could be so stimulating . . . so pressing . . . so. . . ." *Sexy.* "Like I really feel the need now to probe even deeper. Why don't you come home with me and we can. . . . "

No such luck. He was tied up all night with the Indians. Velvet-eyed Camilla in her red beret, tapping her cane on the floor, and dozens more weathered old souls, one after another talking about the good old days before the white man.

Growing realization. I'll be as honest as I can about this. All I wanted to do at that moment was to take that particular white man back to my trailer. Take off his clothes . . . and mine . . . and forget about Indians and land claims and hideous social conditions. But the hours ticked away. And my hair went limp. I felt embarrassed about my silly fantasies. That's all they were. Fantasies. There was no connection between the Romance of the North and my tired lonely existence as a Northern Nurse. I'd been tricked somehow. So like old Bun probably did a hundred times before me, I went home alone.

I've tried not to even think about Greek Night. Let alone talk about it.

Nancy and I cooked up *dolmathes* with cabbage instead of grape leaves, and pork *souvlaki*, and Greek salad without the *feta* cheese and black olives; wearing the Greekest things we owned; listening to Melina Mercouri, planning our four hundredth trip to Europe. The candlelight glowed softly around the table, the music blocked out the endless wind outside. Suddenly, the door flew open and there was Lorraine's big shiny face leering at us through the candlelight. Bulgy, lurid Lorraine and gin-running Ray just come for a visit, just come to see how we were enjoying our *petite soirée.*

"Got anything to drink besides this horse piss?" Meaning the fruit punch. "What kind of a nurse are you if you don't have any medication? You must have something! I mean, what do you do here every night if you're not drinking? The two of you. That's the sixty-four dollar question here at Snake. Play scrabble? Play with each other?"

Now why did they say that? Why did they even think that? Why did they have to destroy the only real comfort we had?

Heather is silent, reliving this painful memory, almost grieving.

Nancy left a week after that. Went back to Thunder Bay to work in a junior high school. Said she didn't like being away from her home and family. Said she missed her boyfriend. She left me all of her books including a cookbook called *Two Hundred Ways To Make Hamburger Sing.* Isn't that a funny title?

Heather looks vulnerable, almost in tears, suddenly trapped.

Oh, it's sweltering in here! I've got to get some fresh air.

Heather exits.

End Act One

Hubert Pantel
Laurel Paetz as Heather Rose
Prairie Theatre Exchange, Winnipeg, 1986

Act Two

Heather Rose enters. There is a new sense of urgency about her.

Heather: I realized when I went out just then that I still haven't been
very honest about this. It's all still a bit romanticized, polished up.
I haven't got to the heart of this. And if I don't, you'll never
understand. . . .

Snow. Snow white.

Sometimes, during the winter, my fantasies weren't much different than my reality. I'd see a raven or I'd dream a raven . . . and
each evoked the same aloneness, the same gaping separateness.

I'd see an Indian boy a mile out on the lake, walking towards me,
a boy with a red toque and a fur parka, perfectly placed in the
light between the sky and the world, walking across the lake,
across a bright white desert. His legs would move but he never
seemed to get any closer . . . or further away.

Mary Kwandibens told me—that was before she stopped talking
to me—that winter was a time of holding on, that the soul went
underground to lie like a woman long and straight upon a bed of
ice, to sleep and be restored, to rise up new and refreshed in the
spring like a young girl.

But that makes winter seem like a time of peace and it wasn't. It
was a horrible onslaught.

Heather writes the word: ALCOHOL *on the board.*

I do know something about alcohol. On New Year's Day, I joined
with two of the teachers in a rum toddy, to welcome in a brand
new year. If only I could describe how *good* it tasted. Hot, fiery,
sensual, merry, hospitable. For the first time in my life I felt . . .
witty!

"A little rum? Why not? To warm our cockles, wherever the hell
they are!" *Laughs.*

Leslie Walters, the new gym teacher arrived at the end of February. I beat Lorraine over to her trailer with my bottle of Bluenose.
I desperately needed an audience.

"Oh, it's not a bad place, if you don't mind scraping ice from your bedroom window in the morning just to see out." *Laughs.*

"What d'you want to know? Heather Rose tells all. The church? The natives got restless and there was a big shoot-up one night. I sound like Annie Oakley myself! It really does look like hell, doesn't it? I guess everyone prays in private now. . . . I'm not exactly a practising anything. The last thing I practiced was the flute in grade ten. *Laughs.*

"Run into Ramsay yet? He's part of the landscape here like the garbage around his store. He's harmless unless you've got a heart and soul. What else do you want to know?

"The Indians? Hard to know what they're thinking. Blow hot and cold like the frigging winds. Pardon my French. They're a broken people. It is really sad, given how beautiful the land is up here and all but . . . like it's not an *ideal* reserve, eh, otherwise none of *us* would even be here, I guess that's how you gotta look at it. Hey! Don't look so glum! Lighten up! Want another drink? Don't mind if I do. Don't mind if I do. Don't mind if I do."

With difficulty, an admission.

After being witty, with Leslie Walters, or just with myself—I thought I was the best audience of all—I put a towel over the bathroom mirror. It made the mornings easier.

Indians.

I remember when I was small, Mom told us not to talk to any of the men who changed buses at the corner by our school. They were Indians. From Munsey Reserve who worked at the mill. I wonder if I'm prejudiced towards Indians because of that?

Our next door neighbours had a daughter named Donna who studied archaeology at UBC and married an Indian. I remember Donna's father sitting in the back yard with my dad. I was under the picnic table. He was drinking a lot and he was crying. I remember him saying that digging bones with Donna was one thing, but he sure as hell didn't want one of them plugging her.

Heather smashes table. Very agitated.

Where is Miss Jackson? This is just like it was up there. No one to tell things to. To help straighten things out. I needed help. I did! Heather Rose! I planned on talking to the fly-in shrink when he came to see the Snake Lake crazies, tell him about the drinking, how I was losing my temper in front of the patients, the missed days at work.

"Doctor Allen," I rehearsed this, "I'm finding the isolation here sort of . . . getting to me."

But after Mabel Turtle told him about her husband appearing in a vision and Albert Loon describing the animals running around inside his head, and all of us sitting on orange plastic chairs around the great white doctor, and the wind howling and the windows like teeth rattling and the room spinning, all I could do was excuse myself and run out of the room—just in time to get to the bathroom.

What did he know about those people? About spirits on Snake Lake, about visions, and animals running around inside your head and long nights and dark days and crying jags and ravens that laugh at you and freezeup and no mail and . . . what the hell did he know?

All those fucking high-paid whites coming through to help the Indians—not little me! Flying in and out, in and out, in and out, consulting on this, consulting on that, flashing their million dollar smiles, stalking about the reserve from plane to community hall, to band office, to plane, with their Indian friends, being helpful and advisory, then back in the air. Once a month old Blue Eyes came and went, his tan always the same. Perfect. Probably used a sun lamp. Hope he gets skin cancer. Probably played squash, told women in satin shorts about his latest junket to desolate Indian reserve . . . about what losers we all were. . . . There was no help for me, except my rum toddies. Want another one? Don't mind if I do.

Heather seems to be reliving something painful. She is hearing Camilla's singing and sort of rocking back and forth.

Oh this is hard.

The occupation of Heather Rose.

"Mary? Mary? What is Camilla doing here, Mary? Why is she singing like that? Mary?"

Something registered in Mary's big dark face but I didn't know what. She used to make me bannock in the mornings, but not anymore. Not after I yelled at her for leaving the station unlocked. It was only for half an hour, but I yelled at her, in front of her daughter Naomi, and called her a stupid . . . Oh God!

"Mary! Answer me! I'm the nurse here. You're supposed to be helping me!"

Camilla Loon was holding a sit-in. An occupation. She was going to occupy the nursing station 'til her new leg and teeth arrived. She'd waited eight months and was tired of waiting. She was going to stay right there on that orange chair as a reminder. That she had been depending on me.

Jesus Christ, I was angry. That's right. Angry. Was it my fault that her new leg had gone to a bush camp by mistake and by the time it was shipped back, it wasn't fit for a moose to strap on? Or that the second leg got waterlogged sitting in a leaky warehouse. Or that the Department's policy was that they were only allowed new dentures every four years, so that they wouldn't be filling orders every time an Indian got drunk and dropped. . . . Hey! I didn't make the rules!

Was it my fault that the goddamned plane took the leg to the wrong place. That half the time, the plane couldn't land because of the wind . . . that things got lost in snowstorms or landing strips or alcoholic blackouts; that pilots forgot shifts or their windshield wipers wouldn't work or they couldn't take off or didn't care enough to.

"So! You think you're going to *occupy* the nursing station. Well it is *my* nursing station. My orange chairs that you stick your Bazooka gum on. My tile floors that you spill your ice cream sandwiches on. I change the toilet paper in the washroom, scrub the waiting room at the end of the day after dozens of you sat with your big snowmobile boots and silent dark eyes waiting . . . for service."

Well if I was going to service them they would have to take what I had to dish out.

"You know what really bothers me about you people? You expect me to stitch you up, give you pills, send you out to the hospitals, wipe your bloody noses and I have never once heard anyone say what you're supposed to say when someone does something *nice* for you.

"What do you say? You say 'Thank you!' To just once hear 'Thank you Miss Rose' would be music to my ears! But instead I get silence. Dark eyes. Secrets. Why is that?

"I never know what you're thinking. Never know what you really want from me. Should I stand on my hands, tell jokes, disappear? Are you glad, sad, mad when you see me? Do you like me, hate me, laugh at me, pity me, blame me?

"ANSWER ME!

"You know what I think you are? I think you're all snobs. Yes, SNOBS.

"You think you're the only ones with a goddamned history. Whenever I've tried to talk about my family . . . about being Scottish . . . things my grannie told me, little stories, or some beliefs . . . whenever I've tried to share my life . . . nobody shows any interest. Nobody gives a good goddamn about me!

"And you never bloody LOOK at me! Look at me! I know you watch me, but you won't look at me. And you talk about me, don't you? Don't you?

"You've been talking to your chief. He came to see me, said he'd heard about problems with the new nurse. NEW! That's a laugh! I feel about as NEW as the frozen dog shit all around this place.
You don't come right out and SAY things. You never let things really pour out like we do! We whites! You don't do that, do you? It's all indirect with you. Well, I'm tired of it. Tired of this goldfish bowl . . . big brother, sister, aunt, uncle watching me . . . judging me, as if I've done something wrong, as if I'm responsible for the pitiful states of your lives. . . . Jesus! When in fact I've had the charity and decency to try and help you. And I told your chief that. And I told him that I didn't want to see the next sad-eyed dark-skinned Indian coming through the door. That I wanted to see a smiling, bouncing, blonde-haired, lacy, pregnant white woman . . . who would yack away about how her baby was kicking inside, and the little clothes she was buying.

"And you know what else I told him? I told him that if he didn't like the quality of my nursing care, he could kiss my ass! And that goes for the rest of you!"

Heather looks mad, then slowly changes to look shaken, sickened by what she's said. Sits down heavily.

I became attached to a particular label on a bottle of white rum. A perfect picture of a perfect ship on a perfect horizon.

What I especially liked was the way the sky kind of lit up the background. That's one of the redeeming graces about Snake Lake. In winter. The sky. And the ravens.

I spent two weeks drawing ravens. Ta hell with nursing.

Heather digs through paper bag, brings out sketches of ravens, holds them up for people to see.

Black ink on thick white Medical Services paper . . . white like the whiteness all around me.

Ramsay came by. Like a mongrel dog that's caught wind of a scent. Just for a visit, he said. Looked at me, at my bottle, then he laughed, . . . no, he snorted.

"That's not a fucking ship," he said, "that's an eye. The iris of a blue-eyed woman."

Took off his snowmobile suit. Then he asked me to sit on his lap. And he kissed me. Said he brought me some stamina. And we . . . partied. For two weeks.

I didn't go near the nursing station. For two weeks. Sick leave.

The onslaught.

Expansively, drunkenly.

The North has always fascinated me. Ever since I was very very young. Its wildness. Its mystery.

Begins singing camp song.

Land of the silver birch,

Home of the beaver,
Where still the mighty moose,
Wanders at will. . . .

Laughs.

"Who the hell is Will?" Ramsay'd say, and I'd laugh every time.

Blue lakes and rocky shores,
I will return once more,
Boom did ee ah ah . . . boom did ee ah ah . . .
Boom did ee ah ah . . . boom!

And so it would go . . . me telling him about our house on Highland Crescent with the grey shutters and the Queen Anne's lace
on the trellis and the dance competitions at the Tam-o'-shanter
and him telling me about eating lard sandwiches in Timmins. And
then we'd flip on the *Edge of Night* and watch Mrs. Turner get
leukemia and her husband get caught in a homosexual roundup of
a subway men's room.

Gets to her feet.

"Wanna see me dance, Ramse?"

*Heather attempts to dance the Highland Fling, but loses her balance,
trips, perhaps falls to the floor.*

To Ramsay. "Don't laugh you ignorant pig. Colleen Stewart and I won
the Junior Girls for that dance when we were fifteen. And my
parents took us out for dinner after, too . . . I can't remember the
name of the place! How could I forget? That was the nicest restaurant I ever went to."

Phones Mom and Dad.

"Hi Mom? Hi. Yeah hi. Yeah it's me. Hi. Sure, get him on the
extension. Why not? The more the merrier. Listen, the reason I
called is 'cause I can't remember the name of the restaurant we
went to after I won the Junior Girls. *Shouts.* Oh God! Of course! It
was the Latin Quarter. *To Ramsay.* It was the Latin Quarter. *To
parents.* Yeah, I've got someone with me. Yeah . . . for dinner. *To*

Ramsay. What time is it? *Laughs.* Is he male or female? I guess you could call him male! So what else? I got your postcard from Malaga and the castanets. Yeah, real cute. I said CUTE. Why the hell did you go to Malaga anyway? Why don't you stay where you belong. Right here in Canada. If you want to see colourful culture, you could come North for a weekend, see the Indians. They're poor, sick, unhappy, uneducated, fucked over . . . oops . . . sorry about that! Good photo opportunities. And I'm sure the storekeeper would honour all major credit cards. I sound like I've been drinking? *Laughs.* Yeah well I have. I've been drunk for two weeks. Because it's too insane here to stay sober. God you sound far away. I don't know when it started happening . . . but I've fallen apart. Completely apart. *Listens, face changes, voice becomes more vulnerable.* Well I'll try to. I know you do. I know. I love you too."

Turns to Ramsay.

"Get out."

I had to get my ducks in a row. People have difficulties and then they rally. They get back on track. People think they'll never recover and then six months later, they can't even remember what they were upset about. They pull themselves together.

"Hold on Heather, get your ducks in a row." That's what Dad always said. I was bushed. That happens in the North in the winter. And six months later, I'd laugh about it.

I cleaned the trailer. I cleaned the walls. Cleaned the shower curtain. The kitchen drawers. Sewed the hems and all the lost buttons.

People throw themselves into work. Work is supposed to get people through the rough spots. It was all still there waiting for me. Camilla was still there, her eyes a long way away. And Mother and Grandmother. Still smiling at me. *To photos.* I had such a steady diet of nurses. Clean, competent, responsible, healthy women. How did you manage? Who cared for you? Bandaged you? Hold on Heather. And the wind still howling and ripping around outside the nursing station. And Annadora's laughter still inside my head. Hold on Heather. And the big cheese poster still on the wall and the t-bone steak, the wet lettuce . . . and a dozen messages from Miss Jackson like little pink petals all over the desk.

Heather steels herself.

"Hello, Miss Jackson? Hi. Heather Rose. Just fine. 110 percent! Just catching up on my paper work. I see you've been calling, but I've had the flu. A bug. Some kind of a bug. I'm all right now though, really. The chief called you? No, I'm all right really. I've got my ducks in a row. I was derailed temporarily but I'm back on track. *Shouts.* Jesus Christ! I said BACK ON TRACK! Why the hell can't they get decent telephones in the North.

"You what? You want me to come out? No. I'm not coming out. I'm staying right here. I have a job to do here and I'm going to do it. There is no question that these people need medical attention. No question at all. I have five vaccinations to do this week and there's always lots of business on the weekends. I don't care who you talked to. I won't. I can't. Go back to what? There's nothing for me to go back to. It's all distorted now, twisted. . . . *Listens.* Who do you think you are? God? Parachuting little people hither and yon, then scooping them out again whenever you please. It makes them crazy.

"Fuck you, Miss Jackson. There's an old woman here with a wooden leg and I've got to make hot meals for her. There's an ancient Indian with a wooden leg occupying the nursing station and Nurse Rose is going to join her."

Crossfade. The sound of Camilla Loon singing.

Break up. The breaking up of winter—that winter that I thought would never end.

Break up.

That's what they call it when winter finally ends. Because the ice on the lake begins to break up like a hundred million ice cubes.

Outside, the sound of drums coming from the community hall. There was a powwow going on. A coming-through-winter festival.

Darkness everywhere. Dark except for the flashlights going back and forth, back and forth in the darkness . . . and the glow from the community hall.

When I looked out into that darkness there was a glare from the window and I looked . . . different. Looked like a photograph of me . . . only as an old woman.

Heather sighs and takes a plastic bag from her paper bag. Holds it up for audience to see.

This is how they do it. Like this.

Demonstrates gasoline sniffing to audience.

They brought Naomi in. Found her in the corner of the washroom at the community hall. Yellow fluid all over her face. Her beautiful face. Wearing her red satin jacket, her mother behind, carrying her navy blue mitts.

Camilla's song continues under. Heather's face is transfixed as she remembers Naomi's body being brought into the nursing station.

"Oh Naomi, what have you done? What have you gone and done?"

At orientation I'd learned all about this . . . but not the horror.

"Naomi, wake up! Say something if you can hear me. Talk! Look, your mother and Camilla are here! Talk!"

And I was shouting her name over and over and slapping her face.

"Naomi! Hey! *Claps hands.* Hey! It's good to talk. I always talk when I'm having troubles. That's what I do. Talk! Talk. Please, Naomi. Tell me what you did today before you. . . . Hey!"

But she was floating in another world.

"Hey, what do you want to do when you grow up? When you finish high school?"

She was drowning.

"Hey! You're in love, aren't you Naomi? With Clarence Loon. I know because I've seen you holding hands with him. Think of him. Live for him. For Clarence. Live for me. Please Naomi!"

But her eyes were closing.

"No! I demand you open your eyes. Damn it! Open them! Naomi. Hey! It's spring. Rise up! You're supposed to RISE UP! It's your legend. You're not allowed to die, Naomi. To give up. You can't do that. You've got to survive. We've got to survive. That's all that matters. . . . "

Naomi's heart stopped.

Heather puts her head down, cries. She looks up at the audience, wearily.

Miss Jackson's not coming. But what did I think would happen here? That I would somehow be able to unload this. I can't. It's inside me now.

Camilla's artificial leg arrived on the same plane that I left on. But not her false teeth. And that's about it, I guess. The occupation of Heather Rose.

Lights go down on Heather.

End

Inside Out

by Pamela Boyd

Enquiries and permission to produce should be addressed to:
Celia Chassels, Gary Goddard Assoc., 696 Yonge Street, Toronto,
Ontario, M4Y 2A7

First Performance

Inside Out was premiered February 28, 1986, at Tarragon Extra Space,
Toronto, under the direction of Jackie Maxwell, with design by Shad-
owland and lighting by Kevin Fraser. The cast was as follows:

Ellen Ross — *Pamela Boyd*
Voice of Arran — *Margaret Carmichael*

The set is a bright, sunny kitchen in a rented Toronto house. It is colourful and attractive but obviously done on the cheap, and suicidally clean. It contains all the usual things a kitchen contains, as well as a table, two chairs, a high chair, a large stuffed armchair on a small carpet in one corner, down left a toy basket full of toys and blocks and a potty. Down right corner there is a phone with a long cord and an answering machine on a small table by the armchair. An exit stage left leading to bedrooms and front door. Door stage right to backyard.

Ellen is 35, determined and runs on nervous energy. Whenever the action allows, she wipes the table, counter or fridge. This is almost subconscious. At no point does she indulge in self-pity.

Arran is 18 months, and is a life-sized, stuffed, caricature puppet. All Arran's movements are obviously done by Ellen. This is not a puppet show, however. Arran should be treated roughly, like a doll or a real child. Arran's reality comes through the relationship the actress playing Ellen builds with him and not *through any fine-tuned or sleight-of-hand puppeteer dexterity.*

He has a metal ring at the back of his neck which can be attached to a retractable hook at Ellen's waist. He has velcro on his hands so that when his arms are wrapped around Ellen's leg he can hang on. This also allows him to hold onto bottles and toys etc.

The voice, sound and noises of Arran are done off-stage by another actress, and it is very important that this noise and babbling is constant whenever he is awake. *He has a recognizable vocabulary of eight to ten words, but the actress doing Arran must also develop her own vocabulary of sounds. He understands most of what Ellen says to him, however.*

*All tantrums, diaper changes, etc. marked by a * need a certain amount of improvisation as the business is complicated and cannot help but vary a certain amount in performance.*

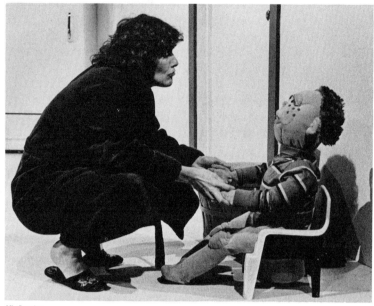

Nir Bareket
Pamela Boyd as Ellen
Tarragon Extra Space, Toronto, 1986

Scene One

Lights up. Ellen enters from L. wearing a housecoat. She turns on the radio and we hear the news as she fills the kettle and puts it on, takes bread from the fridge and puts it in the toaster, fills a baby cup with milk from the fridge, puts coffee from the fridge into the coffee filter, and exits L. to fetch Arran.

Arran all the while can be heard off stage yelling: "up, up, Mummy, up", etc. and shaking his crib.

Radio: *A CBC type voice.* A second baby has died of a mysterious illness that struck Winnipeg's Health Science Centre last week. The hospital said the baby had been in critical condition in the intensive care nursery and had not been expected to live. The name of the baby has not been released. *Pause.*

The department of statistics released its latest unemployment figures today. Unemployment across the country is down point one percent this month everywhere except in Newfoundland. Unemployment is up in that province to eighteen percent. *Pause.*

Here are the headlines again: A Norwegian cruise ship, The Royal Viking King, was sunk by a Soviet submarine yesterday afternoon in the Gulf of Riga. It had apparently strayed into Soviet waters and was sailing near Saaremaa Island, a sensitive strategic Soviet air base. Tass, the Soviet news agency, said the Norwegian ship did not respond to attempts made by the Soviet submarine at radio communication. Over nine hundred passengers and crew members are still missing. The United States is calling for an emergency meeting of the United Nations Security Council to discuss what it calls the heinous Soviet action.

Ellen re-enters carrying Arran, puts him on the potty and squats facing him. They grunt at each other through the rest of the newscast.

The Prime Minister's office has approved further cruise missile testing in Canada. Our government told the U.S. government last night that it can go ahead with five more test runs in Northern Alberta this winter. The decision surprises no one.

And now the weather: It is another sunny mild fall day outside our downtown studios this morning. High today sixteen with a ten percent chance of rain. Low tonight nine, and let's hope it lasts through to the weekend.

Radio goes to music.

Ellen: Push, Arran, pooooosh the poop out.

Arran: Poooooooooooooooo

They grunt some more. The kettle whistle goes off. Arran stands up and cheers and claps. Ellen looks into the pot.

Ellen: No poop.

The toast pops and the kettle whistle goes off.

Arran: Toes, toes.

Ellen: Toast's up . . . oh! and there goes the kettle.

She hooks Arran onto her waist and wraps his arms around her leg. During the following she turns off the radio, turns off the kettle and pours the water through the filter. Arran follows her around, generally getting in her way.

Ellen: My God. More baby deaths. Winnipeg now. Well, at least they can't blame it on Nurse Susan what's-her-name this time. Poor wee tykes . . . but if it were murder who could blame them, really . . . a miserable kind of life with some sort of nasty heart disease . . . or was that just the Toronto bunch? . . . Arran, let go. Don't you want some toast? Let go.

She unhooks him and puts him in the high chair and gives him a spoon.

Ellen: Here play with this. *He bangs it on the tray.* No, don't play with that, it's too noisy. Here.

She takes it away and gives him his bib. During the following she gets the toast and peanut butter, spreads the toast and cuts it.

Ellen: Euthanasia on babies . . . would I do it . . . would I? . . . Ye gods, how would I know, I'm not even awake yet, and what does it matter anyway, we're all going to be blown up in a nuclear holocaust. You know, Arran, if you can do your poop in your pot before we go out, you can go without your diaper. Think how comfy that would be, no nasty diaper, just like playing in the garden in the summertime, but you have to concentrate while you're sitting there and really try.

She ties his bib on; gives him his toast and milk. She gets a pear for herself and sits at the table.

Ellen: Now.... Unemployment down. That's good. That means more people have got jobs and a roof over their heads for the winter ... only a tiny bit though, except Newfoundland, it's up, eighteen percent ... eighteen percent, that's awful, that's almost one fifth of the population. That can't be right, it must be eight percent.... No, I'm sure they said eighteen percent; that's terrible.

Arran: Daddy? Daddy?

She gets up as she answers him and pours herself a cup of coffee and sits again.

Ellen: Daddy's gone to work to keep a roof over our heads. He got up while we were still sleeping. He's gone to work ... to have a shower on T.V. and tell all the people how well Head and Shoulders gets rid of his dandruff ... which he doesn't even have.... Let's see now, what else? ... Oh yes. They're going ahead with more of the cruise missile tests, the shits ... those poor Albertan suckers.... Damn them! Damn! Damn! Damn!

Arran: Da! Da! Da!

Ellen: Oh good. No, Arran, damn is a bad word. Mummy shouldn't say damn and neither should Arran.

Arran: Da! Da! Da!

Ellen: No, my love, no.

Arran dumps his milk on the floor.

Ellen: Arran, you little bu ... that was really vicious. That was a mean thing to do!

She gets a cloth and wipes it up.

Ellen: That's it, no more milk. I can see you can't be trusted.

She goes out left and comes back in with the mail.

Ellen: There was something else ... something about Vikings....
No.... Vikings? ... No ... it was a disaster of some sort....
What was it?

Arran throws his toast on the floor.

Ellen: Don't throw it on the floor, Arran, it gets the floor all dirty.
She picks it up and puts it back on his tray. Or was it a shooting? ... It was something important.... Damn, what *was* it?

Arran: Da!

Ellen: Oh dear. *She sits down and begins to go through the mail.*
Bill.... Bill.... Bill.... A cheque! ... six hundred and forty-
three dollars and ninety-six cents! *She kisses it.* Oh, you beautiful
baby. We can pay the rent, Arran.

He throws his toast on the floor.

Ellen: Don't throw it on the floor! ... All right, that's it.

*She picks the toast up and puts it on the counter. Arran stands up in his
chair and screams.*

Arran: No!

Ellen: Sit down then and behave yourself.

Arran: No. Toes. Toes.

Ellen: Sorry, you have to sit down first.

Arran: Toes. Toes.

Ellen: No sit down, no toast. Sit down, then toast.

They glare at each other, he lets out another scream, then she lifts him down to the floor. He screams. She sits down and ignores him.

Ellen: I'm not listening. If you want your toast you have to behave properly. *She sips her coffee. Arran quietens down.* It had something to do with Vikings, I'm sure.... What on earth could it have been? ... Gone. ... Good, Ellen, brain decay.

Arran: Pee-pee! *He is sitting in a large puddle.*

Ellen: Pee-pee on the pot! *She whips him onto the pot.* More pee-pee?

Arran: Pee-pee.

Arran cheers and claps. Ellen looks in pot.

Ellen: No pee-pee. You should have done it in the pot, you dingbat.

She grabs a diaper and wipes up the floor.

Arran: Toes? Toes?

Ellen: Yes, if you sit properly in your chair.

Arran: Up. Up.

Ellen: All right.

She lifts him into his chair and gives him his toast. The phone rings.

Ellen: Oh yeah! The outside world.... Hello. *She brings the phone to the table, sits and talks.* Oh, good morning, love. What time did you leave? I didn't even hear you.... When will you be done? ... Great. And then you'll be home? ... Listen, I need to get out tonight, I've got a severe case of cabin fever.... Oh, one hundred and eight degrees.... Yes, and catching.... Well, I want to see Susan's show. You said you could get tickets, right? ... and dinner?!! No, we can't afford it.... Oh, what the hell, we can use the Visa. Oh, no wait, it's okay, it's okay. The rent came in with the mail this morning ... a cheque for six hundred and some from that commercial .... No, the deodorant, I think.... Fabulous, I'll reveal my legs ... well, I can shave.... With you making that kind of money I can buy long underwear when it gets cold.... *To Arran.* Okay sweetheart, are you all done? ... Wait, I'll put you

down. *He stands up in his chair. She shouts.* Just wait, Arran! ...
Into phone. Oh, sorry. ...

While continuing her conversation, Ellen takes Arran's bib off, carries him to the sink and washes him, running the tap loudly. She carries the phone with her.

Ellen: What? ... Who's in town? ... Jason Gold? You're kidding, but he's the guy I've been thinking of, the one I told you about. ... No, of course he knows nothing about it, but he will, it's just his kind of script. Oh, if I could just get in to see him it would save putting it in the mail. What's he doing in town? ... Casting what? ... A feature?! Well, well, well. ... Arran, hold still!! ... Is it a good part? ... Great, tell your agent to leave room for me. ... I said, tell your agent to leave room for me. Arran, *stop* it, you're getting me all wet. ... Oh, sorry. ... What? ... Of course I know him. We were great buddies at one times, but it was a while ago now. ... What? ...

She turns off tap and puts Arran down and gives him some toys.

Ellen: Well, he can be quite tricky, likes to think he's an intellectual, but really, he's just a big softy underneath. ... Because. ... Because I'm an exceptionally perceptive person. Listen, how can I get hold of him? ... Oh, great, wait ... pencil ... crayon. Okay, shoot.

Arran: Cutty, cutty, cutty.

Ellen: Just a second, Arran. *She writes on the fridge.* 9-2-8-3-0-5-6. Fantastic. Thank her for me will you. I'll call right away. ... *To Arran. Please,* Mummy. *Picks up toy.* Windwindwindwind. ... What? ... Oh right, sorry. See you at noon then. ... Bye. *She hangs up and re-dials immediately.* Whoopee!

Arran: Cutty, cutty, cutty.

Ellen: *She winds his toy again. Please,* Mummy, windwindwind. ... Hi, Marg, it's Ellen, are you guys in tonight? ... Great, can you take Arran? ... Yes, cancel that divorce, we're going out. ... Dinner and a show. ... Yes, please, if you don't mind, about six? ... Great, thanks, see you then. Bye. *She hangs up and replaces the phone.* Right ... ten to nine ... dishes.

She whips round the kitchen, doing dishes and general clean-up at top speed as she speaks to Arran.

Ellen: Mummy and Daddy are going out tonight, Arran. You're going to Paul's house after your supper. You're going to sleep at Paul's house. Mummy and Daddy will come and get you while you're still sleeping, okay. Maybe Paul's mummy will cut your hair, that would be nice, wouldn't it? *She wipes table.* What a nice sunny day. Let's pack a lunch and go to the pa.... Oh my God, the bastards. *She plonks down in a chair.* The Soviets, they've sunk a ship ... a Viking ship? ... No ... a Norwegian ship, that was it. The Soviets have sunk a Norwegian cruise ship ... how absolutely awful.... How could they do that, the bastards? ...

She begins to wipe the table furiously, then the counter and finally the fridge.

Ellen: Reagan is going to "come" right in his drawers.... The bastards ... you just don't do that sort of thing.... Oh no, the number! *She peers at it.* 9-2-8-3-0 ... 5-6 ... 8-6.... Oh my God, is that a five or an eight? ... I'll have to try both.

She glances at Arran and goes to the phone and dials.

Ellen: 9-2-8-3-0 ... 8-6.... Plumbing service?! Sorry, I've got the wrong number.... Must be a five. *She dials again, glancing hopefully at Arran.* 9-2-8-3-0-5 ... okay El, real cash ... 6.... Oh! Good morning, is Jason in yet? ... And what time do you expect him? ... Ah ... are you his assistant? ... And she's not in yet either.... What's her name again? It's gone right out of my head....

Arran: Mummy ... mummy ... mummy ... mummy....

Ellen: Eileen Scott, yes of course.... No, thanks, I'll catch them at nine-thirty. Thank you. Good bye. *She hangs up.* What *is* it, Arran?

Arran: Ju, ju.

Ellen: *Please*, Mummy, juice. You must try to be polite, sweetheart, especially to those you love.

She gets him some juice in a bottle from the fridge.

Ellen: Oh no, ... Scott ... Irene? ... No ... Elain ... yes, Elaine
Scott, that was it.... I think.... nine-thirty; right.... Clothes,
diaper. Come on Arran, diaper time.

*She fetches clothes and a diaper. She catches Arran up and they have a
chase around the table till she eventually catches him and pins him on
the floor.*

Ellen: Okay, you little monkey, Mummy's going to catch you. Come
on, you nut case.... It's not summer anymore, you have to wear
clothes.... Arran, stop it! Come on now, hold still ... Arran,
don't ... don't wiggle ... hold *still.* ... Patience, El.

*She has the diaper partially on by this time and proceeds to dress him,
to great opposition.*

Ellen:

Taffy was a Welshman.
Taffy was a thief.
Taffy came to my house
And stole a piece of beef.
I went to Taffy's house,
Taffy wasn't in, ... Okay, pants
I jumped upon his Sunday hat
And poked it with a pin.

Taffy was a Welshman.
Taffy was a sham.
Taffy came to my house
And stole a leg of lamb.
I went to Taffy's house,
Taffy was away,
I stuffed his socks with sawdust
And filled his shoes wi ...

Arran kicks her in the breast.

Ellen: Oooowww!! You little bast ... *The phone rings.* Hello....
Who? ... No, are you trying to get the Denato's? ... You've got
the wrong number.... Yes, that's the number you've dialed, but

they don't have this number anymore.... I know, but they haven't had this number for about eight months. Call directory assistance.... 401 ... no, no that's the highway ... 411.... That's all right ... goodbye. *She hangs up.* Come on, love, almost dressed.

She fetches Arran's shoes, jacket and hat. She picks him up and sits him on the table.

Ellen: Now, just hold still.

Arran: Cutty, cutty, cutty.

Ellen: All right, all right, I'll get it for you. *She picks up the truck he is yelling for and gives it to him, talking alternately to him and to herself.* It's called a front-end loader ... hold *still* ... for building things with.... I *should* have left a message ... stupid ... roads and houses and things. They picks up loads of sand and dirt and stuff ... other foot ... OTHER FOOT ... and dump it on things ... I think ... front-end loader.... *She picks up the toy and looks at it.* Fork-lift? ... hat ... jacket ... other arm ... zipper.... Reagan is going to go nuts.... Good.... Done.... Now, you go outside and do some front-end loading while I get dressed.

She opens the door, sends him out and stands watching him.

Ellen: I wonder what he'll do ... take the stairs backwards, love ... yes, that's right ... he's capable of anything ... good boy. *She closes the door and stands watching for a moment longer.* He wouldn't retaliate would he? ... No, don't be stupid, how could he retaliate. You're over-reacting ... go get dressed, you dumb broad.

She goes off left and comes back on in T-shirt and underwear, carrying jeans and socks. She dresses, watching Arran through the window, and rehearsing her conversation with Jason.

Ellen: Hello Mr. Gold, my name is Ellen Ross. We met four years ago at a workshop in Winnipeg. I've written a screenplay about ... I've written a screenplay about ... well I guess it's a sci-fi fantasy. I'd very much like you to look at it. Would it be possible ... *sighs*.... Hello Jason, this is Ellen Ross from Winnipeg.

Listen, I've written a screenplay. It's a futuristic fantasy about teenage alienation and despair and I want you to direct it. . . . Jason, hello, how nice to talk to you again after all this time. It's Ellen Ross . . . the screenwriters' workshop in Winnipeg. . . . I'm the one you were screwing . . . oh dear God, this sort of thing's supposed to be instinctive, please let the right words come.

She looks out the window one more time at Arran.

Ellen: Okay sweetheart, just five more minutes. *She dials.* Jason Gold please. . . . Morning, can I speak to Jason, please. . . . Already? . . . Um . . . no, I don't think so. Are you Elaine Scott? . . . *Eileen* Scott, I'm sorry. My name is Ellen Ross.

Arran is by this time banging on the door and screaming. Ellen checks to make sure he is okay, then sticks one finger in her ear and closes her eyes in concentration.

Ellen: I'm a . . . a writer and an old friend of Jason. I've got a script . . . pardon me? . . . Oh, that's my son, he's having a tantrum. . . . No, no that's fine, but thank you. Anyway, I've got this script I want him to look at. Do you think you could squeeze me in for fifteen minutes or so while he's in town? . . . You could?!! That's wonderful!! . . . Yes, sure, five o'clock today would be perfect. Thank you very much, Elaine . . . Eileen, oh dear, I'm sorry. . . . Thank you, yes, see you at five. *She hangs up.* Good heavens, I've got no more copies. . . . I'll have to go to the printer's. . . . Whoopee!!!!! It worked. *Glancing up.* Thanks Buddy.

She jumps up and opens the door for the now hysterical Arran. He jumps in at her.

Ellen: I'm sorry my love, but it was worth it. Mummy's going to be rich and famous any day now and we'll all go to Antigua for Christmas. *She sits down with the still screaming Arran and speaks to him guiltily.* I'm sorry you're upset sweetheart, I really am, but sometimes Mummy has got to talk on the phone. Come on, it's not as bad as all that. Cut the blackmail . . . please. *She begins a "fingers-walking-up-the-leg" game.*

There was an old woman and what do you think,
She lived upon nothing but victuals and drink.

Victuals and drink were the chief of her diet,
And yet this old woman could never keep quiet.

Lots of laughter and tickling.

Ellen: Come on, let's go to the park. We'll pick up a lunch at the deli to celebrate . . . but first . . . *She reaches for the phone and begins dialing. Arran gets hold of the cord and tugs on it, yelling. She puts it to his ear as she dials.* Boy oh boy, someone upstairs is looking after us today. A cheque in the mail, a date with Daddy, an appointment with Jason Gold, and the sun in the sky . . . too bad the news isn't so hot. *She takes the receiver from Arran. He makes a tremendous fuss.* Marg, hi, it's Ellen . . . oh . . . would you talk to Arran for a sec? *She puts the phone to his ear. A moment's silence then he blows a raspberry into the phone. Ellen takes the phone back.* Charming . . . listen, I've just got an important appointment downtown at five. Can we make it four-thirty instead? . . . Great, thanks, you're a trouper. I'll take Paul for a long shift next week for sure. . . . Okay, bye.

Arran: Bye. *She hangs up.*

Ellen: Okay sweetie pie, let's get out of here. *Carrying Arran with her she gathers up her things.* Mummy's jacket . . . Mummy's bag . . . cheque book . . . cheque . . . diaper . . . script. *She sits Arran on the table beside her bag and puts her jacket on.* What do you want for lunch m'dear? Cream cheese on a bagel? Corn beef on rye? Hey, how about creamed shrimp? Maybe we'll splurge.

Arran: Toes, toes.

Ellen: Okay, note for Daddy. *She gets a crayon and writes on one of the bills.* Lunch in park . . . bring champagne! There, that'll keep him guessing. Now, let's go . . . oh, where's your hat? *She picks him up and opens the door.* There it is. *She puts it on him.* You have to keep your hat on, love. Don't you know you loose seventy percent of your body heat through your head? *She is about to close the door. . . .* Oh, good heavens, the phone machine, fancy new answering machine and I keep forgetting to put it on. *She crosses to the machine and puts it on.* Depress answer button . . . there, that's right, isn't it?

The phone rings.

Ellen: Oh! . . . Okay machine, do your stuff.

Machine: *We hear Tom's voice.* Hello, you have reached Tom Michaels and Ellen Ross. No one is available to take your call at the moment but if you leave your name, phone number and the time of your call we'll get back to you as soon as possible. Please wait for the beep.

Arran: Daddy, Daddy.

We hear the beep, a beat of silence and then the loud buzzing tone.

Ellen: No, no! Don't hang up, you're supposed to leave a message! . . . Big help that is . . . probably Hollywood calling. Let's go Arran. *They go out and close the door.* Do you want to ride or push the stroller? No, no, we've wasted enough time already, you'd better ride. Keep still, Arran, and keep your hat *on.*

Screams off into the distance.

Scene Two

Three hours later. A scattering of clothes and dishes gives evidence of Tom having been and gone. Chatter and laughter from off. "Daddy, Daddy" etc. Door opens. Arran is hooked onto Ellen's waist.

Arran: Daddy?

Ellen: Daddy? Daddy? . . . No Daddy . . . Daddy's dishes, Daddy's clothes . . . Daddy's note. *Reading the note.* "Gone to meet Claude for a drink. See you later. Love Daddy."

She puts the note down, disappointed.

Ellen: . . . sorry about lunch, Ellen . . . Claude? What's Claude doing in town? Claude's here from Montreal, Arran. Well I guess we'll see Daddy after nap.

She unhooks Arran and proceeds to take off clothes and diaper.

Ellen: Have you had that poop yet? Let's get that diaper off and you can sit on the pot.

Arran: No.

Ellen: Yes.

Arran: No.

Ellen: Yes.

Arran: No.

Ellen: * Yes. Now hold still . . . hold still! . . . Arran! Why do you have to do this . . . every time . . . just co-operate for once. . . . Arran . . . don't . . . it's so much easier if you just. . . . All right, now, sit on the pot, read your book, and *do* something. I'll clean up after Daddy.

After putting Arran on the pot and giving him a book, she hooks him back onto her waist, wraps his arms around her leg and proceeds to clear up Daddy's mess.

Ellen: Claude. What's Claude doing in town? . . . No love, go sit on the pot. . . . Do I get to see him this time? . . . I can't walk when you hang onto my leg . . . Arran! . . . Go sit on the pot and poop!

Arran: No!

Ellen: All right. No poop. Nap time.

Arran: No! *Screams.*

Ellen: Yes! Let's get a diaper on you.

She picks him up, picks a diaper up and exits. From off.

Ellen: * Arran! Stop it! . . . Now just hold still! . . . hold *still!* . . . Arran, stop it . . . don't kick me . . . stop it! . . . There, now, give it a rest, loud mouth, and go to sleep.

She re-enters while he is still screaming. She flips the switch on the answering machine to rerun the messages, puts the coffee on to heat and hangs up their jackets. She takes three scripts out of her bag, puts the two new manuscripts on the table and the original in a drawer in the table. Meanwhile, the answering machine replays the first of a series of hang-ups and annoying buzzing noises.

Ellen: There we are now, five hundred naps and all my savings in one folder.

Second buzz. The coffee boils over. She jumps up and pours a cup.

Ellen: Oh good, boiled coffee.

Third buzz. She looks at the machine.

Ellen: Good investment that, you never have to miss a call.

She looks in the direction of Arran's screaming.

Ellen: Oh, shut-up . . . *he does.* . . . Thanks.

She gets a pen from her bag and writes on one of the script folders.

Answering Machine: *Portuguese voice. Está . . . está . . . Maria . . . Maria . . . quero falar com Maria . . . Maria Denato. . . . Quem é aquele senhor. . . . Maria, estas aí, Maria. . . . Não sei, é muito* *estranho há qualquer coisa que não esta bem.*

Ellen: Ellen Ross, 57 Maple Grove, Toronto.

Answering Machine: *Stilted, as if unaccustomed to answering machines.* Oh . . . oh . . . Tom, I mean Ellen, this is your mother . . . ah . . . oh, the time. . . ah, it's . . . I don't know the time, just after breakfast in Brandon. . . . Ah . . . I just needed to chat, dear. Call me when you get in. Goodbye. . . . Oh, I've bought you some make-up, it was on sale. . . . I hope it'll be useful. I'll post it off this morning.

Click. Buzz. Ellen sits tensely looking at the machine.

Ellen: Chat. . . . Oh Mother . . . so get a job. *She reaches for the phone and begins dialing.* What am I doing? I'm not calling her in the middle of the day.

She hangs up, replaces the phone to the table by the arm chair and turns off the answering machine. She returns to her manuscript on the table and begins to flip through it.

Ellen: Oh dear . . . looks so tacky. . . . *She tosses it on the table and looks at it.* Would I bother with something that came to me looking like that? . . . No, what is this, some sort of frustrated housewife? . . . I should have had it professionally typed. . . . Ooooooh, so bloody unlikely, how can seven weird kids and a dog survive all the upheaval of . . . it's ridiculous. . . . Oh, stop it, El, that's not the point, you know it isn't. That's not even what it's fundamentally about. . . . You're going to throw away five hundred naps on ridiculous and tacky? No! . . . Oh, Jason, if you're the same man I remember, you'll understand.

She picks the manuscript up and hugs it tightly.

Ellen: My seven brave heroes, you're beautiful, I know you are and you can speak for yourselves. So, come on, El, you're going to give it to him. You're going to talk intelligently about it, and you're going to be charming to the man.

She puts it back on the table.

Ellen: So get your head out of the diaper pail and get your act together.

She exits left to the shower.

Ellen:
   Hickety Pickety my fine hen. She lays eggs for gentlemen.

We hear the shower running for a couple of minutes, then the phone rings. Ellen rushes in with her house coat on and a towel wrapped hastily around her head. She grabs the phone.

Ellen: Hello. . . . Oh, wonderful . . . ah, I don't speak Italian. . . . I'm sorry, *no comprendi.* . . . You've got the wrong number!!

She slams down the phone and exits.

Ellen: I don't believe it!

The phone rings. She runs back in again and grabs it.

Ellen: What do you want from me?!!! . . . Oh. Sorry. What's happening? . . . I'm sorry, I'm sorry. I keep getting calls for those Denato people and I was in the shower. . . . No, it's all right, I'm out now. What's happening, am I going to get to see Claude? . . . But . . . but we're going out . . . but I thought you had tickets. . . . Well, poop! . . . Because we haven't been out for. . . . I am calm. . . . Yes, I'm sorry, all right. I'm glad Claude wants to see Arran, and I want to see Claude. I'll throw something together, but we've got to go out soon. . . . Could you pick up something for dessert and some wine? . . . Please. . . . Thank you. . . . Well, *I* don't know, *you* choose, *you're* going to eat it. . . . I'm not mad. . . . I'm sorry, I don't mean to, I'm disappointed, that's all. . . . Oh well, *c'est la vie,* I guess. . . . Oh, . . . *dit . . . dit bonjour, cheri, à Claude . . . et dit . . .* um . . . *je suis trés contente . . . à voir . . .* no . . . *à regarder* . . . oh, you do it, tell him I'm looking forward to seeing him. . . . Yeah, sure, keep on truckin' partner. See you later . . . WHEN? . . . good, at five then . . . bye.

She hangs up.

Ellen: SHIT! . . . Shitshitshitshitshitshitshitshitshit!

She goes to the fridge and stands looking in. She takes out two trucks and a ball.

Ellen:
> Hickety Pickety my fine hen. She lays eggs for gentlemen.
> Sometimes nine and sometimes ten. Hickety Pickety my fine hen.
> What the hell are we going to eat? . . . chicken curry. . . .

She takes out frozen chicken and puts it on the counter, then turns to the phone.

Ellen: Baby-sitter.

She goes to the phone and dials. Arran wakes and starts screaming.

Ellen: So much for that shower. . . . Hi, it's me. Cancel all of the above, we're not going out, we don't need a baby-sitter. . . . No . . . too complicated to bore you with, but I'm giving a dinner party instead. . . . Yeah, well, ours is not to reason why. . . . I don't know, maybe tomorrow, maybe Saturday, maybe never. I gotta go. . . . Okay, thanks anyway, bye.

She hangs up.

Ellen: Oh stop bitching, El, it'll be nice to see Claude. Coming Arran.

She exits.

Ellen: Well that was an awfully short nap.

She re-enters carrying Arran. He is very bitchy.

Ellen: Well, what do you want? Do you want to go back to bed?

Arran: No!

Ellen: Do you want some juice?

Arran: No!

She tries to soothe and comfort him. He screams. She tries to put him down. He screams. He is pointing.

Ellen: Apple?

Arran: No!

Ellen: Pear?

Arran: No!

Ellen: Truck?

Arran: No!

Ellen: Radio?

Arran: Uh, uh.

Ellen: No, Arran, that's not a toy, you know you can't have that. How's that diaper, have you had that poop yet? *She pulls out the back and has a sniff.* No poop. Let's get this thing off and you can sit on the pot.

Major tantrum as she tries to get the diaper off.

Ellen: * Arran don't do this! . . . Stop it! . . . Keep still! . . . Keep still! . . . Come *on*! . . . Arran! Don't kick . . . don't kick . . . just keep still! . . . etc. etc. *She stops abruptly.* Oh my God, I've cancelled the baby-sitter!!!

She heads for the phone. Stops. She can't hear a thing above Arran's screaming. She picks him up and carries him off.

Ellen: Don't you hit me!! I don't want to know about it. When you're civilized you can come back.

She re-enters, heads for the phone. Stops.

Ellen: Oh God, what am I doing. That's not fair.

She turns. Stops.

Ellen: Yes it is. That *is* the right thing to do.

She shakes off indecision with difficulty. Dials. Waits.

Ellen: Come on! . . . Where the hell has she gone? . . . Shit!!

She hangs up. The phone rings. She grabs it.

Ellen: Hello. . . . You've - got - the - wrong - number!!!

She hangs up.

Ellen: Maybe *they* want to babysit!

She thinks for a moment, remembering the number. Dials.

Ellen: Jose, hi, it's Ellen. . . . Fine thanks, how are you? . . . Listen, I'm in a jam, are you guys in this afternoon?

During this call she goes to the fridge, carrying the phone with her. She gets juice and pours some into a bottle, then replaces the juice in the fridge.

Ellen: The flu? Oh, the poor kid, how is he? . . . Oh dear . . . how miserable . . . the poor little guy. Well listen, I'm desperate, this is really important. It's only from 4:30 to 6:00, I'm going to have to take a chance, if it's okay with you.

Arran appears sheepishly at the doorway. She sees him.

Ellen: No, Jose, you're right, I'd better not. Thanks anyway. I hope Mick gets better. Bye.

She goes to Arran and squats at his level.

Ellen: Hi Arran, are you feeling better?

Arran: No.

Ellen: Would you like some juice?

Arran: Rais, rais.

Ellen: All right, I guess you could have some raisins.

She gets a bowl of raisins and puts them on a chair. She stands him beside them and proceeds to take off his diaper, unimpeded.

Ellen: You're so nice when you're not screaming, I like to hug you. . . . What a dumb-ass thing to do. Maybe he can see me tomorrow. . . . What a nice quiet boy, eating his raisins. . . . Surely he'll remember me, give me a break. . . . Still no poop. We'll leave your diaper off and you can use the pot when you want.

She fetches the phone and dials.

Ellen: Marg, please be there . . . where have you gone so fast, my love? . . . *Please* Marg. . .

Arran: Rais.

She moves Arran onto the rug.

Ellen: Oh no sweetheart, eat them here, don't take them on the rug, they're too sticky.

Arran squeals and wiggles.

Ellen: Oh. It's all right. It's all right. Relax. Take it easy.

She goes to the phone and dials.

Ellen: Please, Elaine, don't let me down now, we're so close. . . . Elaine Scott, please. . . . *Eileen,* yes, sorry, Eileen Scott. . . . Eileen, hi, it's Ellen Ross, listen, something has come up and I can't make it today. Is there any way you could fit me in tomorrow instead? . . . But I thought he was here till Saturday? . . . Oh, I see, so it's now or never. Damn!! . . . No, it's not that simple, you see I've . . . um . . . I've lost my babysitter. My husband said he would be home by five, but I can't be sure, and I don't know how to get hold of him, so you see. . . . Oh no, I couldn't possibly bring my son with me . . .

At this point Arran begins yelling, "Mummy, mummy, poo, Mummy, poo, poo", and continues through the rest of the phone call. Ellen registers the commotion, but not what he is saying.

Ellen: No, that's ridiculous, I'd never be able to concentrate. Look, is there some way I could talk to him on the phone? . . . He must have *some* time between now and when he leaves town. What about my appointment time? . . . Yes, I know he's very busy, but we . . . we're friends, we've worked together. . . . Well, no, it was a while ago, but that doesn't matter, he *will* remember me . . .

By this time, really rattled, Ellen has moved over to Arran and picked him up with one hand in an attempt to keep him quiet.

Ellen: No, I *can't* just mail it to him, I *must* speak to him personally. . . . Please try!!! . . . I'm sorry, Elaine, I didn't mean to yell . . . *Eileen*, I mean. Oh dear, I *am* sorry, you're such a nice person, and Eileen is so much nicer a name than Elaine, I don't know why I keep calling you Elaine, I . . . you will!!? . . . Oh, thank you, thank you, what time? . . . Five-thirty. If I'm not there by five-thirty, he'll call me here. . . . Oh, 653-2117. . . . You're wonderful. Thank you very much Eileen. Goodbye.

She hangs up.

Ellen: Well . . . that's that. . . . POO?!! Did you say poo, Arran? *She looks in the pot.* Oh no. *She glances around the room.* Where Arran? . . . Show me, where did you poo, Arran?

He leads her to the rug.

Ellen: Oh no, not on the rug!! . . . Oh Arran, it's all over your leg!! . . . Wait, Arran, hold still.

She grabs a cloth to wipe him off. He struggles and yells.

Ellen: * Don't kick, Arran, you're getting it all over me!! . . . Arran, stop it. . . . Arran, don't . . . don't . . . STOP IT!!

She gives him a shove and he falls over. A beat of silence then he starts screaming. She takes a moment to regain control of herself, then goes to him, picks him up and sits in the chair.

Ellen: I'm sorry, love, I didn't mean to push you, I really didn't. I'm just running out of patience, that's all. It doesn't mean I don't love you. I do love you, I just don't like getting poo in my hair, especially just after I washed it. . . . Kiss and make up?

Arran: No.

They sit in silence for a while.

Ellen:

There was an old woman who lived in a shoe,
She had so many children she didn't know what to do.
She gave them some broth without any bread,
Spanked them all soundly and sent them to bed.

She tries to tickle him.

Arran: No.

Ellen: I'm sorry, love. . . . There's been a change of plans, sweetheart. You're not going to Paul's house. Mummy's not going out. Daddy's going to bring Claude home for dinner and we're going to have a little party. Do you remember Claude? He's Daddy's friend. So . . . Mummy has got to do some cooking. Do you want to go outside and play in the dirt with your trucks now?

Arran: No.

Ellen: Are you sure? It's a nice sunny day, it might be fun in the dirt?

Arran: No.

Ellen: A pound of flesh . . . right . . . Mummy loves Arran.

She kisses him and begins, softly, to hum the tune to "Jesus Loves Me", and to rock Arran on her lap. Fade to black.

Scene Three

It is five-thirty. Dinner is ready on the stove. The dishes for dinner are ready, set on the counter. Ellen and Arran are dressed and tidy. They are playing with trucks and cars on a simple structure of ramps and platforms made of blocks and boards on the floor.

Arran: Mummy, Mummy.

Ellen: Put it up yourself then ... look, you put this block on top of this one and then the ramp on top ... no, you bimbo, it doesn't work that way, you have to put it this ... that's right, now you can run your trucks down.

Arran: Cutty, cutty.

Ellen: Truck, Arran, truck ... voom-voom.

Arran: Zoom-zoom ... pane.

Ellen: Okay, plane next. Push it hard love, and it'll go all the way.

Arran: Pane, pane.

Ellen: Well look, you have to push it hard.

Arran: Pu pu pu

Ellen: That's right, poooosh!

Arran: Poooooooooo

Ellen: No, that's what you do on the pot, silly. . . . Good one!

Arran: Yeaaaaaaaa

Ellen: Yeaaaaaa

Arran: Bike.

Ellen: No, we have to wind the bike. Windwindwindwind. Let's see if it'll go all the way down the ramp ... voom.

Arran: Zoom-zoom.

Ellen: No, Arran, let me do it. Mummy can do it better.

Arran: No! No!

Nir Bareket
Pamela Boyd as Ellen
Tarragon Extra Space, Toronto, 1986

Ellen: But Arran, you can't balance it. Let me do it. Let Mummy do it. Let go, Arran.

Arran screams. She catches herself.

Ellen: I'm sorry, sweetheart, you do it.

He does. It falls.

Arran: Mummy?

Ellen: It's tricky, love, you have to wind it and then you have to balance it too. Like this, see . . . no, like this.

Arran: No!

Ellen: I've got a good idea, let's do the cruise missile. Where's your plane? . . . Okay, here comes the nasty old cruise missile buzzing over North America loaded with deadly, nuclear bombs, heading for Toronto. . . . Bzzzzzzzzzzzz . . . BOOOOOOOM!

She crashes the plane into the block structure and demolishes it.

Ellen: Everybody dead! Everything gone! Yeaaaaaaaaaaaaa!

They both cheer and clap. Arran grabs the plane and copies her.

Ellen: Oh my God, what am I doing?!

She stands and watches him for a moment, then wanders.

Ellen: Quarter to six. No Daddy, no Jason.

The phone rings. She glances at Arran then answers it.

Ellen: Hello. . . . Oh Mother, hi . . . no, I'm sorry, I just haven't had a moment all day and I'm expecting a very important phone call any minute. Can I call you back? . . . I promise I won't forget. . . . I'll call you right afterwards. . . . I'm sorry, Mum, but it really is very important. . . . Thanks, bye. *She hangs up.* Good timing, Mother.

She wanders, glances at the clock.

Ellen: Where the hell is Tom? . . . Well, Arran, it looks as if it's going to be too late for you to eat with us. I'll make you an omelette in a wee while.

She wanders to the mirror and looks critically at herself.

Ellen: You know, if you don't look at my face, I look like a young person, on the verge of a brilliant career . . . if you don't look at my face. . . . If you do, I look like a more mature, tired person, who might be interesting. . . . Then I open my mouth . . . and nothing comes out. . . . I look like a boring person who never reads the paper. . . . Maybe I should get a hair cut.

The phone rings. She jumps, then conscious of not drawing Arran's attention, she answers it.

Ellen: Hello. . . . Yes, Eileen. . . . Yes, certainly I'll hold.

Arran: Mummy, mummy, gup?

She takes two plums from the fruit bowl and gives them to Arran.

Ellen: No, sweetheart, Mummy's on the phone. Would you like some plums? . . . There you are, your favourite . . . that's a good boy.

She moves away from him, still looking at him, willing him to stay quiet.

Ellen: Take the stones out, love, don't eat the stones. . . . Jason, hello, you may not remember me. We worked together four years ago at a workshop in Winnipeg. . . . Yes, that's right . . . the reason I'm cal . . .

Arran has got a stone stuck in his throat. She watches in suspense, waiting for him to dislodge it.

Ellen: Sorry, yes, I'm . . . Arran!!

She drops the phone and runs to him, grabs his arms and yanks them above his head. Nothing happens.

Ellen: Oh, my God . . .

She whips him upside down and starts thumping him on the back.

Ellen: Come on! COME ON!

Nothing happens. She rights him and sticks her finger down his throat.

Ellen: I can't get it! I can't get it! . . . COME ON!!!!

The stone pops out.

Ellen: Oh my God! Thank God!!

She is holding him, looking into his face.

Ellen: Breathe. . . . Come on, breathe, Arran. . . . Breathe, damn you
. . .

She is shaking him.

Ellen: Breathe . . . BREATHE!!

He does, and starts to scream.

Ellen: Oh, my God. . . . Thank God, thank God, thank God!!

They cling to each other, rocking and crying. When he begins to quiet down she sings to him.

Ellen:
   Hushabye, don't you cry
   Go to sleep a little baby.
   When you wake, you will find
   All the pretty little horses.
   Dapples and Greys
   Pintos and Bays
   All the pretty little horses.

The phone begins to beep its off the hook signal. Ellen looks at the phone for a moment, then without releasing Arran, she pulls the cord out of the wall. Lights fade to half.

Ellen: I love you, Arran.

Arran: Mummy.

Fade to black.

Scene Four

It is seven-thirty, dark outside. There is evidence of Arran's supper about and the usual mess of toys and blocks etc. As the light fades up we hear Ellen, singing the end of the lullaby, off.

Ellen:

> Speed bonny bonnie boat
> Like a bird on the wing
> Onward the sailors cry.
> Carry the lad
> That's born to be king
> Over the seas to Skye . . .
> Night, night, God bless, Mummy loves you.

Arran: Kiss?

Ellen: All right, one more . . .

Arran: Ju, ju?

Ellen: Juice? You don't need a bottle, you're a big boy now.

Arran: Ju, ju.

Ellen: No, Arran, you're too big for a bottle, besides, it's bad for your teeth.

Arran: Peas, peas.

Ellen: Peas? Don't be silly, you don't want peas at this time of night. Now, lie down and go to sleep, there's a good boy . . . night night.

Arran starts crying. Ellen comes in carrying an armful of toys and books and drops them in the toy basket. She begins to clear up the toys, dishes etc., desperately trying to ignore the crying. She comes to the phone cord.

Ellen: Well shit, no wonder he hasn't called.

She plugs the phone in and begins to put away the blocks. As she picks them up one of the mechanical cars starts up again. It scoots across the floor.

Ellen: Oh for Pete's sake stop it. He's gone to bed.

She chases it, reaches for it and drops her armful of blocks, almost throwing them in irritation as they fall. She throws herself down in a chair, head in hands, listening to Arran's crying. She looks up suddenly.

Ellen: Peas?!! ... he said "peas"! *She jumps up and runs to him. From off.* Arran, did you say peas? Oh my sweetie pie, you said peas.

She enters with him. He is in a sleeper. She goes to the fridge and gets him a bottle.

Ellen: Oh my sweety, what a bad Mummy I am, you probably have a sore throat after all that choking. Of course, you can have a bottle, especially when you're so polite. Oh, Arran, what a clever boy.

She hugs and kisses him and takes him off to bed. From off.

Ellen: All right, now settle down. . . . Night, night, Mummy loves you.

She re-enters and slumps into the chair, listening to the silence. She looks around the room, then at the clock.

Ellen: Seven-thirty . . . it doesn't matter. It does *not* matter . . . peas. *She looks at the phone.* Two bloody hours, he's going to kill me. "What the hell do you think we bought an expensive answering machine for?"

She puts all the blocks and toys back into the toy basket and then begins to wipe the table, and stops.

Ellen: Stop it.

She wanders to the door and stands looking out. She opens the door and breathes deeply, looking at the night.

Ellen: Cold now . . . brain's stopped. . . . LEMME OUT!! . . . Calm . . . calm. . . .

She closes the door.

Ellen: Today's gone . . . let it go . . . tomorrow's a new one. . . . One at a time ol' girl, one at a time . . . we'll chalk the whole thing up to Murphy's law. . . . Who the hell was Murphy, anyway . . . and where does he get off naming a law after himself? It's a dumb law anyway. *She picks a wine glass up from the table.* Thank you. I'd love one.

The phone rings. She looks at it for a moment, replaces the glass.

Ellen: I'm sorry dear, the phone was unplugged. I couldn't help it.

She answer the phone.

Ellen: Hello. . . . I'm sorry dear, the phone was unplugged. I couldn't help it. . . . No, no, don't panic, it was after five-thirty, besides, that's your agent's job, not mine. . . . Allow me a screw-up from time to time, I'm not Supermum. . . . Because it's been ringing like a fiend all day long, mostly for the Denatos, and when Arran got a plum stone stuck in his throat I couldn't. . . . No, no, just a bad scare, nothing to worry about. . . . No, I'm lying to you, he stopped breathing, turned blue and now he's retarded. What do you think I am, totally irresponsible?!! . . . You implied it. For God's sake, Tom, give me a break! . . . Yeah, yeah, so you're sorry. . . . Yes, it *is* a big deal. Do you remember way back at eight o'clock this morning I told you I had cabin fever? What do I have to do, smash windows before you'll believe me?!! . . . Just . . . just tell me what the hell's going on. . . . Oh, you've had dinner. Swell, scrap the dinner. . . . What?!! . . . You had dinner with Jason Gold? . . . I don't believe it. . . . I see . . . hmmmm . . . oh . . . you and Claude. . . . Well, that's lovely, just lovely. Did you get a job? . . . Wonderful. . . . By the way, I did not get to see him today. . . . That's putting it mildly. . . . If you're so sorry all the time, maybe you should start proving it. . . . That's your problem. . . . I know, Tom, it's never your fault. . . . Sure, you could come home now if you don't mind a butcher knife in the gut. . . . Of course I'm mad, it's been a crappo day, in more ways than one. You can take the whole thing and blow it out your ass!!!

She slams down the phone, then slams on the answering machine.

Ellen: You two just waltz into Jason's office and out to dinner with him, while I sit here cleaning SHIT off the floor and making an *ass* of myself on the phone. I'll bet you had a good laugh over that at the happy hour. Sorry??!! Bull!!! You don't even know the meaning of the word. You try being Johnny-in-the-sink for a while and let me waltz about town being Johnny-on-the-spot, then we'll see how sorry you are. . . . "Keep on truckin' partner"! . . . I must have crossed the bloody continent a dozen times by now. Trouble is, partner, you're in a bloody limo and I'm on a God-damned tricycle.

The phone rings.

Ellen: SHUT UP!!! GO AWAY!!!

Answering Machine: Hello. You have reached Tom Michaels and Ellen Ross . . . etc. etc.

Ellen: *As the taped message continues.* I'm not your *mother*. I'm your *wife*. You have some responsibilities towards me too, you know. *I'm not your mother!!!!!!*

Beep from the answering machine.

Answering machine: Ellen, it's your Mother again. You haven't called me back. Please call, darling, I know you're there—you're always there. Please call, I need someone to talk to.

Click. Buzz. Ellen laughs.

Ellen:
I had a little wife, the prettiest ever seen,
She washed up the dishes and kept the house clean.
She went to the mill to fetch me some flour,
And always got home in less than an hour.
She baked me my bread, she brewed me my ale,
She sat by the fire and told a fine tale. . . .

Here's to you, little wife. *She toasts her. Pause.* So, he leaned over, ever so gently and kissed her on the lips. There was a moment of suspense and then her eyelids fluttered open and he took her in his arms. The instant she saw him she loved him. There was great rejoicing in the land and the very next day they were married and lived in perfect happiness ever after.

She sings and dances.

Ellen:

Some day my prince will come.
Some day I'll find my love.

She stops, suddenly, and looks intently at one of the chairs for a moment. Then she sits on the second chair and addresses the first.

Ellen: I've been there . . . I know despair. I know the road from panic to hopelessness to despair, and it's wrong. . . . I see them out there, on the buses, in the school yards, on the streets, in their clothes and their hair and their make-up like death's heads. . . . And I look into their eyes and they're utterly innocent . . . and it hurts. What have we done that our children dress like the dead? It's wrong, I know it's wrong. Our children must *never* give up, they must *always* hope, because they are the hope and life of the future. I want to give those children back some hope, I want to tell them that struggle and conflict may not be evil, because from out of struggle and conflict can come clarity and growth, wholeness and peace. . . . So, I've written this, and I want you to film it. . . . Oh! . . .

Her concentration is suddenly broken.

Ellen: Oh my, Jason. . . . I'm sorry, what a fool I am, blabbering away as if . . . and Tom, oh dear, I'm really not prepared for this. A nice surprise he says. If I'd known you were going to bring home a celebrity, I'd have brought out the crystal and put on my *Cordon Bleu* with the *bleu* trim. Oh-oh, we don't have a thing in the house to drink. Did you remember to pick up some wine, Tom? No, of course not. Oh well, never mind, we can have a nice glass of cold water with dinner. We even have some ice in the ice tray, fancy that. Actually, we don't have any crystal, but we will have when my Mother dies—she has lots. She's very healthy though, and not about to die, although I could kill her. But I don't really have time. I've been very busy lately, toilet training my son. He's eighteen months. See, here's our family portrait.

She fetches it.

Ellen: That's him there, the one with the diapers on, and that's Tom.
He'd just had a hair cut, you can see the tan mark. And that's me.
My mother thinks I should wear more make-up. I don't. I think
it's dishonest. I like to look my age. I think it gives a woman dig-
nity, don't you? After all it's not what you look like that counts,
it's what you do.

She returns the portrait to the fridge and slams it down.

Ellen: No, no, I've been doing a lot of writing lately. See here's my
typewriter. It's a pretty good typewriter, but the "H" sticks, so I
type in cockney. My screenplay's not in cockney though, it's in
Canadjun, I guess. That's what I've been writing, between
diapers, a screenplay. See, here it is. It's pretty good, considering,
and heavy, too, but the typing's not too good. I hope you can find
time to read it some day. I'd like you to direct it. I think we'd
make a good team. . . . Oh, but what about you?

She returns the typewriter to its place, then sits at the table.

Ellen: You look great, haven't changed a bit, what I can see of you.
No need to ask what you've been doing. Great celebrity now,
dozens of divorces, feature films all over the place, you must be
very proud . . . and hungry too, no doubt. I almost forgot, dinner.
I'll just dress the salad.

She goes to the fridge and takes out the salad.

Ellen: I usually make my own salad dressing, but I didn't have time
today. I hope you don't mind store-bought.

She pours liquid detergent on the salad and tosses it.

Ellen: I've made a nice chicken curry. Oh, it's nothing really, just
something we like. Tom thinks I don't make it hot enough, don't
you, Tom, but I like to taste the things in it. I hope it's all right for
you. Perhaps if I made my own curry powder it would be better. A
good cook would. . . .

How much muck would a good cook cook

If a good cook could cook muck. . . .

We buy it already made up as curry powder, then of course it sits in the cupboard for months on end and loses its hotness. It does, you know. You should only buy small amounts at one time and then it retains its bite. Tom bought a pint jar of the stuff about two years ago, didn't you, Tom, and we're still using it. It probably tastes like pablum by now. There . . .

She is finished tossing. She gets two plates and two spoons and slams them down in front of the two men, one presumably in the high chair.

Ellen: Now . . . I'll give you both a little bit to start and you can come back for seconds if you're not too full. I know, I'm probably talking too much. It's an occupational hazard, you know, home all day long with the baby, then you get out with intelligent adults and run off at the mouth like somebody's mother. Brain atrophy's another. Hopefully it's not chronic.

She begins to cram food into their mouths.

Ellen:
There was an old woman who thought she was bright.
But her brain was a traitor and took off in flight.
She opened her mind, took everything in
But it all came out in a garbled din. . . .

I do try, though, to keep myself alive, mentally that is. I've forgotten how to read, so I don't read the paper, but I do listen to the radio. It doesn't always go in, and if it does, it doesn't always stay in. That's called the drafty brain syndrome—it's a follow-up to pregnancy. Today, however, was a particularly good day for the ol' grey matter. I listened to the news and then I gave myself a quick quiz. But I only scored eighteen percent and that's not even one-fifth of the population. So many awful things going on in the world—babies with heart disease being torpedoed by Vikings. What do you suppose Reagan will do? I know one thing for sure, he's going to need a diaper change. But, dry pants or wet, it's quite terrifying to think what he might do. And then there's our very own P.M. out cruising in Northern Alberta. I don't know what he thinks he's going to do if he ever scores, push a button maybe, and then, poofters . . . silly bugger. Ah well, I try.

She clears the dishes from the table.

Ellen: But then, it's not what you actually *do* that counts, it's what
you *are*, because what I *do* doesn't amount to a thimble-full of
piss in a diaper bucket. . . . Oh, don't get me wrong, I don't piss in
the diaper bucket, it's my son that does that . . . well, he doesn't
actually piss in the bucket either, he pisses in the diapers, which
go in the bucket, although he's supposed to piss in the pot. Poo
too. He pooped in my hair today. You've probably noticed that I
smell slightly off. Well, that's why. My son shat in my hair. No,
he didn't actually squat on my head. No, no. He's a manipulator,
that's true, but I'm not a total fool. He shat on the floor and then
wiped it on my head. But I do *try*. I *try* to keep myself up, show
off my attributes, write the odd screenplay. I've written one
recently, against great odds, great odds. It's about *hope* and *faith*.
Bringing up children in this day and age should be enough, you
say. Should be fulfillment. Should be fulfillment. Perhaps I'm a
freak. Perhaps we're all freaks. We're all freaks. We're all freaks.
We're all freaks. Bringing babies to life doomed to imminent
death. Doomed to imminent death. Imminent death. It's animal
nature. We're all animals. We're animals. We're animals. Just
animals. When faced with extinction propagate in a frenzy. A
frenzy. A frenzy. A frenzy. When faced with starvation, eat its
young. Eat its young. Eat its young. Eat its young.

*Her tirade is suddenly broken as a prolonged infant's cry fills the
kitchen. Pause. She holds an imaginary baby close to her face and
shoulder, soothing and comforting it.*

Ellen: My baby! . . . my baby my baby my baby my baby my baby
my baby my baby my baby hush hush hush hush hush hush hush
my love my love hush hush Mummy's here Mummy's here. *She
is stroking and rocking the baby.* Hush hush Mummy's here
Mummy loves you Mummy keeps you safe hush hush hush. . . .

Barely audibly she begins to sing to it.

Ellen:
   Hushabye don't you cry
   Go to sleep a little baby.
   When you wake you will find

All the pretty little horses.

She kneels down on the floor and places the "baby" gently on the floor in front of her.

Ellen:
> Dapples and Greys,
> Pintos and Bays,
> All the pretty little horses.
> Hush hush hush. . . .

She slowly reaches for a pillow on the floor beside her, hesitates momentarily, then abruptly places it on the baby's face and holds it there. As she sees what her hands are doing, slowly realization dawns. She takes her hands away in horror and lifts her face to the audience in a silent scream.

Arran: *From his room off.* Mummy . . . Mummy . . . Mummy.

Ellen: Arran? . . . Arran?

He rattles his crib.

Arran: Mummy.

Ellen: Arran.

She goes off to fetch him.

Ellen: *From off.* Arran. What are you doing awake at this time of night?

Arran: Huc, huc, kiss.

She enters with him.

Ellen: Did you wake up just for a hug and a kiss? You are a monkey, and Mummy loves monkeys. MMMMMmmmmmmmmmm. . . . Boy, you're getting to be such a heavy boy, you know that? You're going to grow up to be a big, strong, beautiful boy. Now you go back to sleep. It's the middle of the night.

She sits holding him in the chair. She looks over at the pillow, still lying on the floor. She looks back at Arran, in her arms.

Ellen: I love you Arran. *Pause.* You are a child of God.

Arran: Mummy.

Ellen: Yes, Mummy too . . . Mummy too.

Fade to black.

Whiskey Six Cadenza

by Sharon Pollock

First Performance

Whiskey Six Cadenza was premiered at Theatre Calgary Feb. 10, 1983, under the direction of Rick McNair with design by Terry Gunvordahl. The cast was as follows:

Mr. Big — *Robert Benson*
Mama George — *Joyce Gordon*
Leah — *Kim Horsman*
Johnny Farley — *Robert Metcalfe*
Mrs. Farley — *Rita Howell*
Cec Farley — *Barney O'Sullivan*
Will Farley — *Duval Lang*
William Windsor — *Stephen Hair*
Dolly Daniel — *Jacquie Presly*
Gompers — *Earl Michael Reid*
Old Sump — *David Marriage*
Widow Popovitch — *Rita Howell*
Constable — *Duval Lang*

Characters

Mr. Big: a man in his 60's
Mama George: his wife of about the same age
Leah last name unknown: girl in her late teens
Johnny Farley: young man about 20
Cec Farley: a miner and Johnny's father
Will Farley: a miner and Johnny's older brother
Mrs. Farley: Johnny's mother
Dolly Danielle: Will's girlfriend, same age as Leah
Gompers: an employee of Mr. Big
William Windsor: a.k.a. Bill the Brit, member of the
Prohibition Police
Old Sump: elderly miner
Widow Popovitch: older woman (double with Mrs. Farley)
Constable: seen, no lines (double with Will)
Voice of the Trainman

Blairmore Marching Band are shadows only

Time

Act One—the fall of 1919.
Act Two—the spring of 1920.

Place

The Crowsnest Pass, straddling the Alberta/British Columbia border
and the Canada/U.S. border.

Playwright's Note

*The opening and closing dance sequence and voice-overs, as well as
the stage directions referring to the refracted, fragmented images,
reflect production components of the Theatre Calgary premiere. These,
plus the gossamer depiction of the Crowsnest Pass, are options which
not every production need choose to exercise. I think of them as strong
indicators of the play's ambiance, and nothing more or less than that.
Terry Gunvordahl's wonderful set did many things, not the least of
which was the creation of Will's ghost on stage with, and yet not with,
Dolly sitting and dancing in Act Two.*

George Gammon
Barney O'Sullivan as Cec Farley, Robert Metcalfe as Johnny, Duval Lang as
Will; back: Rita Howell as Mrs. Farley.
Theatre Calgary, 1983

Act One

The front of the stage is filled by a gossamer depiction of the Crowsnest Pass. The view is of an open expanse of rolling foothills with mountains as misty peaks. We are looking westward. Nestled in a crook of the landscape, the smudgy and vague outline of a small, distant town that might-have-been, Blairmore. All is as if seen through a soft rain. The light grows on the gossamer depiction so that the image is well-established. A plaintive note is heard, repeated and faint, from a player piano. Light builds behind the image, exposing it as no more than a gray, dusty, cobwebby affair much as a spider might spin in the entrance of an abandoned mine-shaft. The cobweb parts. We see what was formerly obscured, the player piano playing, as well as skeletal bits and pieces of the town of Blairmore, primarily a Farley area and the Alberta Hotel area. In the Alberta Hotel, a chair is knocked over. Images and figures often appear fractured, refracted, fragmented. Behind the town, surrounding it, is the gossamer depiction of the rolling hills, the misty mountains, but seen from a different perspective— from what was once the main street of Blairmore. The landscape extends into the infinite, giving an impression of viewing eternity through a glass, a telescope, a microscope, a kaleidoscope.

The music from the player piano quickens in tempo slightly, growing in volume. The figures, now complete, now fractured, refracted images, of Mr. Big and Leah, Will and Dolly, Cec and Mrs. Farley, Gompers and Mama George; Sump dances alone. Occasionally they change partners. Bill the Brit watches, dancing with no one. Johnny is absent.

Voice-overs are heard, they sound like the wind, blowing softly, stirring tumbleweeds, increasing, and dying.

Mr. Big: *Voice-over.* And around . . . and around . . . and around . . .

Leah: *Voice-over.* My head . . .

Mr. Big: *Voice-over.* And around . . .

Leah: *Voice-over.* It's whirling . . .

Mr. Big: *Voice-over.* And round . . .

Mrs. Farley: *Voice-over.* And dip . . .

Mr. Big: *Voice-over.* T'gether . . .

Dolly: *Voice-over.* And out . . .

Will: *Voice-over.* And round . . .

Mama George: *Voice-over.* Ohhhhhhhh . . .

All: *Voice-over.* Ohhhhhhhh . . .

Leah: *Voice-over.* Whirrrrl . . .

Gompers: *Voice-over.* And dip . . .

Dolly: *Voice-over.* Whirrrrrrl . . .

Mrs. Farley: *Voice-over.* Ohhhhhh . . .

Cec: *Voice-over.* And out . . .

Mr. Big: *Voice-over.* And out . . . and round . . . and round . . . and
out . . . and round . . . and out . . .

Leah: *Voice-over, faint, as the image of Mr. Big and Leah is the last
to fade from view. . . . And . . . dip. . . .*

*Silence. Lights fade to black as small round green light alone in
blackout grows in brightness. Blast of train whistle followed by sound
of distant but approaching train. Green light changes to red light.
Headlight of train shines directly into audience. It grows in size to the
sounds of the train as it draws nearer, slows down, and stops at station.
Steam from the engine floats in front of headlight.*

Trainman: *Voice-over.* Blairmore! Blairmore! Is that it? . . . No
more for Blairmore?

Sound of train increases as it readies to pull out.

Trainman: *Voice-over.* Board! All aboard!!

*Sound of the train pulling out. Its headlight grows brighter, brighter,
blindingly bright and larger as the train departs as if through the audience. Sound fades with the departing train. The stage is left in darkness
except for the residual steam from the engine, and the red light. The
red light turns green. Faint whistle from train.*

In the drifting steam the faint figures of Mr. Big, Leah, Gompers, in one grouping; Johnny, by himself, can be made out. They have gotten off the train. Johnny passes billfold to Mr. Big. Mr. Big, Gompers, Leah exit, with Mr. Big and Leah stopping to exchange a backward glance with Johnny, who watches them depart. He stands a moment in thought, takes a deep breath, glances towards home and Mrs. Farley.

Johnny draws closer to Mrs. Farley, watching her, listening.

Mrs. Farley:
In darkness, sings.
Somebody's boy's in temptation
Away from the shelter of home,
Far from a mother's protection
And weary and sad and alone.

There are pitfalls oh in plenty
Awaiting his soul to destroy,
Oh voter speak out at election
And help to save somebody's boy!

Light slowly builds on her.

Somebody's boy may be your boy,
His eyes just the same shade of blue,
Someday your tears may be falling—
The breweries don't care if they do.

'Tis theirs to ruin and trample,
To crush out all hope and all joy
Oh voter speak out at election
And vote to save somebody's boy!

Mrs. Farley: *Glances down at her song book. She speaks to herself in an absent-minded way.* Praise the Lord . . . ame. . . . *She catches sight of Johnny; she can't believe her eyes.* Johnny? . . . Johnny? . . . John-ny! You're home. You are home, you're home!

Johnny: That's it.

Mrs. Farley: And just look at you. . . . Oh you've grown!

Johnny: I have.

Mrs. Farley: But you're thin.

Johnny: I am.

Mrs. Farley: You've got so big, and you've got so skinny.... Now did you never eat?

Johnny: I ate.

Mrs. Farley: And why are you standin' there? Aren't you comin' in, aren't you gonna sit even?

Johnny: I'm in, Mum.

Mrs. Farley: Well sit then.

Johnny: Gonna stand a bit.

Mrs. Farley: Oh I did miss you, Johnny—and I prayed for you, yes I did, I just love you and miss you so much, thank the Lord, thank you Lord for . . . and now I'm gonna cry.

Johnny: Don't cry.

Mrs. Farley: Don't you be lookin' at me cryin', don't you be doin' that. You could be sittin', you could be lookin' like you're gonna stay a while—did you never eat?

Johnny: I ate, Mum.

Mrs. Farley: You never wrote.

Johnny: I wrote.

Mrs. Farley: Not proper letters, not continuin'-like letters, not every week you didn't.

Johnny: No.

Mrs. Farley: You never wrote like you should.

Johnny: No.

Mrs. Farley: Like you promised.

Johnny: I had nothin' much to write about.

Mrs. Farley: You coulda wrote that.

Johnny: Ah-huh.

Mrs. Farley: It woulda been somethin'.

Johnny: I know, I just didn't get down to doin' it, that's all.

Mrs. Farley: Not even to tell us you were comin'.

Pause.

Johnny: Where's Pop?

Mrs. Farley: At the mine—and William—same shift. *Her attention drifts from Johnny for a moment. He watches her. She looks at him. . . .* You've not come back, are you?

Johnny: Guess they'll be surprised to see me, eh?

Mrs. Farley: You've not come back? I mean it's just for a visit, eh Johnny?

Johnny: So, ah, how are they, Will and Pop?

Mrs. Farley: Your father's coughin' and spittin' and dyin'—but still workin'.

Johnny: I don't want you to start in on that, Mum.

Mrs. Farley: I as'ed you a question—are you come back?

Johnny: I tried, I did try, Mum, but I . . .

Mrs. Farley: You tried!

Johnny: If you'd listen . . .

Faint blast from a mine whistle.

Mrs. Farley: Don't need no listenin'! Him who can't write a letter is tellin' me to listen? You listen, Johnny! You . . .

Johnny: Don't cry.

Mrs. Farley: And haven't I the right?

Johnny: There weren't no jobs east.

Mrs. Farley: If you cared nothin' for me, you should care somethin' for yourself. Why are you come back?

Johnny: Do you think I wanna work in the colliery?

Mrs. Farley: There's your father dyin' of the lungs; there's William who'll end up just the same—if he don't go like his brothers Teddy and Robert, workin' the same shift . . .

Johnny: I remember.

Mrs. Farley: The two of 'em, your brothers too, Johnny, caught and crushed and chokin' to death when the air give out. One hundred and eighty-nine dead at Hillcrest—now did they die for nothin', Johnny?

Johnny: You know it's not what I want but I got no choice, Mum!

Cec enters black from the mine.

Mrs. Farley: There he is! There! Now is that what you wanna be? Look at him! The black worked right through the skin and the blood and the heart and the lungs and the brain! That's not a man, Johnny, that's a thing, a utensil belongin' to Dominion Colliery! *Exiting.* Can't even tie his shoe without spittin' a clot.

Pause.

Johnny: 'Lo Pop.

Cec: You're taller.

The two regard each other. There seems to be a desire on their part to embrace in greeting but some other subtle but stronger force preventing them. Cec busies himself with removing his black work clothes.

Cec: Yup, 'bout what? Two inches?

Johnny: Dunno. Maybe.

Cec: They says you's supposed to stop 'bout eighteen.

Johnny: Musta been that eastern air.

Cec: Robert now, he grew some after that, and he never had a tetch a eastern air. He thrived on dust, that Robert did.

Johnny watches his father undressing. Silence for a moment. His father looks at him. Awkward silence between them for a second before Johnny speaks.

Johnny: Where's Will?

Cec: Out back throwin' some water on hisself outa the pump. Got hisself a girl and she don't mind the callused hand, but she surely don't care for the black. Gonna scrub the skin right off he is, and not do a damn bitta good. *He laughs.*

Will enters looking dampish. He and Cec will change their clothes during the scene. Will sees Johnny.

Will: Well je-sus.

Johnny: God damn.

Will: Well je-sus god damn and holy shit, what're you doin' here, boy?

Johnny: What the hell does it look like, boy?

Will: It looks like my baby brother! Arrrrrrrrr!! *He bellows and holds out his arms. He and Johnny embrace.* What the hell are you doin' here?

Cec: *Feeling considerably more at ease now that he's no longer alone with Johnny.* He heered a rumour all the way back in Tronna, he heered some fella out here in Dominion Colliery got a foolproof way to get the black off so's he come to see.

Will: Just like huggin' a picket offa a fence, boy, you're all straight lines and angles.

Cec: I told him that rumour's all horseshit, can't nobody get the black off.

Will: You seen Mum?

Johnny: Ah-huh.

Cec: Oh he seen her all right.

Johnny: Yeah.

Cec: And she give it to him, good and proper.

Will: Are you come back then?

Johnny: I ah ...

Cec: Well there he is standin' there ain't he? The favourite is come home.

Johnny looks at him, saying nothing.

Will: That right, Johnny?

Johnny: I guess so.

Cec: And she don't like it, not a bit.

Will: *To Johnny.* Hey.

Cec: Ain't no escapin' the mines.

Will: Buck me up, buckeroo.

Johnny: Yeah.

Cec: Filled his head, she did, but it comes down to the same in the end. And didn't I say it when you left, boy? Didn't I say it?

Will: Ain't the end a the earth.

Johnny: No.

Cec: Shoulda heard her, Will. Held his father up as a bad example she did. Here I was, nothin' but a damn utensil, wasn't that what she said, Johnny? No better than a spoon, only worse cause I'm coughin' up the clots on the shoes, Will ... and don't you be laughin' cause the same thing is gonna happen to you! Only worse! That's what she says, boy, your mother says it. *He laughs.*

Will: Hell, I thrive on the dust.

Johnny: Like Robert and Teddy did?

Cec: Now that's your mother in you, that is. *He gathers up the clothing and exits with it.*

Will: Hey.

Johnny: Nothin' changes.

Will: Don't pay him no mind. He's glad to see you, he just can't say it.

Johnny: Sure.

Will: And you him—so why the hell don't *you* say somethin'?

Johnny: I will.

Will: It's real good to see you, boy, welcome home. *They embrace. Will whispers.* The mines ain't the end a the earth, boy.

Cec re-enters with clean clothes for himself and Will. Cec is not so particular about removing the black as Will.

Cec: She's pourin' over the good book lookin' for helpful verse.

Will: You wanna see somethin' fine?

Cec: What?

Will: Look at that. *Holds out a hand.* I still got the calluses ... but ...

Cec: What?

Will: White.

Johnny: Red.

Cec: *Examines Will's hand.* What the hell you use on that?

Will: Lye.

Cec: Lye?

Will: I used the lye and the bleach.

Cec: Jesus christ, Will, that hand's gonna rot.

Will: But you can't see the black now can you?

Cec: You didn't use no lye on that?

Will: Sure I did. *He winks at Johnny.*

Cec: *Catches him.* Ha! He's always merry-makin', this one. This boy'll be laughin' when he's lyin' in bed coughin' his lungs into a hankie he'll be laughin'.

Will: I'd bawl if I thought it'd help.

Johnny: Pop says you got a girl.

Cec: He even give her a picture.

Will: I got girls up to my armpits.

Johnny: A particular girl.

Cec: Go on Will, you tell him.

Will: Could have.

Cec: Tell him her name.

Will: You watch it.

Cec: It's Dolly.

Will: Tread carefully there.

Cec: Dolly Danielle.

Johnny: A Frenchie?

Cec: A bohunk.

Will: A blonde.

Cec: You remember the Yakimchuks?

Johnny: Ah-huh.

Cec: Well this here's the one that used to be Polly.

Johnny: Polly Yakimchuk?

Cec: And...

Will: I'll take it from there.

Johnny: Polly with the braids all round the head?

Will: Uh-huh.

Johnny: Legs like matchsticks and knees like grapefruit?

Cec: Them grapefruits' moved up a bit.

Will: *Warning.* Uh uh.

Cec: And she don't like the black.

Will makes a motion as if to hit his father.

Cec: Eeeehhhhh would you hit an old man, would you hit your father there Will?

Will: You betcha.

Johnny: How did Polly Yakimchuk get to be Dolly Danielle?

Cec: She went to Tronna.

Will: I'll take it from there. It's like this, Johnny boy. She's like you, kinda like you, for this girl's got a particular hatred for coal. It's true she don't like the black, and what she don't like even more is the thought of the men crawlin' thro' seamy little spaces in the bowels a the earth, and more than that, is the ponies.

Johnny: She don't like the colliery ponies?

Will: You don't want to get her talkin' 'bout them ponies, Johnny.

Cec: That's the truth.

Will: It brings her to tears.

Cec: And it bores you to tears.

Will: She's a sensitive girl.

Cec: Tell him 'bout changin' her name.

Will: I'm gettin' to that.

Cec: Only a bohunk'd think a French name's a step up in the world.

Will: Shut up, do you hear?

Cec: Ohhh, no jokin' 'bout Dolly Danielle.

Will: To make a long story short, she goes to Tronna, she comes back from Tronna, and while in Tronna, she changes her name.

Pause.

Johnny: Is that it?

Will: Pretty well it. *Pause.* You see it kinda makes her feel like she didn't come from here, like she kinda chose here 'stead of endin' up here.

Johnny: Oh.

Will: She's a sensitive girl.

Cec: Is that what she told you?

Will: I can see for myself.

Cec: Lemme look at you—right enough—you got a thin layer a dust right over them eyeballs.

Will: You old . . .

Mrs. Farley: *Off-stage and faint, singing.* Somebody's boy in temptation. *Going flat.* Away from the shelter of—

Johnny, Will and Cec listen for a moment.

Johnny: I was hopin' she'd got over rampagin' for Temperance.

Cec: She needs a cause to keep goin'.

Will: She'd have a man so dry you'd have to prime him to spit.

Cec: She's in a state, she is.

Will: You can tell 'cause her throat tightens up—

Cec: Resultin' in that ... She'll move into the hymnary next.

Cec: What'd I tell you?

Mrs. Farley:
Away from the shelter—
Shelter of—
offf
Away from the shelter of home
Far from a mother's protection
And weary and sad. (*Flat again.*)
and alone
Alone
Alooone.
There are pitfalls oh in plenty
(*Flat.*) ty ty plenty
Pitfalls oh in plenty
Awaiting his soul to destroy
(*Flat.*)
Oh voter speak out at election
And vote to save somebody's boy.

With renewed vigour.

Mine eyes have seen the glory
Of the coming of the Lord
He is stamping out the vintage
Where the grapes of wrath are stored.

Creeping in is the sound of a marching band, building in volume.

Johnny: Still prayer meetings on Wednesday and service on Sunday?

Cec: And temperance on Thursday.

Mrs. Farley:
He is loosening the Vengeance of His terrible swift Sword.

The marching band is fairly loud.

Will: Like clockwork.

Cec: I thank the Lord she more or less give up on us.

Will: She ain't intercedin' on our behalf no more. If we're to be saved it'll be by the direct intervention a the . . . the Lord.

Mrs. Farley:
His Truth goes marching on
Glory, glory, Hallelujah!
Glory, glory, Hallelujah!
Glory, glory, Hallelujah!
His truth goes marching on!

The sound of the marching band is quite loud, fragmented images of trumpets, trombones, light glancing off brass instruments. Finally, Mrs. Farley can no longer be heard, only the marching band.

Will: . . . Hisself . . . What the hell is that?

Cec: It's . . . it's the Blairmore marchin' band!

Will: Key-rist! Had me worried.

Cec: This ain't no practice night.

Will: So what the hell's it out for?

The marching band is outside the house, still playing.

Cec: It's stopped outside.

Will: Front a the house.

Cec: Here comes Old Sump—he ain't no band man.

Will: And Gompers, ain't that Mr. Big's man Gompers?

Old Sump, followed by Gompers, approaches the house.

Old Sump: Cec! Cec, you home t'ere, Cec!

Cec: Pray to God your mother don't see Gompers comin' here.

Old Sump: Cec!

Will: He'll have to smite her ears as well as her eyes.

Old Sump: Cec!

Will: Whata you want, Sump?

Cec: *Whispers.* What the hell you doin' here, Gompers?

Old Sump: Come for Johnny.

Will: For Johnny?

Cec: Eh?

Old Sump: *To Johnny.* I wanna shake your hand.

Cec: What the hell for?

Old Sump: 'E's a 'ero, 'e is.

Will: He's a what?

The band is continuing to play outside the house.

Cec: *Yelling.* Hey! Could you play somethin' soft—and maybe religious?

Gompers: Come on.

Johnny: Wait a sec.

Gompers: He says bring you, I bring you.

Johnny: Who?

Gompers: Mr. Big.

Johnny: Who?

Will: He's the rumrunner, Johnny.

Cec: What is happenin' here?

Will: Damned if I know.

Old Sump: Up you go. *They lift Johnny onto their shoulders.*

Will: Where're you goin'?

Old Sump: T'Alberta Hotel, you're invited!

Cec: What the hell—

Will: How come?

Old Sump: 'E's a 'ero!

He nearly drops Johnny.

Gompers: Suuuummp!!

Old Sump: Oh t'at was close, t'at was.

Cec: The Alberta Hotel?

Gompers: Mr. Big!

Old Sump: At t'Alberta Hotel! Are you comin'?

Sump, Gompers and Johnny exit. The sound of the marching band and the glint of instruments fade.

Mrs. Farley: *Off-stage and faint.* Johnny?

Will: Why'd the rumrunner send Gompers to bring him?

Mr. Big, dimly lit but light growing, draws himself a beer at the Alberta Hotel. Mama George wipes the bar. Leah hums softly, pushing back a strand of hair. Leah activates the player piano, which plays in the background.

Mrs. Farley: *Off-stage, faint.* Johnny!

Cec: There'll be booze.

Will: At the Alberta Hotel.

Mrs. Farley: *Off-stage, faint.* Johnny!

Will & Cec: We're comin'! *They exit.*

Scene shifts to the Alberta Hotel.

Mr. Big: You'll see, Mama, just wait till you see him.

Mama George: But to give him your wallet . . .

Mr. Big: It was that or lose it to a pair of American thieves.

Mama George: It coulda been stolen by him.

Mr. Big: You haven't seen him, Mama.

Mama George: That's true.

Mrs. Farley: *Off-stage, faint.* Johnny!

Mr. Big: Now if I'd had a son . . .

Leah: 'Stead of a daughter?

Mr. Big: 'Long with a daughter. . . . This boy's got character, Leah, same as you've got character.

Mama George bustles off-stage.

Leah: *Smiles.* Character.

Mr. Big: And I am a judge a character. That 'bility to judge is not somethin' you cultivate, it's somethin' you're born with. Now the first time I saw you I knew right here. *He touches his heart.* Same thing with him. And that's why I passed him my wallet. You see I could tell just by lookin' at him— as soon as I looked at him— somethin' like you, the first time I laid eyes on you. Can't you remember the first time I laid eyes on you?

Leah: What kinda character could I have had at eleven?

Mr. Big: Whata you mean?

Leah: I mean I was only eleven.

Mr. Big: Go on.

Leah: I mean what kinda character could you see in me at the age of eleven?

Mr. Big: I could discern your potential to love, and to be loved, to be honest, to be loyal, to trust, to be worthy of trust, to . . .

Leah: All that at the age of eleven?

Mr. Big: Was I wrong?

Mama George re-enters with food for the party.

Mr. Big: Eh Mama, whata you say?

Mama George: Mmmn?

Mr. Big: I was talkin' 'bout Leah.

Mama George: Judge a character, that's what I heard.

Mr. Big: Was I right about Leah?

Mama George: Sounded more like a litany for a dog than a daughter.

Mr. Big: A chosen daughter.

Leah: Mama's right, Mr. Big.

Mr. Big: And I chose her because a my great capacity for judgin' character.

Leah: You felt sorry for me.

Mr. Big: Well anybody would've, but that wasn't it.

Leah: Now look—Mama's feedin' seventeen cats in the kitchen.

Mama George: Never in the kitchen.

Leah: From the kitchen, in the back, you know what I mean, and where did they come from?

Mr. Big: I know what you're sayin' but that isn't it either.

Leah: So how's a man who can't pass a mewling cat to sidestep a cryin' kid?

Mr. Big: But you were not cryin'! That's one of the first things I noticed.

Leah: I was cryin'.

Mr. Big: Inside you were cryin'—cryin' out—not a tears kinda cry but a passionate suffusion that . . .

Leah: *Laughs.* Oh Mr. Big, what stories!

Mr. Big: It's true.

Mama George: He believes it.

Mr. Big: And another thing! . . . No shadow. Here's this scrawny little girl-child walkin' along without castin' a shadow.

Leah: It was rainin', Mr. Big.

Mr. Big: For you! For me there was a radiance all round you, and it was comin' from you. From you, Leah. And I didn't stop for more than a . . . it coulda been a hundred years, or a second, or no time at all! Like an instantaneous gatherin' up, like God descendin' to take his Chosen up into heaven in a fiery chariot!

Leah: Are you God, Mr. Big?

Mr. Big: At that moment I was. Invincible, Leah.

Mama George: He was.

Mr. Big: And when I come home, I said, Mama, look Mama.

Mama George: I thought it'd be a ring with a real diamond in it like the pearls that he gave me before.

Mr. Big: That you keep in the box.

Mama George: I look silly wearin' those kinda things.

Mr. Big: But it weren't none a those things. It was somethin' more precious. The most valuable thing I could give her . . . that I never gave her before.

Pause.

Leah: It gets better every time you tell it. . . . What was it really like?

Mr. Big: Can't you remember?

Leah: No.

Mr. Big: It was just like I said.

Leah: *Smiles.* You.

Mr. Big: And this boy the same. Not exactly the same, but a certain kinda sameness. That's why I passed him my wallet.

Mama George: Didn't I tell you, it's risky travellin' by train?

Leah: 'Specially when you're carryin' cash.

Mr. Big: Six thousand dollars! I could tell just by lookin' at him not a dime'd be missin'.

Mama George: Next time you take the MacLaughlin.

Mr. Big: What . . . and have the Brit stuck to my bumper from here right into Lethbridge?

Mama George: The poor man.

Mr. Big: Bill the Brit a poor man?

Mama George: He's just doin' his job.

Mr. Big: We will be outa business the day he starts doin' his job.

Mama George: I still say . . .

Mr. Big: Mama George listen! Are we agreed I'm a great judge a character?

Mama smiles.

Mr. Big: Agreed. Well, when I peruse Sergeant William Windsor, known to some as Bill the Brit . . .

Leah: *Savouring the word.* Pah-ruuse.

Mr. Big: Read, scan or study.

Leah: I know.

Mr. Big: Now when I peruse Sergeant William Windsor a the Prohibition Police . . . there's a void. A vacuum. The man has no character.

Leah: Everyone has some sorta character.

Mr. Big: Not Bill.

Leah: Despicable maybe but . . .

Fragmented image of William Windsor, a.k.a. Bill the Brit, is first seen. Bill approaches the Alberta Hotel, observing it before entering.

Mr. Big: The first time, Leah, I saw William Windsor . . .

Leah: Was he castin' a shadow?

Mr. Big: Sur-rounded by shadow—and imprinted on him comin' was the western hemisphere, and on him goin' the eastern!

Leah: What?

Mr. Big: If you split him down the middle, you'd have a map a the world—predominantly covered in red . . . The Empiah!

Leah: *Laughs.* Oh.

Mr. Big: And all a those red parts were throbbin', this angry red pulsin' and throbbin'!

Leah: Sounds awful.

Mr. Big: It was like lookin' at a movin' planet a boils.

Leah: Make him stop.

Mama George: Now who could do that?

Mr. Big: Honduras and Hong Kong!

Leah: What about 'em?

Mr. Big: Strategically located, and hideously hued!

Bill the Brit enters. He looks more like a Boy Scout than a policeman.

Mr. Big: Aahhh, Sergeant Windsor.

Bill: What?

Mr. Big: A pleasure I'm sure.

Bill: Ah-huh. . . . Which bloody tap have you got runnin' today?

Mr. Big: Beg pardon?

Bill: I said, is it the two percent beer you're pourin' . . . or the hard stuff?

Mr. Big: Two percent's legal tender, Sergeant Windsor. . . .

Bill: Mmmn.

Mr. Big: But if you're lookin' for a drink a bootleg liquor, you better go elsewhere.

Bill: What?

Mr. Big: I said, this is a law-abidin' establishment.

Bill: You're a wily old dog . . . but I'm onto your scent.

Mr. Big: Do you think I'd have it otherwise, Mr. Windsor?

Bill: Sergeant Windsor to you—and you bloody well would, if you could.

Mr. Big: So . . . is it the sarsaparilla . . . or the two percent legal brew you've a thirst for?

Bill: I'll take . . . *He considers.* . . . the tap on the right. . . . *Leah draws him a glass. He observes closely.* . . . Now the left. . . .

He watches intently. Leah glances at Mr. Big, then draws a second glass for Bill, and gives them both to him. He tastes first the one, then the other. He's disappointed as both are legal drafts. He continues to drink from both.

Mr. Big: Tell me . . . do ah . . . two glasses of two percent legal beer constitute four percent beer, hence an indictable offense?

Bill: You're workin' somethin' with those taps—and don't you think I don't know it.

Mr. Big: Ohhh, never have I underestimated your perspicacity, Sergeant Windsor.

Leah stifles a giggle.

Bill: Mmmm. *Drinks his beer.*

Mr. Big: Shall I take a liberty?

Bill: Mmn?

Mr. Big: I'd like to ask you something.

Bill: *Suspicious.* What's that?

Mr. Big: Well . . . there you sit . . .

Bill: Mmn.

Mr. Big: A member of the rulin' class . . .

Bill slowly nods his head in quiet assent.

Mr. Big: Stalwart a the British Empire . . .

Bill: Right.

Mr. Big: Steeped in Raleigh, Drake, and Clive . . .

Bill: India.

Mr. Big: Correct. Trafalgar, Waterloo, Bleinheim.

Bill lifts his glass in a silent toast to the noble fallen.

Mr. Big: And here you sit, isolated in a colonial outpost, surrounded by Ruthenians, Silesians, Bukovinans, Austrians, Russians, Galicians, Moldavians . . . and Irish . . .

Bill: British subjects.

Mr. Big: But didja know the classification Canadian-born's been accepted in this year's census?

Bill: Same thing—British subjects.

Mr. Big: True . . . I suppose.

Pause.

Bill: Was that the question?

Mr. Big: Mmn?

Bill: The liberty you were takin' to ask . . .

Mr. Big: Ah yes. Here, 'tis you must bear the mantle a British decency—Justice! Fair play and pluck! Eh Sergeant Windsor?

Bill: Is that the question?

Mr. Big: You stand lone against the sky preserving the prairies and British civilization from the inroads of barbarism!

Bill: Right.

Mr. Big: Would I lie? And what I want to ask is this. How is it that in the plebiscite, with the Drys urgin' "YES TO PROHIBITION", the electoral slogan of the Wets was "BE BRITISH, VOTE NO TO PROHIBITION"?

Pause.

Bill: You think you got me, don't you?

Mr. Big: Caught in a conundrum, Sergeant Windsor?

Bill: I'm not nowhere but here . . . stuck in Blairmore and dealin' with the likes of you.

Mr. Big: Did you yourself vote in the plebiscite? Oh, forgive me. To address such a question to you.

Bill: You're bloody right.

Mr. Big: This obsession with the bloody . . .

Bill: What obsession are you talkin' about?

Mr. Big: Does it come with the Empire?

Bill: That's something you'll never know.

Mr. Big: But to return to the question at hand.... Of course you voted! It would be un-British not to! How did you vote?... And that's the question.

Bill: That's nobody's business but my own.

Mr. Big: Ahhh.

Bill: And if you had any sense a the basics a democracy, you wouldn't ask!

Mr. Big: Therefore I extrapolate: you're British therefore you voted and being British you voted No. No to Prohibition!

Bill: You don't know how I voted.

Mr. Big: The slogan Sergeant Windsor, "BE BRITISH AND VOTE NO". Would you cast aside your heritage for YES?

Bill: No...

Mr. Big: Ah!

Bill: But...

Mr. Big: Could the slogan be erroneous in its assumption a the British character?

Bill: In some....

Mr. Big: Would this cast doubt on the veracity of all British comment?

Bill: No.

Mr. Big: I refer to history, William Windsor!

Bill: History?

Mr. Big: Published accounts a valiant struggles against the knavish conspiracies a Latin Popes!

Bill: Oh.

Mr. Big: I'm talkin' dates, William Windsor, can't even these be trusted!

Bill: What are you saying?

Mr. Big: I'm speakin' a dissimulated information regardin' the nefarious activity a benighted savages in Africa, Asia, the Americas, and Anglo-Saxon efforts to overcome same!

Bill: What the bloody hell are you talkin' about?

Mr. Big: *Sings.*
Rule Britannia!
Britannia rule the waves!

Did you vote dry to preserve your job, William Windsor, or did you vote Wet—Yes or No—and even now as you sit here sippin' my legal draft, are you engaged in the activity a policin' an unjust and damnable law that you yourself voted against!? *Pause.* Aaaaahhhh . . . what it must do to your soul, William Windsor.

Pause.

Bill: Which of the mongrel races do you originate from?

Mr. Big: Canadian, sir.

Pause. Bill looks at Leah.

Bill: What's she doin' here?

Mr. Big: She lives here.

Bill: No women.

Mr. Big: In their livin' room?

Bill: What livin' room?

Mr. Big: This livin' room.

Bill: What livin' room?

Mr. Big: Perhaps not your kinda livin' room, but the Alberta Hotel is our home, Mama's and Leah's and mine, and such as it is, this is our livin' room.

Bill: No operatin' a business from your livin' room. I could charge you for that!

Mr. Big: A business?

Bill: You're sellin' beer, aren't you?

Mr. Big: Did you pay for your beer?

Pause.

Bill: I could get a score a people to swear they bought beer in this room.

Mr. Big: Oh those occasions I am runnin' a business . . . and should you ever catch Leah or Mama on the premises, of course they must be charged.

Bill: You can't run a business one minute, and a livin' room the next.

Mr. Big: You've presented irrefutable proof that I do.

Bill: But you can't.

Mr. Big: But I do.

Bill: What I'm sayin' is there's a law against it!

Mr. Big: Ahhhhh. *Accepting Bill's statement.* What law would that be?

Pause. Bill gets up to leave.

Mr. Big: Sergeant Windsor? . . . Has the local constabulary apprehended the two responsible for the hold-up on today's train outa Lethbridge?

Bill: Why do you ask?

Mr. Big: Well my good man, I was a passenger on same, and I lost forty dollars to the tip of a gun.

Bill: Forty dollars?

Mr. Big: Correct, sir.

Bill: Mmm.

Mr. Big: Have . . .

Bill: We caught 'em crossin' the border.

Mr. Big: I see.

Bill: Story has it they're American rumrunners, come up and paid a big man in these parts for a load a booze. Six thousand dollars worth.

Mr. Big: What a sum.

Bill: And they hoped to steal it back offa that man on the train he was takin'. A double-cross you could say.

Mr. Big: And were they in possession a six thousand dollars?

Bill shakes his head.

Mr. Big: Their "big man" musta travelled some other route.

Bill: *Nods his head.* Suure.

Sound of the marching band approaching. Glint of light on brass. Fractured images. Eventually the figure of Johnny appears on the shoulders of Will and Gompers, accompanied by Cec, Dolly, and an exhausted Old Sump.

Mr. Big: Six thousand dollars ... and I thought it a tragedy to lose forty-five.

Bill: Forty-five?

Mr. Big: *Smiles.* Forty in bills, and five dollars in change, forty-five in all. Approximate.

Bill: Approximate.

Mr. Big: Ah listen ... I'm plannin' a wee celebration—in our livin' room, this evenin'. Would you care to join us, Sergeant Windsor?

Bill: Celebratin' what?

Mr. Big: I'm extendin' an invite.

Old Sump: *From outside.* Are we t'ere t'en?

Will: Jesus, Johnny, think light.

Widow Popovitch: *Running on to join them.* Vait! Vait! Ve should make d'entrance togetter.

Bill starts to leave.

Mr. Big: Maybe later? ... Any time.

Dolly: Leah!

Martial music galore. As Bill steps out of the Alberta Hotel to view the motley herd, Old Sump cuts the sound from the band. A brief squawk from a horn instrument. Mr. Big laughs. Dolly rushes in to Leah.

Dolly: Wait 'til you see him.

Leah: Who?

Dolly: His brother.

Leah: I've already seen him.

Dolly: You have?

Leah: Uh-huh.

Dolly: A best friend is someone you don't hide nothin' from.

Leah: Here they come.

The crowd rushes in as Mr. Big greets them and Mama pours drinks.

Mr. Big: Good man, Gompers. A precise delivery. . . . And Will Farley, beast a burden to your brother . . . and what a brother.

Will: How do.

Sump: *To the off-stage band.* Thanks for the hot air, now bugger off.

Mr. Big: Get your man a whiskey, Dolly. He's earned it. *To Johnny.* Don't go, boy. Here, beside me, right here beside me.

Will: *Whispers.* Hey, Johnny?

Dolly: Come on, Will. *She yanks him over to the bar.*

Mr. Big: You've a fine son, Mr. Farley, I wish I'd the same. I envy you this boy.

Cec: How'd him and you . . .

Mr. Big: He's got potential. . . . We'll drink to that, if your good wife doesn't . . .

Cec: What she don't know won't hurt her.

Mr. Big: Nicely put.

Dolly: *Holds up a glass.* For you, Cec!

Cec: I'm acomin'!

Mr. Big: And Widow Popovitch, a pleasure, Widow.

Widow: Why don't you haf dat Leah help vit da mama?

Mr. Big: But she's helping with me.

Widow: And den I vould not haf d'opportunity to do so, eh? *She laughs and moves to help Mama at the bar.* Mama, look at dese hands, dey are crying out, put dem to vork!

Mr. Big: And Sump.

Old Sump: Ah-huh.

Mr. Big: Have you survived the Frank Slide and both minin' disasters a 1914 to succumb on my step to simple exhaustion?

Old Sump: I'll revive wit' a drink.

Mr. Big: A drink for Old Sump!

Old Sump: T'boy looks lean enuff but 'e still wears on you after a mile.

The widow gives him a drink and he drains it.

Old Sump: I feel me strengt' comin' back . . . not *totally* back . . .

Mr. Big: Another, my friend?

Old Sump: I t'ink it would help.

Dolly and Leah in one conversation, Mr. Big and Johnny in another.

Mr. Big: Now let me get a good look at you, boy.

Dolly: Well?

Leah: Well what?

Johnny: What do you see?

Dolly: Well what do you think?

Leah: 'Bout what?

Johnny: What is it?

Dolly: Tell me.

Leah: You mean him?

Mr. Big: I see a fine lad.

Dolly: He's not as cute as his brother.

Mr. Big: A lad to be proud of.

Leah: You think not?

Dolly: Not half so cute.

Johnny: You can't tell that from lookin'.

Leah: No?

Dolly: No.

Johnny: Can you?

Mr. Big: Some can—and some can't.

Johnny: Oh.

Leah: Is so.

Mr. Big: I can.

Leah: And nicer too. . . . Here you are. *Hands him a drink.*

Johnny: Thanks.

Mr. Big: It's an elegant distillation.

Will: Hey Johnny, there's things you been keepin' from us, boy.

Mr. Big: All in good time, eh, Johnny?

Will: Me and the old man, we was wonderin' how the two a you . . .

Mr. Big: And a notable tale it is, Will.

Will: Yeah?

Mr. Big: But first lubrication . . .

Old Sump: Can I have a t'ird, t'en?

Mr. Big: You not only can, you must!

Old Sump: T'ose are t'words t'at bind me to you. *He's off for a third drink.*

Johnny: And second?

Mr. Big: Illumination.

Will: Illumination—you got that, Johnny?

Johnny: Ah-huh.

Will: Well—Pop and me'll just keep workin' on the lubricatin' part. . . . Johnny?

Johnny: In a minute.

Leah: Do you want me to get you another?

Johnny: I ain't hardly touched this one yet—but thanks all the same.

Mr. Big: I owe you, young man.

Johnny: You don't owe me nothin'.

Mr. Big: But I do. You did me a service.

Johnny: Wasn't much.

Mr. Big: And when a service is done, a debt is incurred . . . you'd agree?

Johnny: I guess . . . in general . . . yes, I'd agree.

Mr. Big smiles.

Johnny: Did I say somethin' funny?

Mr. Big: I'm a judge a character, Johnny—and I liked the way you handled that query.

Johnny: You did?

Mr. Big nods.

Johnny: It don't necessarily mean that I agree you owe me.

Mr. Big: I understand what you meant.

Johnny: And if you did owe me, which you don't, the booze for Pop and Will—and myself—and the general celebration and all, well, that's more than paid off the debt. Which you don't owe me. If you get what I mean.

Mr. Big: I do. Precisely.

Johnny: Good.

Mr. Big: And the perambulation I arranged with the marchin' band, you don't mention that?

Johnny: Well, to tell you the truth, I been ridin' that train straight out from Tronna, and what them Pullman benches started, them bony shoulders finished. My be-hind's so raw you could. . . . Oh . . . I beg your pardon, Miss.

Mr. Big: My daughter, Leah.

Johnny: Nice to meetcha. *He stares at Leah.*

Mr. Big: You were sayin'?

Johnny: Mn? . . . Oh. Nothin'. . . . Just . . . nothin'.

Mr. Big: I'm int'rested, boy.

Johnny: I . . . I ain't got nothin' else to say, I don't think.

Mr. Big: So . . . home from Toronto . . . for a visit?

Johnny: No, I come back you could say.

Mr. Big: Couldn't find work.

Johnny: That's it.

Mr. Big: How'd you pay for your ticket?

Johnny: I . . .

He looks down at his hands. Pause. Mr. Big squeezes his shoulder.

Mr. Big: It's all right. You're a good boy. I can tell.

Johnny: I tried.

Mr. Big: I know.

Johnny: I walked them streets applyin' for jobs a dog wouldn't take . . . worse than the mines.

Mr. Big: You think so?

Johnny: No. Not worse than the mines, but you see . . . I could never get nothin' steady and now the soldiers is back and nothin' steady for them and . . .

Mr. Big: And what?

Johnny: And . . . I give up. That's what I done. I give up. Ain't got no choice. I had to come back.

Mr. Big: You been over to the colliery?

Johnny: Not yet.

Mr. Big: But those are your plans.

Johnny: There ain't nothin' else but the mines.

Mr. Big: And are you lookin' forward to that?

Johnny stares at Mr. Big. He says nothing. Mr. Big leans closer to him.

Mr. Big: There's a radiance round you, boy, and those with eyes can see it.

Johnny: *Smiles.* That's 'cause I ain't got the black from the mine yet. Any radiance Pop had is all gone, and Will's is just peekin' through in spots.

Mr. Big: I'm talkin' incandescence, boy . . .

Johnny: Yeah?

Mr. Big: Look at Leah.

Johnny: Ah-huh.

Mr. Big: Can you see it?

Johnny looks at Leah, tilts his head, squints his eyes a bit, looks at Mr. Big, back at Leah. Leah smiles.

Leah: Sometimes he just talks like that.

Johnny: Ah-huh.

Mr. Big: Can you see it?

Johnny: Aah . . .

Mr. Big: Can you?

Johnny: Bit maybe.

Mr. Big: Same thing with you. I can see it. A luminous aura. That's how I knew I could trust you. . . . I'm a man a influence, Johnny. Do you know what I'm sayin'?

Johnny: No.

Mr. Big: I'm talkin' gainful employment, and a position right here, by my side. Like a son, Johnny.

Mr. Big moves away from Johnny to address the gathering. Leah touches Johnny's arm.

Leah: You'll get used to him. He's just kinda like that.

Johnny: *Nods his head.* Yeah. Okay.

Mr. Big: Ladies and gentlemen!

The player piano begins playing very softly of its own accord. It provides an accompaniment to Mr. Big's speech.

Mr. Big: Ladies and gents of the flourishin' city of Blairmore!

Cec: City you says!

Mr. Big: Says city I do! For the future is as clear to me as the past! Destiny calls to Blairmore. . . .

Will: Oooooooo-eeeeeeeee!

Mr. Big: Ooooooooooo-eeeeeeeeee! And this tiny town will feed and fatten on the efforts a citizens such as ourselves to achieve one day a state a such metropolity it'll make Tronna no more than a cow pie, and its environs nothin' but road apples!

Old Sump: Watch where you step, ooooo-eeeeee!

Widow: And vere vill you place in da scheme a tings den?

Mr. Big: Where fortune and destiny dictate.

A round of applause.

Mr. Big: But tonight is not one dedicated to paeans a future exploits, no matter how well deserved and inevitable they be. Tonight I speak of a courageous deed executed by this young man here!

The player piano grows a bit in volume with appropriate music as Mr. Big sets his "train cars" with a couple of chairs. The others, at first reluctantly, but then with growing enjoyment, play the roles he assigns.

By the time the widow enters as the conductor there is much fun and games; it is no longer necessary for Mr. Big to direct or assign. Everyone is into it.

Mr. Big: Picture ... if you will ... the interior of the railway car from Lethbridge....
This seat here ... and here ... and here.... And here ... sits Johnny, gingerly but alert, fourteen days on the rails from the mysterious east, but within sight and smell a home and mother.... Forgive me, Mrs. Farley! To mention your name in these surroundings is to render less than your due, which is prodigious for producing such a boy as Johnny!

And here ... a lady with a dark brow and piercin' eyes and a countenance to turn the hens off their nests for a fortnight. Now Dolly, it's a challenge to your art a make-believe. And by her side a child.... *Places Will in chair next to her.* ... with little of the cute and cunning ways of children. But rather the sad inheritor of all those traits least amiable and features most repulsive from both maternal and paternal lineage. Coupled with these, a voice like a rasp and in possession of a small drum. To even contemplate, much less act upon, the intention of inflicting this tot on one's fellow man in an enclosed space.... Ah truly there are things answerable only when the dead awaken.

... And here ... my Leah ... and close at hand, my Gompers ever faithful, ever watchful, ever ... ever Gompers.

And myself.

Well outa Lethbridge.

The sound and motion of the train begins among those on it. It picks up speed.

Mr. Big: Past Pincher Creek.... Into the Crowsnest.... Past picturesque log cabins cut from virgin lodgepole pine.... When suddenly from the end a the car ...

Widow: *Enters the train car swaying to the motion of the train.* Blairmore! Blairmore! Next stop Blairm.... Dat child's a menace, ma'am.

Cec and Sump enter the train car. Sump has a gun he's got from behind the bar.

Widow: Blairmore! Nice trip, Mr. . . .

Cec: Everybody calm and nobody gits hurt!

Dolly: Aaaahhhhhh!

Old Sump: *To Gompers.* Don't try nothin' funny.

Widow: Da safety a da passenge . . .

Old Sump: Shaddup or I ventilate t'chest!

Dolly: Aaaaaahhhhh!

Mr. Big stands up with his wallet behind his back. Johnny plucks it out of his hand and shoves it into the back of his pants under his jacket. They never stop responding to the train's motion.

Cec: *To Dolly.* Your money or your grapefruit!

The child, Will, bites his arm.

Cec: Ahh! Git this kid off! Leggo!

Old Sump: You! *To Mr. Big.* I want da wallet!

Cec: Help! *As Dolly and Will beat at him.*

Old Sump snatches a billfold Mr. Big offers.

Old Sump: Come on, let's go!

Cec: Help!

Gompers makes a grab for Old Sump. Sump gives him a whack with the gun.

Gompers: Ouch! Hey!

Old Sump grabs Cec. They make their way to the end of the train car. Dolly, Will, the widow and Gompers advance on them with murmurs of protest.

Old Sump: Back! Back! Don't make me fire! Back! Ready, Floyd?

Cec nods. Sump fires three real shots in the air as Cec opens the "door". The two of them jump supposedly from the train, rolling as they hit the dirt. Dolly, Will, the widow, even Gompers, break out of character as they realize the shots are real.

Will: Holy shit!

Cec: Je-sus, Sump, whata you got there?

Old Sump: T'bar gun.

Cec: That's some real, that is.

Old Sump: Didn't t'ink it'd hurt none.

Johnny returns Mr. Big's wallet to him. Mr. Big puts his arm around Johnny's shoulders.

Mr. Big: Thank you, Johnny.

Johnny nods, accepting his thanks.

Dolly: I was scared.

Mr. Big: In a tight corner, you're a man I'd have at my back.

Widow: Dis ear, dere is notin' dere, maybe not ever again.

Old Sump: Eh?

Will: She says you bust one a her ear drums.

Old Sump: Half a what you hear ain't wort' listenin' to anyways.

They all get fresh drinks.

Mr. Big: For you. *Gives a drink to Johnny.*

Cec: You hear that, Popovitch?

Widow: Vit dis ear I hear it. Vit dis, notin'.

Bill appears on the run.

Gompers: Then stand to the other side a Sump. *He turns her bad ear towards Sump.* That way you'll not miss a thing.

A roar of laughter. Bill rushes into the Alberta Hotel.

Bill: All right everyone! Hold it!

They obey.

Mr. Big: Delighted you could join us, Sergeant.

Bill: I heard somethin'.

Mr. Big: Convivial folks rejoicing!

Bill: Sounded more like a shot.

Widow: Oo vas shot?

Will: Somebody shot?

Old Sump: Murder!

Cec: Help, police!

Bill: Hold it!

Mr. Big: This is surely distressing news . . . have you apprehended the villain?

Bill: I know the villain all right.

Mr. Big: Quick work.

Bill: I've got him 'tween a stone and a hard place.

Mr. Big: Congratulations.

Bill: I'm impounding the contents . . .

Mr. Big: A toast . . .

Bill: . . . a the glasses!

Mr. Big: . . . to Sergeant Windsor!

Bill: Hold it!

They down the contents of their glasses as Bill makes a futile attempt to grab a glass or two for evidence.

Bill: You! Hey! Come on there!

Bill gets Dolly's empty glass. Several of the company are repressing their reaction to downing overproof whiskey in one gulp. Bill runs his finger round the inside of Dolly's glass. The widow plucks the glass from his hand as he tastes the residue on his finger.

Mr. Big: My god, man, I'd no idea you craved it so.

Bill: Whiskey.

Bill grabs Leah's glass. He runs his finger round the glass.

Mr. Big: A beer for Bill the Brit!

Bill: Sarsaparilla.

Mr. Big: Profuse apologies, sir.

Mr. Big presents Bill with a glass of legal two percent brew. Mama has switched the taps back. All get a two percent beer which they sip with little satisfaction and some discomfort.

Bill: Two percent.

Mr. Big: A legal draft.

Bill: I had the evidence right here. *He holds up his finger.*

Widow: *Grabbing Bill's finger and giving it a suck.* Mmmmn—sch!

Bill: Ah, you revoltin' old . . .

Cec: Hey!

Sump: T'at's enuff!

Bill: But she . . .

Cec: Watch it!

Bill: What the bloody hell . . .

Mr. Big: Bear with the rustics.

Bill: It's your doin'.

Mr. Big: Oh no. It's a Canadian custom—like kissing the hand of a king.

George Gammon
David Marriage as Old Sump, Stephen Hair as Bill the Brit, Rita Howell as
Widow Popovitch
Theatre Calgary, 1983

Will: He's right.

Will grabs Dolly's hand, gives a quick kissy suck to her finger.

Cec: I do it myself.

Old Sump: Every time we meets t'members of t'colliery head office, we all does it!

Will, Dolly, Old Sump, the widow, and Cec start a mad round of quick kiss/suck of any and all fingers, dropping curtseys and murmurs of obeisance or patronage. Johnny and Leah are amused. Johnny takes Leah's hand. He pauses, then kisses the back of it. She smiles at him. Mama George notices. Mr. Big does not.

Mr. Big: It's a mark of respect.

Several make grabs for Bill's hand. He tries to shake them off, nevertheless several succeed in quick kissy sucks.

Bill: Get away! Get away there! Aaaahh! Get away!

Car headlights flash on the window, two short, one long honk from a car horn. Mr. Big and Gompers exchange a look.

Will: It can't be!

Old Sump: But it is!

Bill: What is?

The headlights are extinguished.

Dolly: Didn't you hear it?

They rush to peer in the opposite direction to that of the car.

Cec: Oh no!

Widow: Vight here in Blairmore!

Bill: What is it?

Dolly: Didn't you hear it?

Will: Look!

Bill: Where?

Dolly: There.

Cec: Oh my god.

Old Sump: It's t'em.

Bill: Who is it?

Dolly: Didn't you see 'em?

Will: And tomorrow is pay day.

Cec: Today is pay day!

Bill: Who is it!

Old Sump: Why it's t' . . . *at a loss.*

Cec: It's the . . .

Dolly: It can't be . . .

Will: That gang from Montana . . . two honks and a toot!

Old Sump: T'ey're headin' for t'colliery office.

Will: They're after the payroll!

Cec: Help, police!

Bill: If this is some kinda ruse.

Mr. Big: Are we to inform Manager Wheatley a Dominion Colliery you thought it not worth checkin' out?

Pause.

Will: A workin' man could lose his job for that kinda oversight.

Pause. Bill exits on the run. The company laughs.

Mr. Big: Switch the taps, Mama.

Mama George: The whole buncha you ought to be ashamed.

Mr. Big: *Checking outside.* Poor man, eh Mama?

Car lights flash on, off.

Will: He only got five horses and three cars.

Cec: To patrol all Southern Alberta.

Gompers draws on gloves.

Widow: He vill vun all d'way to d'colliery.

Old Sump: 'uffin' and puffin'.

Mr. Big: *Prepared to leave.* A drink to the man's dedication. A *proper* drink, Mama.

Mama switches the taps, pours the drinks.

Mr. Big: Excuse us my friends.

Old Sump: You'll be back t'en?

Mr. Big: In a while.

Gompers stands ready to go.

Mr. Big: Remember ... celebrate—enjoy—else my wrath'll fall directly on you.... You Sump and Will and Cec ... Dolly, Widow, Johnny ... Mama too ... and Leah, even you!

Old Sump: We swears to celebrate.

Several: Amen!

Mr. Big and Gompers exit in the direction of the car.

Old Sump: Now—as I was sayin'—t'legal draft tastes just like bunny pee.

Will: And when'd you drink that, Sump?

Leah, with a look to Johnny, drifts over towards the piano. Johnny follows.

Old Sump: Be you buried four days you drink most anyt'ing.

Dolly: Where'd you get the bunnies?

Old Sump: Was your own piss you drunk, but we likes to call it bunny pee.

Will: Bunny pee?

Old Sump: T'ere's ladies present.

Will: Bunny pee?

Old Sump: T'beer tastes like piss.

Will: Ah-huh.

Old Sump: So's I was lookin' for a genteel way a sayin' t'at.

Johnny: You was sayin' . . . he's always like that?

Leah: Who?

Johnny: Him. Mr. Big.

Leah: Most always.

A single note on the piano, low, hardly distinguishable as such, could almost be the sigh of the wind, a stirring of the heart, a ting of a glass from the bar. There are four rough groupings: Johnny and Leah apart from the others, Will and Dolly not so much so, Cec and Old Sump in close proximity but not with the widow and Mama. The note, and sometimes a couple of notes, repeat on the piano at intervals during the following. Lights move back and forth across the figures picking out first this grouping, then that, a fluid dance of soft light with the voices, the piano, the people.

Will: You're not upset by that, are you?

Dolly: By what?

Will: "Piss".

Dolly: I heard it before.

Will: That's good.

Widow: I'm vatchin' dem, Mama. You vatch vit me.

Leah: Do you wanna stand or do you wanna sit?

Johnny: What do you want?

Leah sits. Johnny sits.

Will: God but you're pretty.

Dolly looks away.

Will: I mean it.

Old Sump: I'm t'inkin', Cec, didja know t'at? Didja know what I'm t'inkin'?

Cec: 'bout piss?

Old Sump: In a way. I was t'inkin t'at t'Lord said to me t'ree times—no, m'boy, don't wantcha. . . . Worked in t'mines all me life, and I never got no lungs t'at I know of, and t'ere you be losin' boys right and left . . .

Cec: And they was good boys too.

Old Sump: T'at t'ey were.

Cec: Teddy named after her father, and Robert strong as a bull.

Old Sump: Didn't do him no good when it come to it.

Cec: No sir.

Old Sump: T'ere ain't none of it makes a helluva lot a sense . . . didja ever t'ink t'at?

Cec: Nope.

Old Sump: Just as well. Don't do to dwell on 't.

Will: Look at my hands, Dolly.

Dolly: You got nice hands.

Will: You wanna know what I used on em? . . . I used the lye, and the bleach.

Dolly: Really?

Will: Uh-huh.

Dolly: I don't think that would be good for you.

Will: I do it for you. It stings like hell, eats the skin right off, that's why it's so red.

Dolly: Do you think you should?

Will: I don't give a damn if it hurts. I do it for you.

Dolly: I wouldn't want you to do something that wasn't good for you because a me.

Will: It's 'cause I know you don't like the black . . . have you still got that picture I give you?

Dolly nods.

Johnny: I can see you're not a great one for talkin'.

Will: Lemme hold your hand, Dolly.

Leah: If I've got somethin' to say, then I say it.

Johnny: Ah.

Leah: Besides, you're not so talky yourself.

Johnny: I toldja I been away for a while on my own. . . . You get to talkin' more to yourself when that happens.

Leah: With Mr. Big, it's hard to keep up.

Johnny: My mum's a big talker—a course not like him—she's more a your . . . ordinary talker.

Widow: Dey're talkin'.

Mama George: Mmn. *Assent; she's noticed.*

Widow: I said dey're talkin', da two a dem, look at dem talkin'.

Mama George: I heard ya.

Leah: Are you gonna take that job?

Johnny: What job?

Leah: The job that he offered you.

Johnny: He just said employment.

Leah: Workin' for him.

Johnny: He said a bunch a stuff, a person don't know what he means and what he don't mean. *Johnny looks over towards his father, who is quite drunk.*

Cec: Too good for the mines, filled his head with garbage. *Cec and*

Johnny catch each other's gaze. .... Good enough for Will, good enough for me.

Johnny: *Back to Leah.* What's he do, 'sides talk?

Leah: *Gets up.* Lotsa things.

Johnny: What'd I be doin'?

Leah: What he told you.

Cec: *Staggers to his feet, bursts into song.*
My father was a miner,
My mother she is dead,
And I am just an orphan child,
No place to lay my head. ...

Old Sump: *Joins Cec in song.*
All thro' this world I wander
They drive me from their doors
The two of them precariously prepare to exit for home.
Someday I'll find a welcome
On Heaven's golden shore!
They're out the door.
Now if to me you'll listen
I'll tell a story ...

Resounding crash as Cec falls, dragging Sump with him.

Old Sump: Popovitch!

Cec: Christ.

Widow: I go.

Cec: Popovitch!

Will: I'll see to 'em.

Widow: You go vit your Dolly. I valk dem up and down and den home.

Old Sump: Popovitch!

Widow: When you're not'in' to no one, you're dead. Dey keep me alive. *She joins Sump and Cec, moving them off.* You break my ear den you call for Popovitch! Get up! Get up! Get going! Popovitch vill drive you like pigs!

The widow, Sump, and Cec disappear from sight, an oblique image flashes and they're gone. Will and Dolly prepare to leave. Johnny looks at Leah, who's standing.

Johnny: Where're you goin'?

Leah: To bed.

Johnny: Stay.

Will: *With his arm around Dolly.* You comin' Johnny?

Johnny: Go on, I'll catch up.

Dolly: Good night.

Leah: 'Night Dolly, 'night Will.

Will and Dolly exit from the Alberta Hotel. Will is whistling. They stop. Will kisses Dolly. They make their way off, Will whistling.

Johnny sits watching Mama and Leah restore a bit of order. Mama tidies. Leah looks as if she might leave.

The reflected and softly blurred image of Dolly and Will kissing. Will's whistling heard faintly from off-stage. The image fades. Whistling continues, growing fainter for slightly longer.

Johnny: Do you gotta go right now?

Leah: Why?

Johnny: I thought maybe we, you and me, we could . . . sit and talk.

Leah: What do you wanna talk about?

Johnny shrugs.

Mama George: Went thro' a whole keg, imagine that. *She places a small light so it may be seen outside.* Course it doesn't take long, fact it takes a lot less than a body'd think, just the same, I'm always surprised. . . . He's taken to you.

Johnny: Oh?

Mama George: Yes he has. Ask her. She'll tell you.

Johnny: I will.

Mama George: If you need tellin'. And do you know who she is?

Johnny: I think so.

Mama George: A chosen daughter. . . . And now who'd you be?

Johnny: Me?

Mama George: Ah-huh.

Johnny: Johnny Farley.

Mama George: You're a fine lookin' boy all right.

Johnny: Who're you?

Mama George: Mama George. With or without incandescence, a body'd be lookin' twice at you, eh, Leah?

Leah: Looks aren't everything.

Johnny: Are you related to him?

Leah: Mama George is Mrs. Big . . . course we don't call her that.

Mama George: Can only be one Big in a family.

Johnny: That ain't his real name—Mr. Big.

Mama George: His chosen name, that's what it is.

Johnny: Mr. George, is that his real name?

Mama George: Glasses, glasses, more glasses . . . the two of you stay, I'll see to these. *She exits with glasses to be washed.*

Pause as Johnny and Leah eye each other.

Johnny: So . . . is it George?

Leah: Does it matter?

Johnny: No. . . . What's your last name then?

Leah: Unknown.

Johnny: What?

Leah: Last name unknown.

Johnny: I thought you was their daughter.

Leah: Their . . .

Johnny: Chosen daughter, ah-huh. . . .

Leah: What're you thinkin'?

Johnny: Nothin'.

Leah: You must be thinkin' somethin'.

Johnny: No.

Leah: What're you thinkin' you don't wanna tell me?

Johnny: Nothin'.

Leah: I'd tell you if you asked me.

Johnny: What're you thinkin'?

Leah: I'm thinkin' . . . you *are* better lookin' than your brother.

Johnny: We wasn't even talkin' 'bout that.

Leah: I know.

Johnny: You wasn't livin' here when I left.

Leah: No.

Johnny: Did I tell you I went to Tronna?

Leah: Dolly went to Tronna.

Johnny: I heard.

Leah: She said it was awful.

Johnny: She's right.

Leah: She had to do awful things. And then she came back here even though her mum was already dead and her dad died after she left and there weren't none of her family left, she still came here. . . . Why do you think she did that?

Johnny: I guess it was home.

Leah: With nobody left.

Johnny: A place can be home, the sky and the hills.

Leah: I'm lucky.

Johnny: How's that?

Leah: 'Cause that will never happen to me.

Johnny: What?

Leah: What happened to Dolly in Tronna. It coulda happened to me but it won't . . . and do you know why?

Johnny: Why?

Leah: 'Cause he gathered me up, like God descendin' to take his Chosen up into Heaven in a fiery chariot! *Johnny is staring at her. She stops and looks at him.* And the same thing can happen to you, if you let him.

Pause. Johnny leans over and kisses her. Pause. He kisses her again. These are little kisses, not passionate ones.

Leah: You shouldn't do that.

Johnny: Why not?

Leah: Because.

They sit in silence.

Leah: D . . .

Johnny: Don't talk.

They sit in silence.

Leah: We gotta talk sometime.

Johnny: It's a nice place, this. I feel good sittin' here. Feel right sittin' here.

Leah: If it weren't for him and Mama, I wouldn't have anyone.

Johnny: You'd have me.

Leah: You just met me.

Johnny: But it don't feel that way, does it.

Leah: I feel funny, that's all.

Johnny: I feel . . . like I . . . like I knowed you—and him—for a hundred years, don't you feel that?

Leah: I dunno.

Johnny: Say you do. I knowed you do. I said it 'cause I knew you could feel what I was feelin'. I wasn't afraid to say it.

Leah: I am.

Johnny stares at her.

Johnny: I . . .

Leah gets up and starts to leave.

Johnny: Leah! . . .

Leah: What?

Johnny: Do you think I should take this job?

Leah: It's up to you.

Johnny: Do you want me to?

Leah: I dunno.

Johnny: Either you do or you don't.

Leah: Well I don't then.

Johnny: You're lyin'.

Leah: Well I do then.

Johnny: Well I will then.

Leah: All right then. *Leah starts off.*

Johnny: Leah!

Leah: What?

Johnny: I just wanted to look at you before you left.

Leah: Well?

Johnny: You look real nice.

She starts to exit.

Johnny: Leah!

Leah: What?

She stops and turns to him.

Johnny: Good night.

Leah: *Looks severe for a moment, then smiles.* Good night. *She exits.*

Johnny: *Watches her go, then softly.* Oooooooo-eeeeeeeeee. Oo-ee.
*He slowly looks round at his surroundings. He walks to where Mr.
Big formerly stood, strikes a pose reminiscent of Mr. Big's. He
speaks softly.* Ladies and gents a the flourishin' city a Blairmore
. . . *He laughs.* Says city I do. *Pause. Serious again, he goes to the
bar. He pours a glass from the tap.*

Mr. Big and Gompers approach the Alberta Hotel.

Johnny: Like a son . . . like a father . . .

Mr. Big: Is the count right?

Gompers: Yes sir.

*Johnny takes a large swig from the glass. He spews it out. Mr. Big and
Gompers enter the hotel. The light is dim; they are unaware of Johnny,
who watches them. They busy themselves with lowering two kegs from
the rafters.*

Mr. Big: I want you in the forward car with the goods. I'll be right
behind. Now remember, any sign a the Brit, and go like hell for
the border.

Gompers: Which border?

Mr. Big: Any border you got a hope in hell a crossin' 'fore he
catches up. And praise the Lord for the Whiskey Six. *Their focus
is on their work.* . . . It's been my experience . . . a little prayer . . .
never hurt . . .

*A clink of glass from Johnny. Mr. Big and Gompers tense, turning to
scan the bar. Gompers makes a move. Mr. Big places a hand on his
arm.*

Johnny: . . . It's me.

Mr. Big: *Relaxing, nods to Gompers to continue.* Ah, so it is. *He
moves to Johnny at the bar as Gompers works.*

Mr. Big: Mama set the lamp, I thought . . . *Runs a finger through the spewed drink.* Did she switch the taps? What you do is . . . replace the glass on the shelf to the left a your knee if you'd care for an illegal draft or a whiskey . . .

Outside the Alberta Hotel, slightly distorted, is a fractured image of Bill in uniform, a bit more formal than his original scoutish uniform. Bill himself appears in the shadows observing the hotel. A stir in the shadows behind him. After a moment we see that a second figure is there—Mrs. Farley. Bill turns to whisper to Mrs. Farley. Mrs. Farley nods. Bill seems to assure her. The two of them gaze at the Alberta Hotel. Mrs. Farley scurries off.

Johnny moves the glass, looks at Mr. Big, then pours another drink from the tap. He tastes it, looks at Mr. Big, and laughs.

Mr. Big: Bit better?

Johnny: Lot better.

Mr. Big: Now that's a secret, boy . . . not a word, even to Gompers.

Johnny: What's a . . . what's a Whiskey Six?

Mr. Big: Six cylinder MacLaughlin, fastest car on the road. A most seductive vehicle. *He blows out the lamp, and looks out onto the street. He can see Bill the Brit.* Do you drive, Johnny?

Johnny: I could learn.

Gompers looks out the window onto the street with Mr. Big. Mr. Big continues his conversation with Johnny. The two kegs are ready to be moved out.

Mr. Big: Do you believe . . . it criminal to eat a cucumber sandwich, Johnny?

Johnny: No.

Mr. Big: Nor is it a crime to drink a beer. . . . Prohibition will never last, boy.

Johnny: It won't, eh.

Mr. Big: For it's based on a lie.

Bill the Brit gives up and exits from his post of observation. Mr. Big nods to Gompers who moves to the kegs. Mr. Big turns to Johnny.

Mr. Big: And a lie cannot endure.

Johnny: Where do you want that?

Mr. Big: Edge of the bar for now.

A groan of effort from Gompers. Mr. Big and Johnny move to help him.

The kegs are awkward to move. They work in silence for a second except for the slight sound of exertion. Light is fading on the Alberta Hotel.

Johnny: Jesus.

Mr. Big: All right?

Johnny: I never knew booze was so heavy.

Mr. Big: Tell me, Johnny. Can you keep a man sober thro' coercion a law? Can a man be made moral by threatin' punishment? Now what are your thoughts on this, Johnny?

The Alberta Hotel disappears in darkness.

Mrs. Farley: *In darkness.* And in the midst of the seven candle sticks one like unto the Son of Man clothed with a garment . . . and girt round . . . a golden girdle. *Light begins to build on Mrs. Farley. She reads from a book.* His head and hairs were white like wool, white as snow and his eyes were as a flame of fire, and his voice as the sound of many waters and he had in his right hand seven stars and out of his mouth a two-edged sword and his countenance was as the sun shineth in its strength, and when I saw him I fell at his feet as if dead.

Mrs. Farley: And he laid his right hand upon me saying fear not. . . . I am the First and the Last, I am he that liveth and was dead and behold I am alive evermore . . . and have . . .

Sound of Johnny whistling off-stage.

Mrs. Farley: The keys . . . *She shuts the book.* . . . of hell and of death . . .

Whistling grows in volume slightly. Johnny stops whistling, doesn't sneak in, but enters quietly. He stops on seeing his mother.

Mrs. Farley: . . . Do you know what time it is?

Johnny: 'Bout twenty past.

Mrs. Farley: Past what?

Johnny: Five.

Mrs. Farley: In the afternoon, Johnny.

Johnny: I know what you're gonna say.

Mrs. Farley: How could you . . . when I don't know myself.

Johnny: Why don't you just say it.

Pause.

Mrs. Farley: When your father got in, it was light.

Johnny: Yeah.

Mrs. Farley: And William, he was later than that.

Johnny: We had a kinda celebration, Mum.

Mrs. Farley: Both of 'em still weavin' when they left for work.

Johnny: I helped a fella out on the train up from Leth . . .

Mrs. Farley: I know it! I may be the last to know it, it bein' all over Blairmore, but someone, outa the goodness a their soul, or the pleasure they get from sorrowin', someone did tell me, so I do know!

Johnny: . . . Anyways . . . the fella thanked me by havin' a do.

Pause.

Mrs. Farley: I'd a thought you'd be out and over with your father and William.

Johnny: That's a funny thing for you to be sayin'.

Mrs. Farley: I'd a thought you'd be over applyin'.

Johnny: You know how we both feel 'bout me workin' the colliery.

Mrs. Farley: Good enough for your father and William.

Johnny: No it's not.

Mrs. Farley: It's them workin' there this minute pays for supper tonight, and don't you forget it!

Johnny: What's got into you?

Mrs. Farley: Nothin'!

Johnny: Then what's wrong?

Mrs. Farley: You tell me.

Johnny: Wasn't it you three years ago beggin' me to leave this place? Wasn't it you cryin', "Not the colliery, Johnny! Not the mines!" From the time I was little, you whisperin' and beggin' and cryin', "Get out, get away, go? Fly away, Johnny!" Wasn't that you?

Mrs. Farley: But you come back and . . .

Johnny: I had no stomach for starvin' and freezin' and bein' alone.

Mrs. Farley: Better that than . . .

Johnny: Than what?

Mrs. Farley: I love you, Johnny.

Johnny: I don't need no colliery now.

Mrs. Farley: You was always my favourite, always.

Johnny: I said I don't need no colliery, I got somethin' else.

Mrs. Farley: I don't want to hear it.

Johnny: The fella over at the Alberta Hotel offered me somethin' and I'm thinkin' a takin' it.

Mrs. Farley: No.

Johnny: That's why I'm so late gettin' in; I give him a hand last night.

Mrs. Farley: Johnny.

Johnny: So I don't have to work at the colliery.

Mrs. Farley: You'll make me a laughin' stock, you know that!

Johnny: Is that all you care about?

Mrs. Farley: I care about you! I tell you I love you and you never listen!

Johnny: You only love me when I do what you want!

Mrs. Farley: Wouldn't you fight if you saw a person you loved goin' wrong?

Johnny: It's not a crime for a man to drink liquor or sell it!

Mrs. Farley: There's the law, and them that breaks it is criminal.

Johnny: Well then Mum, the whole bleedin' country's criminal—them that works in the mines, them that owns the mines, the lawyers, the judge, and who's to say the god damn Prime Minister don't have a wine when he chats with the King?

Mrs. Farley: And them that sells it is worse than them that drinks it!

Johnny: Why don't you fight what drives Pop to drink instead a the drink?

Mrs. Farley: You are not workin' for that man, Johnny.

Johnny: I'm thinkin' a doin' that. I'm tellin' you straight that's what I'm thinkin'.

Mrs. Farley: Do you know what he is?

Johnny: He's a fella offered me a job.

Mrs. Farley: Offa the train from nobody knows where.

Johnny: Have you made that a crime?

Mrs. Farley: And his wife . . .

Johnny: Don't . . .

Mrs. Farley: Never speakin' to no one . . .

Johnny: Mum . . .

Mrs. Farley: Whose only friend is a Jew . . .

Johnny: Shaddup!

Mrs. Farley: And you know why his wife's so quiet? 'Cause right in that Alberta Hotel, the same roof, the same bed, her husband is keepin' a whore!

Johnny: Who are you talkin' about?

Mrs. Farley: Young enough to be his daughter.

Johnny: I don't believe you!

Pause.

Mrs. Farley: I been sittin' here steelin' myself to say it. You want nothin' to do with her. Or him.

Sound of faint blast from mine whistle; they don't appear to hear it.

Johnny: You're lyin'.

Mrs. Farley: Why would I lie?

Johnny: You'd lie 'cause ... 'cause you'd rather see me dyin' for a livin' in the mines, than workin' in the clean, pure air for a rum-runner.

Sound of a second blast from the mine whistle. This time Johnny and his mother do hear it and realize it is the second blast they've heard. Mama George, Mr. Big, and Leah appear on stage.

Johnny: ... That ain't the end a the shift.

Mrs. Farley's lips begin to move slowly and silently. Sound of a third blast. Gompers appears, then Bill, and finally Dolly.

Johnny: That ain't the end a the shift!

Sound of a fourth, then a fifth blast, as Cec and Sump enter the house.

Cec: Mum.

Johnny: What happened?

Old Sump: Weren't not'in', Johnny ... a piece a timber ... t'bracin' ... it just shifted like.

Johnny: Weren't nothin'.

Old Sump: Not a bit a rock fell, just t'at one piece a timber, it just shifted like, 'gainst t'wall, t'at was all. ... And it caught 'im.

Johnny: Will?

Old Sump: He jumped . . . but he weren't fast enuff.

Cec: Mum.

Old Sump: We got 'im out. We got 'im up. He died when we 'it t'surface.

Pause. Johnny starts to leave.

Mrs. Farley: Johnny? . . . Where're you goin'?

Johnny: For christ's sake can't you reach out to *Pop!* For one lousy minute can't you mourn for poor Will? Will is dead and it's still Johnny, my Johnny. You are crushin' me with your love as sure as Will was caught and crushed by a timber.

Mrs. Farley: John . . .

Johnny: Leave me alone.

Mrs. Farley: You're all I got left.

Johnny: Don't say it.

Mrs. Farley: It's true.

Johnny: Get away.

Mrs. Farley: It's all right to cry.

Johnny: Then why aren't *you* cryin'?

Mrs. Farley: I'll tell you . . . every bit a my bein' is consumed with one thing, to keep some vestige a hope in my soul . . . bargainin' with the Lord to spare one a my sons.

Johnny: Don't.

Mrs. Farley: You think I don't weep? Why none a you here could conceive a my sorrow. Inside a my breast is a deep yawnin' hole and through it rushes a torrent a tears such as you've never seen! I have mourned Teddy and Robert and I mourn Will . . . but I will not mourn you Johnny! He's promised me you.

Johnny: In exchange for them?

Cec: She can't mean it, boy. *He makes a gesture of support which Johnny brushes aside as he turns on his mother.*

Johnny: God damn your church meetings and temperance!

Cec: It's all right.

Johnny: Nothin' is right! I'm goin'. I'm leavin'. I'm rentin' a room from Popovitch.

Mrs. Farley: No.

Johnny: And I got me employment at the Alberta Hotel.

Mrs. Farley: The rumrunner.

Johnny: Right. *He starts out.*

Mrs. Farley: *Yells after him.* And what will you do with his whore?!

Johnny runs across the stage out of sight. We are left with fractured images of him fleeing. They glint as light fades.

Mrs. Farley: John-ny!!

Blackout

David Russell
Wally McSween as Mr. Big, Lee Royce as Mama George, Rebecca Starr as
Leah
Studio Theatre, Edmonton, 1985

Act Two

Plaintive sound from the player piano. Rippling distorted image of Bill the Brit heralds his measured entrance on stage. He now wears a holstered revolver and his appearance is more solid and threatening. In repose he seems dangerous as opposed to silly. He stands at ease but watchful on the stage. He looks off and sees someone approaching. He smiles and removes his hat in greeting. It's Mrs. Farley. She bobs her head in greeting. He indicates she should look down the street.

She does so. Bill observes her, and steps away from her a bit. Mrs. Farley is torn between leaving and staying. She doesn't wish to be seen by Johnny whom she is watching, but she wishes to continue to observe him. He approaches. He sees her. He stops. She stiffens and sails past him like an iceberg in the North Atlantic. Johnny watches her go, catching sight of Bill. Johnny enters the Alberta Hotel.

The player piano melody brightens a bit as light builds on the Alberta Hotel. Leah stands by the piano. A strand of hair has come loose. She's running her thumb over the perforations in a piano cartridge. She stands in a stream of sunlight. Mr. Big sits, his lunch unfinished and forgotten in front of him. He watches Leah.

Mama is present, unobtrusive but busy as always.

Johnny looks at Mr. Big, at Leah; he stands in silent scrutiny.

Mr. Big: Leah? . . . Your hair.

She makes a motion to restore the strand to its place.

Mr. Big: No. Leave it . . . just as you were . . . the head tilted, the eyes . . .

She resumes her former position.

Mr. Big: How far between us . . . Johnny? *Mr. Big's eyes never leave Leah but he has obviously been aware of Johnny.*

Johnny: Eh?

Mr. Big: What would you ascertain the distance to be separatin' me—from her?

Johnny: I dunno.

Mr. Big: Hazard a guess.

Johnny: Fifteen feet.

Mr. Big: Fifteen feet is it, across the well-worn floor a the Alberta Hotel?

Johnny: 'Bout fifteen.

Mr. Big: Or is there stretchin' between us a great and gapin' abyss with a bottom a layered, feathery bones, thin and delicate as the scales of a pearl—and pressin' on t'other side a that—the Vaults a Hell?

Johnny gives a slow shrug.

Mr. Big: Or are we so close there is nothin' between us but a hazy shimmer, insubstantial as a veil a dust motes driftin' in the sun. . . . Eh Johnny?

Johnny: I dunno.

Mr. Big: You don't know . . . well then, try this. Why do I bestride my world like a colossus?

Johnny: Diet?

Mr. Big: Come on, do you know?

Johnny shrugs.

Mr. Big: I've mastered the art a seein' the multiple realities a the universe, and more than that. I have embraced them, though they be almost always conflicting, but equally true. . . . Now, how far is it—fifteen feet, the abyss, or nothin' between us?

Johnny: The car's ready.

Mr. Big: As good an answer as any. *He finishes eating as he talks.* You know, if I could choose one image to carry with me through all eternity, it would be that of Leah, as she stands there today, at this moment, elbow held just so, head tilted, a single strand a hair . . . what do you say, Johnny?

Johnny: That's a long time.

Mr. Big: 'Til Judgement Day?

Johnny: 'Til then.

Mr. Big: Ah yes. And when the good Lord called my name, I'd say, "Look, encompassed there, that's my life."

Johnny: And what would He say?

Mr. Big: Who?

Johnny: God.

Mr. Big: *Laughs.* ... Well Mama, won't be long. *Kisses Mama's cheek.* Give Johnny some a that schnitzel. I'll just get my coat, Leah. *He exits.*

Mama exits with Mr. Big's dishes. Leah has continued to hold, relaxed and informally, the pose Mr. Big has described. Johnny stands staring at her. Eventually she turns to look at him.

Johnny: ... I don't suppose you got any idea a how stupid you look.

Leah: Not your kinda image?

Johnny: Didja ever meet Jack Cottrell?

Leah: Should I?

Johnny: He's a fella from the Creek studied taxidermy by mail. You reminded me a one a his earlier efforts.

Leah: Thank you.

Johnny turns to leave.

Leah: Wait! Please ... why ... do you always sidle outa a room every time that I enter?

Johnny: I don't.

Leah: And if you stay, why are you always so rude?

Johnny: I'm not.

Leah: Or else pretend you can't see me ... I'm not even there?

Johnny: I don't do none a those things.

Leah: Yes you do! And you been doin' them for ages!

Johnny: Look, if you're gonna stand around strikin' affected poses and lookin' stuffed and actin' deaf, I just thought someone should tell you.

Mama is observing most discreetly. On the street, Bill is just a shadow.

Leah: Should be me's avoidin' you.

Johnny: Why's that?

Leah: Cause you said things to me that were lies, and I believed you. You said . . . you don't even like me!

Johnny: I do.

Leah: No you don't!

Johnny: Who said?

Leah: How people act is a lot more truthful than what anybody can say.

Johnny: I was tryin' to act like a friend!

Leah: When!

Johnny: When I told you you looked stuffed.

Pause. Then Leah suppresses a smile.

Leah: You wanna know somethin'?

Johnny: What?

Leah: *Whispers.* I felt stupid. *She smiles.*

Johnny: Well you sure looked stupid—it was okay at first . . . it was when you kept standin' there it got stupid.

Leah: Do you know this is the most you ever said to me since that night? *Pause in which Leah sees Johnny's unease.* But we won't talk about that—you wanna know something else? You do, don-cha?

Johnny: Sure.

Leah: From doin' . . . that. . . . *She cranks and tilts her head in an exaggeration of the pose. . . .* I got a crick in my neck . . . right . . . here.

Johnny: Is it gone?

Leah: Mostly gone. Feel it. *She leans forward for him to feel it. He puts out his hand to feel it and stops.* The muscle's all . . . what is it? . . . What's wrong?

Johnny: So why do you do it?

Leah: I love him.

Johnny starts out.

Leah: Now where are you goin'?!

Johnny: Check on the car.

Leah: You haven't had lunch!

Johnny: Have it later.

Leah: Come back here! What is the matter with you? At first I thought it was your brother—

Johnny: Never you mind my brother!

Leah: But it's six months now. . . . And then I thought it's because a your mother and you not speakin' and that gettin' you down—

Johnny: I don't like people talkin' 'bout that!

Leah: You might not like it, but we all do.

Johnny: Well it's none a your business!

Leah: Why did you say those things to me? You felt like you knowed me for a hundred years, that's what you said, and you liked me, and tried to make me say them too, and now you just. . . . Why did you do that? I'm not lettin' you go till you tell me!

Johnny: . . . It . . . was a bet.

Leah: A bet?

Johnny: Yeah.

Leah: With who?

Johnny: Ahhh, Will, with Will.

Leah: What for . . . to make fun a me?

Johnny: Yeah.

Leah: To make me look stupid.

Johnny: I'm lyin'.

Leah: Why?

Johnny: It wasn't a bet, I just said that.

Leah: What for?

Johnny: I dunno. For fun.

Pause.

Leah: I thought we were gonna be friends.

Johnny: So what kinda friend do you want—a Mr. Big kinda friend?

Leah: Whata you mean?

Johnny: You know what I mean.

Leah: No ... Mr. Big is my friend, more than my friend—if it weren't for him and Mama, I wouldn't have anyone.

Johnny: I'm not talkin' 'bout that.

Leah: What are you talkin' about?

Johnny: I'm talkin' 'bout you and him!

Leah: You don't want me to love Mr. Big?

Johnny: Jesus Christ you're stupid.

Leah: Well you're cruel.

Johnny: *I'm* cruel?

Leah: I don't want you for a friend.

Johnny: Pretty sad state of affairs when the "daughter" a the colossus a Blairmore's gotta look for a friend in the person of her father's employee!

Leah: I *chose* you!

Johnny: 'Cause you don't have no others! Why's that I suppose?

Leah: I have friends.

Johnny: Name one.

Leah: Dolly's my friend.

Johnny: And what's she but another hunka slag same as myself?

Leah: And me, what am I?

Johnny: You know what you are!

Leah: I'm his chosen daughter.

Johnny: Have you got no sense a what's proper, what's right?!

Leah: I'm his ch . . .

Johnny: Whore!

Pause. Fractured image of car. Honk of horn off-stage.

Johnny: Tell me it's just a story.

Mr. Big: *Off-stage.* Leah!

Johnny: A mean story, ain't no truth in it.

Mr. Big: *Off-stage.* Leah!

Sound of car horn off-stage.

Johnny: I wanted to talk to you a million times since that night. I meant every word I said. I mean it more now. *Mr. Big enters. Johnny whispers.* I love you.

Mr. Big: Leah?

Leah: Yes.

Mr. Big puts his arm round her in a warm, not an intimate, fashion.

Mr. Big: Here you are. Well, we'll be seein' you, Johnny.

Mr. Big and Leah exit. Johnny watches them leave.

Mama George: *Softly.* When he brought her home, she was just a tiny wee bit of a thing.

Johnny: Stealin' kids offa streets don't hardly seem right.

Mama George: Papa and I, we never had any.

Johnny: That don't make it right.

Mama George: She was runnin' away.

Johnny: So where was she runnin' from?

Mama George: Papa says her past, and into her future.

Johnny: What do you say?

Mama George: She told me—the William D. Purdy Home for Orphans. It was the sixth time she'd done it—and her only eleven. She'd been beat, her poor little backside and her arms, they had bruises like over-ripe plums.

Johnny: Why are you tellin' me this?

Mama George: Because I want you to understand.... Why shouldn't she love him?

Johnny: There's love and there's love.

Mama George: Well, she'd have run from here if she hadn't been happy.

Johnny: Where would she run to?

Mama George: She'd run before, six times and only eleven.

Johnny: Maybe she was tired a runnin'!

Mama George: He picked her up and he brought her home and he gave her everything, a mama who loves her, a mama she loves, him who adores her—and you.

Johnny: I'm not a thing to be given to people.

Mama George: Maybe he don't realize that's what he's done.

Johnny: Then maybe I don't want her.

Mama George: You don't mean that.

Johnny: Well, a person can't be givin' people to people! He don't own her—nor me—and if her and me ... it'd be our own business, have nothin' to do with him.

Mama George: That's right.

Johnny: But—I'd have to know, you see.

Mama George: Why?

Johnny: You say why, not what ... you know what I'd have to know, doncha?

As Mama moves to leave, Johnny stops her.

Johnny: You say she's like a daughter, more than a daughter, isn't that right? And those, you see, are the words I keep stumblin' on. Is a person takin' advantage of a person here, and which person is that!?

Mama George: Let me go.

Johnny: I gotta know, Mama.

Mama George: Where would you be if it weren't for him?

Johnny: In the mines! And you think I don't thank him for that? I find myself lovin' that man ... and I owe him ... I do owe him—he's ... he's ... like—yesterday when ... when the Brit got onto our tail ... Mr. Big was drivin' ... you know what he did? The road lay ahead, and I thought "trust to the Whiskey Six, B.C. border or bust" and ... and he swings the wheel one hundred and ten degree angle turn! We are off the road, and streamin' over those golden dips and mellow rises ... and the Brit, I swear to God he broke an axle attemptin' the turn ... and Mr. Big, he says "We'll just snake our way into the 'Mericas, I know a man there who's into the marketin' of what slakes a powerful thirst. We'll do business with him." ... It was ... real sunny, no wind for a change ... and we stopped on the top a one a them hills and we got outa the car and we stood there. .... Far as you could see a rollin' sweep a foothills, and us two standin' there, with the car sittin' right on the top a one a them gentle rises, no trail leadin' to it or from it—and over it and us and all and around—the sky, like a big blue bowl. Him, with his foot on the runnin' board, and one hand in his pocket, and he says "Johnny—we are standin' at the centre a the universe, Johnny, everything is in relation to here"— and I believed him. .... And he says "We are the warp and woof in a divine tapestry, Johnny"—and I believed him. I don't know what the hell it means, but I believed him.

Mama George: You love Leah, that's all that matters.

Johnny: No—'cause inside a me, Mama, nestled 'gainst that gratitude is a grain a rot, and if I don't find out, that grain is gonna grow and spread.

Mama George: Then you'll reap a harvest a tears.

Johnny: I gotta have the acquaintance a the whole man!

Mama George: Is that possible?

Johnny: He says himself—a lie cannot endure. I don't wanna be committin' myself to a lie.

Mama George: He says there's many truths.

Johnny: But him sayin' don't make it so. Lies can endure, and with no game-playin', there's truth.

Mama George: But whoever lived without playin' games?

Johnny: I can stand knowin', it's not knowin' that kills.

Mama George: If you love Leah, why does anything else matter but that? . . . I love him, and nothing else matters but that.

Johnny: You've heard a my mum . . . inside a my mum, the milk a human kindness is curdled. She's like a thin mangy old cat that's gone wild. Nothin' left to nourish herself or her own. . . . But she would be rippin' out the belly and tearin' the throat, she would be killin' that tom that came on her kitten. . . . And there you are: warm and plump and lovin', givin', forgivin'. . . . What I'm wonderin' is—are you less than my mum?

Pause. Mama exits. Johnny stands alone, still. He looks out, his eye is caught by the vague shadow of Bill and Gompers. He watches them although he seems preoccupied as opposed to having some strong reaction at seeing them together.

Bill stirs in the shadows. Gompers approaches. Bill nods a greeting. The two of them draw together briefly. Gompers laughs, and leaves Bill. Bill's good cheer disappears as Gompers leaves him. Bill casually saunters off.

Gompers enters the hotel. Goes directly to look out and watch Bill's progress out of sight.

Johnny: . . . What did he want?

Gompers: Nothin'.

Johnny: What did he say?

Gompers: Passin' time, that's all. *He moves to get a drink from the tap.*

Johnny: ... Watch him.

Gompers: I don't need you tellin' me that.

Johnny: Right.

Gompers: *Drains his drink, gets himself another, looks at Johnny.* What're you starin' at?

Johnny looks away. Gompers sips his second drink.

Gompers: ... Did you know the Brit was waitin' for us yesterday?

Johnny: I heard.

Gompers: Seemed to know which route we was takin'.

Johnny: You lost him, didn't you?

Gompers: Ah-huh.

Johnny: Well then, what the hell. He's always stakin' out this route or that. For once he got lucky.

Gompers: Maybe. He's keepin' an eye on the front too, thinks he'll catch us bringin' it out or in.

Johnny: That's why it's stashed 'cross town.

Gompers: He wants it real bad.

Johnny: Ah-huh.

Gompers: He's replacin' his vehicles with motorcycles.

Johnny: So?

Gompers: And they're puttin' machine guns on the front a them.

Johnny: Where'd you hear that?

Gompers: Around.

Johnny: Who from?

Gompers: Do you suppose a Whiskey Six can outrun fire from a Gatling gun?

Johnny: Whata they want to bring guns into it for? They wouldn't open fire on an unarmed car that was just carryin' booze.

Gompers: Lawbreakers is lawbreakers accordin' to the Brit. Murderers, rapists and rumrunners, all the same to the Brit. Principle of the thing he says.

Johnny: What else did he say?

Gompers: Nothin'.

Johnny: You keep the hell away from him.

Gompers: That's important information I got.

Johnny: But what were you sayin' to him?

Gompers: Nothin'!

Johnny: Keep it that way. . . . Come on, we got work to do.

Gompers: How did them that come last get to be first?

Johnny: Drink up.

Gompers: I don't take orders from you.

Johnny: We got six kegs to load and deliver. Are you comin' or not?

Gompers: *Drinks up.* . . . Gatlin' guns, Johnny.

Johnny: If there's guns, they're for show. Let's go.

Gompers: Don't it make you stop and think just a little?

The player piano plays ever so softly creeping in. One chair, the chair that Will sat in during the party in Act One, has light growing on it.

Johnny: No. We'll cut across the foothills, helluva lot smoother ride than the road anyways.

Johnny and Gompers exit from the Alberta Hotel and head down the street.

Gompers: You wanna know why I always win at poker? 'Cause I know . . .

Johnny: You lose at poker, Gompers. And just forget them motorcycles. Think a the jackasses ridin' them.

They disappear from sight.

The piano plays, growing in volume slightly, light building on the chair. Dolly enters. She listens to the piano. She takes a small photograph from her pocket, looks at it, places it flat on the table by the chair. She looks at it. She smiles. She extends her hand towards the chair, an invitation to dance. She dances with her imaginary partner. She is at first somewhat solemn and the dance slow, but it picks up in speed and merriment. It finishes quite merry and quick with Dolly responding, laughing, sharing the dance with a partner. The piano stops, not abruptly but at the end of the composition. Dolly releases her partner, extending a hand as he moves away from her. The light which has followed her dance returns to the chair. Dolly speaks quietly not trying to mimic Will's voice.

Dolly: . . . God but you're pretty. *She smiles.*

Cec enters followed by Sump. The light begins to fade slowly on the chair.

Old Sump: You and me, we know t' difference t'ere, Cec. Cec! I says we know t' difference.

Dolly: . . . I done it for you.

Cec raps vigorously on the bar.

Old Sump: T'ere's one drink and t'ere's two drinks and t'ere's t'ree. A man can have t'ree or four drinks and it don't mean a t'ing.

Mama enters; she will pour two glasses of liquor and refill Cec's flask for him.

Old Sump: Are you listenin', Cec? . . . And t'ere's not'in' wrong wit' a flask. I had me a real nice kinda shiny lookin' one, do you 'member it, Cec?

Dolly: Lemme hold your hand, Dolly.

The light on the chair is gone. Dolly's focus shifts from an inward one as she becomes aware of Cec and Old Sump.

Old Sump: But t' t'ing never went underground, do you hear what

I'm sayin'?

He and Cec down their drinks. Mama refills them and exits.

Old Sump: I said t' t'ing never went underground, Cec.

Cec: What's the time?

Old Sump: First off, you needs your wits about you down t'ere, and number two, where would you be if t'ey caught you?

Cec: What's the time?

Old Sump: Out on your keester, so don't be carryin' t'at t'ing down wit' you.

Cec: Ain't got no watch on you?

Old Sump: Cec.

Cec: Where's your watch?

Old Sump: To hell wit' t'watch.

Cec: What's the time, Dolly?

Cec makes his way over to Dolly, followed by Sump.

Old Sump: What t' hell's time to you, or you to time. We're talkin' important t'ings here.

Cec: Dolly?

Old Sump: She don't have t' time.

Cec: Eh?

Old Sump: Tell him.

Dolly: I don't have the time, Cec.

Old Sump: See?

Cec: Don't anybody have a watch?

Old Sump: No.

Cec: Shit.

Old Sump: No more takin' t' flask down wit' you, and no more a t' drinkin' till you drop—wit' t' exception a Friday and Saturday nights t'at is—and no more a t' 'avin' a short snort 'fore t' shift ... Cec?

Cec: I thought you was workin' this shift.

Old Sump: Well, I am but I am sacrificin' my good sense to keepin' company wit' you.

Cec: Oh.

Old Sump: I don't want you drinkin' alone. *Cec nods.* And I made me a solemn promise wit' your boy, wit' Johnny. I made a promise to be t'ere to catch you when you fall down, t' see you home when I'm able, and t' watch you when we're working t' shift. ... If I knowed then what I knowed now ...

Cec: What's that?

Old Sump: Bein' t'ere is all right but ... good god, Cec, seein' you home. Oh, t'at woman.

Cec: Yup.

Old Sump: She takes a strip right offa me front and down me back.

Cec: Yup.

Old Sump: What t' hell're you "yuppin'" for? You ain't even t'ere. You're out. While I suffer t'at woman's tongue, you lie where I lay you—right on t' floor. ... Do you sleep on t'at floor, Cec? Or do she get you up to t' bed?

Cec: What's the time?

Old Sump: You should be showin' her who wears t' pants.

Cec: Is there someone don't know the answer to that burnin' question?

Old Sump: Well t'en, you gotta reclaim t' pants.

Cec: Who says I want 'em?

Old Sump: It's not right for a woman t' be wearin' t' pants.

Cec: I dunno.

Old Sump: Eh?

Cec: Some got a bent for it.

Old Sump: But t'ey're not to be encouraged.

Cec: I don't want the god damn things!

Old Sump: You're not makin' sense.

Cec: Got a heart like an ax head in winter.

Old Sump: It's t' liquor, Cec.

Cec: Eh?

Old Sump: Saturatin' the cells a t' brain.

Cec: Oh.

Old Sump: Soakin' it up. . . . Let's go.

Cec: Now?

Old Sump: T'at's right.

Cec: We got a couple a minutes.

Old Sump: Shift change now.

Cec: In a minute.

Old Sump: Now.

Cec: What's the time?

Old Sump: Come on, we're gonna be late.

Cec: How do you know?

Old Sump: I got me an interior time-piece! Now come on.

Cec stands up and knocks over a chair.

Old Sump: Jesus.

Cec: I'm all right.

Old Sump: You can't be showin' up like t'at.

Cec: Los' my balance for a minute, that's all.

Old Sump: Siddown.

Cec: I'm all right.

Old Sump: You're not all right.

Cec: I'm fine.

Old Sump: You're pissed.

Cec: I just—

Old Sump: You t'ink I don't know pissed when I see it? Now sid-down and stay t'ere! ... Mama! ... Mama!

Sump exits to find Mama. Cec looks at Dolly.

Old Sump: *Off-stage.* Where's Johnny?

Mama George: *Off-stage.* He and Gompers are 'cross town.

Old Sump: *Off-stage.* Can you send someone for 'im?

Mama George: *Off-stage.* If they haven't ...

Old Sump: *Off-stage.* I gotta git to t' colliery. I can't be clockin' in late. *Enters on the run, calling back to Mama George, who appears for a moment.* Tell 'im Sump's workin' and Cec ain't, tell 'im 'e's 'ere! Now you sit t'ere, Cec, and you wait. *He's out of the hotel flying to work, yelling back....* See to 'im, Dolly!

Silence for a moment, then Cec reaches out and takes Dolly's hand. After a moment he releases it, and looks at his own hand.

Dolly: What's wrong?

Cec: I 'member ... you're the one don't like the black. *He smiles. She takes his hand.* I used to tease him some did. ... He was a real good boy. ... Full a fun. Always laughin' he was. I 'member the time, him and me we was ...

Sound of faint blast from the mine for change of shift. Pause.

Dolly: Go on.

Cec: ... He was just a good boy, that's all.

Ripple image of car.

Mr. Big: *Off-stage, faint.* Leah?

Sound of door slam.

Mr. Big: *Off-stage, a bit louder.* Leah!

Leah enters. She stops on seeing Dolly and Cec.

Leah: Oh . . . 'lo Dolly.

Mr. Big enters. Leah looks at him, goes over and sits with Dolly and Cec.

Leah: What're you two doin' here?

Dolly: I come over to visit.

Mr. Big: Leah?

Leah: I was out for a drive.

Mr. Big: Leah.

Cec: Somebody wants you.

Leah: But I'm back now.

Dolly: Oh.

Leah: Aren't you workin', Mr. Farley?

Cec: He wants you.

Leah: Whatta you want?

Mr. Big: I . . .

Leah: What is it?

Mr. Big: I thought . . .

Leah: You go on by yourself.

Mr. Big: Leah.

Leah: Why don'tcha take Mama?

Mr. Big: I want to take you.

Leah: Why don'tcha take Dolly?—Do you wanna go with him, Dolly?

Dolly: I dunno.

Leah: You go with him, Dolly, it's fun.

Dolly: Are you comin'?

Leah: No.

Dolly: Where is he goin'?

Leah: He'll deliver a keg, then you'll stop for a while and . . . you'll visit the Butlers.

Cec: What Butlers is that?

Leah: You know the Butlers.

Cec: No.

Leah: Yes you do. . . . They got a fluffy white dog and a swing in the front and she always has cake and Mr. Butler and him sit on the porch and drink whiskey—isn't that right, Mr. Big?

Dolly: I don't know the Butlers.

Cec: 'Cause there ain't any Butlers.

Leah: I'd go but I been in that car for an age—my stomach's upset.

Mr. Big: Is that it?

Leah: Well what did you think! I said I felt sick!

Mr. Big: That's what you said.

Leah: And I do. So. Are you just gonna stand there?

Mr. Big: No.

Leah: So!? *Pause as Leah and Mr. Big stare at each other.* I . . . I'm . . . I'm sorry . . . I hurt you, I made you feel bad.

Mr. Big: No.

Leah: We . . . we . . . can go tomorrow.

Mr. Big: That's what we'll do.

Leah: . . . We . . . could go today—later today—if you want.

Mr. Big: We'll make it tomorrow.

Leah: You won't be mad that we don't go today?

Mr. Big: Mad? *He moves to the bar to get a drink for Cec. Some of his former exuberance returns.* A definition of "madness", Mr. Farley!

Cec: Eh?

Mr. Big: *Dementia praecox.*

Dolly: What's that?

Mr. Big: Disordered reason. The question is—do I suffer from it—and if so, what could have caused it.

Leah: I said I was sorry.

Mr. Big: And I believed you. How could I be angry ... *He goes to put his arm round her; there is the smallest apparently not deliberate move away from him on her part. He may be aware of it but he doesn't show it. ...* with you. *He incorporates her rejection —if such it is—into a move to Cec with his drink. As Johnny enters.* Now, Mr. Farley ...

Johnny: He's had enough.

Mr. Big: Haven't you left yet?

Johnny: We were late with the loadin'. ... Come on, Pop.

Cec: I was jus' fine, Johnny; it was Sump wouldn't wait.

Johnny: Sure it was.

Cec: I wanted to go.

Johnny: Come on, I'm takin' you home.

Dolly touches Leah's arm to draw her attention to the photograph.

Mr. Big: Johnny?

Johnny: *Shouldering his dad up.* Yeah.

Mr. Big: I've left a keg in my car out front.

Johnny: What?

Mr. Big: A touch of *dementia praecox.*

Cec: Disordered reason.

Johnny: Shaddup Pop. ... What do you want me to do?

Mr. Big: It'll have to be moved.

Cec: Move it in here, sucker'll disappear like magic.

Johnny: Where to?

Cec: See? *Holds up his empty flask upside down.*

Mr. Big: Pull the car round and ...

Cec: Nothin' left.

Johnny: Shaddup Pop.

Cec: Can't go home dry.

Mr. Big: You best deliver him first.

Cec: Sill kill me.

Mr. Big: And see me when you get back.

Cec: Don' wanna.

Johnny: Right.

Cec: Near the place.

Mr. Big: Unless you want to use it to ...

Johnny: I'll walk him. *Gets Cec out the door with Cec rambling on as they disappear from sight.*

Cec: Sill's gonna kill me Johnny oh god when se shees me that god damn Sump he wouldn't wait all his fault ...

Dolly: It looks just like him.

Leah: Yes it does.

Mr. Big watches Leah and Dolly examine the photograph.

Dolly: Isn't it strange they can do that?

Leah: I suppose.

Dolly: He had it taken for me.

Leah: I know.

Dolly: It wasn't studio-done.

Leah: You told me before.

Dolly: It was when that man with the camera and all came through. He took pictures a the colliery office, and then Mr. Wheatley, who's head of it all, had him and his wife and his family all in a group in fronta his house, and Will, when he heard, you know what he did?

Leah: You told me, Dolly.

Dolly: Well, he went right up to that man with the camera, and he said, "Hey there"—he never said sir—he said, "is that a val'able thing you got there?" And the fella said, "You bet your sweet fanny ass it is," that's what he said, "and mind you don't touch it," and Will said, "Well, if it's val'able, I wouldn't be pointin' it at those ugly mugs there, cause surer than hell it'll break! You wanna capture a visage a heaven on a photographic plate—aim that thing this way." ... He meant a picture of himself so's he could give it to me. And that's what happened. That's how come I got this picture a him.

Leah: Dolly?

Dolly: What.

Leah: ... It's a real nice picture.

Dolly: It is, isn't it.

Leah: ... Dolly?

Dolly: And I got it for all time cause a picture like this lasts forever. When I'm old, he's still gonna be young. ... Do you think when you die, you stay the age that you die at?

Leah: I wish you wouldn't keep talkin' like that.

Dolly: Like what?

Leah: All a that is over, Dolly.

Dolly: I don't think so.

Leah: It's past.

Dolly: But it's still there.

Leah: Where?!

Dolly: It's not gone. Will isn't gone.

Leah: He is, Dolly, and you got to face that!

Dolly: No.

Leah: It is past and over and done with!

Dolly: No.

Leah: You gotta forget about Will.

Dolly: I don't want to.

Leah: You gotta start fresh.

Dolly: I couldn't.

Leah: Why not?

Dolly: Nobody can.

Leah: A course they can!

Dolly: What makes you think that?

Leah: They just can, that's all.

Dolly: But you're who you are and who you were and who you met and what you did and . . .

Leah: *Will . . . is . . . dead.*

Dolly: He's alive right inside a me, and caught in this picture is a little bit a him, and he is sittin' right over there where we used to sit, and in the mine where he used to work, and if you listen real close, which I know we can't but if we could, you could hear him, things he used to say and make everyone laugh, and you could hear us laughin' too!

Leah: Why can't you just leave him?

Dolly: That's what you wanta do, leave everything behind, pretend things never happened, but I don't wanta do that—and you can't do it either!

Leah grabs the photograph of Will from Dolly and tears it into little pieces which she drops on the floor. Dolly moves as if to bend down to—what?—pick them up? Leah puts her foot over them.

Dolly looks at her a moment, then Leah turns and runs off. Dolly looks at the pieces of photo on the floor. She bends and gathers them up as lights fade on the hotel. She runs out of the hotel leaving Mr. Big, who has observed the scene, alone.

Cec: *Off-stage singing.*
Don't weep for me and mother.
Although I know 'tis sad
But try and get someone to cheer—

Light building on Mrs. Farley and Bill in the Farley home. They listen to Cec's approach; Mrs. Farley draws Bill to a place of partial concealment.

Cec: *Off-stage, singing, closer.*
And save my poor old dad.
I'm awful cold and hungry
. . .

Cec and Johnny enter the house.

Cec: *Singing rather loudly.* She closed her eyes and . . . Shhhh! Shhhhh!! Shh Johnny not a sound! She'll be in here like lion 'mong the Chris'ians, shh be quiet, you jus' leave me 'n ge' hell out. You go 'n don' worry 'bout . . .

Mrs. Farley steps into view.

Cec: Too late. Well! I was jus'n den he and we wereoohh 'n then ah so we come along there 'nd I 'n he and then it was jus' 'n thasa 'bou' how it was. *He sits.* So—don' be angry with 'im, be angry with me. Good night, Johnny.

Pause. Johnny turns to leave.

Mrs. Farley: Johnny.

Johnny turns back to his mother.

Mrs. Farley: I . . . I was . . . have you gotta get right back, Johnny? *Pause.* You wanna sit awhile? *Pause. Johnny sits.* I . . . I been missin' you . . .

Bill is present in the shadows. Johnny does not see him.

Johnny: Yeah.

Mrs. Farley: What?

Johnny: Me too.

Mrs. Farley: Here you are, right in town, and I haven't seen you since . . .

Johnny: You seen me.

Mrs. Farley: What?

Johnny: I said you seen me. You seen me lots a times.

Fractured slow image of constable taking shape outside the Farley's.

Mrs. Farley: No, I. . . . *She stops as Johnny stares at her in a silent rebuke. Pause.*

Johnny gets up to leave.

Mrs. Farley: Johnny!

Johnny: What.

Mrs. Farley: You make it real hard for me! . . . Say somethin'.

Johnny: I wish . . . I wish things was different, but they aren't . . . and . . . I don't see what I can do about that.

Mrs. Farley: Things can change.

Johnny: I don't see how.

Mrs. Farley: I know they can. But you gotta have faith, and you gotta *do* somethin'.

Johnny: Like what?

Mrs. Farley: You gotta believe that by doin' somethin' you can change somethin'.

Johnny: What're you talkin' about?

The figure of the constable, with careful observation, can be seen at his post outside the house.

Mrs. Farley: *Smiles.* You're right I seen you. I went outa my way on the hope a gettin' a gawp a you. *She laughs.* And you seen me. I can say you did cause you said so. . . . I never set foot outside a this house my head wasn't full a possible places a glimpsin' you.

Johnny: Not a word to me though.

Mrs. Farley: I . . .

Johnny: How come now?

Mrs. Farley: *Takes Johnny's hand, pressing it between hers.* Because that's over and done with now. It's gonna be different now.

Pause. Johnny removes his hand, gets up, moves away, then turns back to his mother.

Johnny: You gettin' outa temperance and bible-thumpin'?

Mrs. Farley: I just . . .

Johnny: That don't seem likely.

Mrs. Farley: I was wrong.

Johnny: 'Bout what?

Mrs. Farley: Come here and sit down.

Johnny: What're you sayin' you're wrong about?

Mrs. Farley: I got you an offer.

Johnny: Eh?

Mrs. Farley: Not the mines, Johnny. . . . Another job, a respectable job.

Johnny: Doin' what?

Mrs. Farley: You come just at the right time 'cause now we can talk and we can get things arranged and everythin'll be settled.

Johnny: What was you wrong about?

Mrs. Farley: There's people want to give you a chance. It's a real opportunity, Johnny. But people earn opportunities eh? Nothin' comes free. Do you understand what I mean?

Johnny: Clear as a slough in summer.

Mrs. Farley: Now don't be like that! I want you to listen and to . . .

Johnny: And to what?

Mrs. Farley: And to not be . . . to consider what I'm sayin' and not
be. . . . Now what you want is a good job with a future, isn't that
right? . . . Isn't that right?

Johnny: That's right.

Mrs. Farley: Soo? . . .

Johnny: Look Mum . . .

Mrs. Farley: You know Sergeant Windsor now don't you?

Johnny: What about him?

Mrs. Farley: He's a good man, Sergeant Windsor.

Johnny: He'd piss in your pocket and swear it was rainin'.

Mrs. Farley: You said you would listen!

The constable shifts his position slightly.

Johnny: How'd the Brit come into this job thing?

Mrs. Farley: I gotta tell it my own way so you'll—

Johnny: So'll I'll what?

Mrs. Farley: Understand!

Johnny: And what was you wrong about?

Mrs. Farley: Whatever I done was for you.

Johnny: I can do for myself. I . . . I gotta go now.

He turns to leave. Sergeant Windsor enters.

Bill: Johnny.

Johnny: What're you doin' here?

Mrs. Farley: He's come to warn you, Johnny, through me. And to
give you a chance.

Bill: That's enough.

Mrs. Farley: He knows you're not like them others.

Bill: Mrs. Farley.

Mrs. Farley: Tell him.

Johnny: I'm late and I'm goin'.

Bill: I'd appreciate you're hearin' me out.

Johnny exits from the house. The constable outside stops him. Johnny attempts to walk around him. The constable strikes him, knocking him down and giving him a boot as he lies on the ground. Then he grabs Johnny by the collar and flings him back into the house, and reassumes his position. Mrs. Farley, hearing the scuffle, makes a move to go to Johnny. Bill touches her arm. It is enough to stop her. Johnny is on the floor.

Bill: As I was sayin' . . . if you could spare me a moment . . . there's been a time in these parts where people have done as they please. Those times're changin'.

Johnny: What the hell is this all about?

Bill: There's some as think they're above the law, beyond the law. They're gonna learn different.

Johnny: Christ!

Bill: I'm talkin' respect and order.

Johnny: Say it plain. *He wipes his mouth, looks at the blood on his hand, then at Bill.*

Bill: Now I got a proposal to make. I'm makin' it to you 'cause you strike me as a smart boy, a good boy.

Johnny spits on the floor.

Mrs. Farley: Listen.

Bill: The whiskey . . .

Johnny: Ain't got nothin' to do with whiskey! Mr. Big burns your ass and that's it in a nutshell! *Bill smiles.* You hate him 'cause he says that uniform and stupid accent don't make you one bit better than he is!

George Gammon
Earl Michael Reid as Gompers, Robert Metcalfe as Johnny, Robert Benson as
Mr. Big.
Theatre Calgary, 1983

Bill: We'll see if it does.

Johnny: He's a man thinks for hisself and you can't stand that 'cause you let others think for you!

Bill: A moral man don't need to think. *Laughs.*

Johnny: You Don't Know Nothin'!

Bill shakes his head, continuing to laugh.

Mrs. Farley: He's givin' you a chance to start somethin' new.

Johnny: Get away from me.

Mrs. Farley: He's offerin' you a job.

Bill: In return for routes, delivery dates, information.

Johnny: Do you know what he's askin' me to do?

Mrs. Farley: He's askin' you to do what's right.

Johnny: I'm leavin'.

Bill: The man's engaged in a trade that killed your brother, you support him, and you think *I'm* stupid?

Johnny: Dominion Colliery killed my brother 'cause the cost a replacin' rotten timber meant more to them than a man's life.

Bill: He was hung over from the booze. He should've seen it comin', he should've moved quick and fast and easy, and he would've—if it weren't for the booze. Rotten timber didn't kill William. The whiskey killed William.

Pause. Johnny wants to hit him but he doesn't. He turns and exits. The constable watches him go. He makes no move towards him. It is as if the previous encounter between him and Johnny had never happened. Bill turns to look at Cec slumped in the chair. He moves to him, looking down at him. He puts a hand under Cec's chin, tilting his face up.

Bill: ... Hey ... hey ... wake up old man. *He gives Cec a light slap.* Wake up.

Cec makes a murmur of protest.

Bill: *Another light slap.* Come on. *Another slap.* Wake up.

Mrs. Farley stands silent, watching. She does not enjoy what she sees but she makes no protest.

Cec: Don'.

Bill: Wake up. *Another slap.*

Cec: Stop . . . don' . . . wha' . . . wha' the hell. . . .

Bill releases Cec's chin; Cec shakes his head. Bill steps away.

Cec: Oh. Ooohhh. *Puts a hand to his head.* Got the . . . got a terbible head, does it to you you know. *He sees Bill. He looks around checking where he is. Back to Bill.* What a . . . what . . .

Bill: Mr. Farley.

Cec: Tha's right. Mister Brit. . . . Whatta you want?

Bill: I'm wonderin' if you could enlighten me as to the workin's a the taps at the Alberta Hotel?

Cec: You turn 'em to the . . . that way, 'cause it's opposite 'cause they're behind the bar, or the other way, and the beverage flows.

Bill steps closer to Cec, slaps his face with the back of his hand somewhat harder than before, still not a hard blow. Cec goes to get up. Bill shoves him back into the chair. Mrs. Farley turns her back and gazes out on the street towards the constable still at his post.

Bill: And the location a the warehouse where they're storin' the kegs?

Cec: . . . I . . .

Bill: In town or out?

Cec: I dunno.

Bill hits him a bit harder.

Bill: When he's out with the girl, is he makin' deliveries?

Cec: How should I know?

Bill: You're around.

Cec: He don't tell me those kinda things.

Bill hits him harder.

Cec: Whatta you . . .

Pause.

Bill: Now. *He moves. Cec reacts believing he's about to be hit. It's a small move but Bill sees it. He gives a dry smile. Pause.* What do you know?

Cec: Nothin'.

Bill begins methodically to beat Cec, no particular anger, no particular rush.

Cec: I don't know nothin'! . . . They don't . . . I . . .

Bill: Times.

Cec: Dunno.

Bill: Routes.

Cec: No.

Bill: Deliveries.

Cec is silent as Bill delivers two more blows and steps back. Cec falls to the floor. After a moment he speaks.

Cec: The . . . the only thing . . . I heered . . . is . . . he . . . he left a keg out front . . . in the car . . . out front . . .

Bill reaches into his jacket, pulls out a pint of liquor, tosses it to Cec.

Bill arranges his tunic and exits. Mrs. Farley turns to look at Cec who looks at her, then drinks from the pint. He gets up and leaves the room. Mrs. Farley follows him. Bill consults with the constable who checks his gun. The two move off.

Light slowly building on the Alberta Hotel. Mr. Big remains in the position from which he observed the Dolly and Leah scene.

A refracted image of glint on motorcycle and gun fades in and out.

Mr. Big: . . . Mama? . . . Mama! . . . Mama! *She enters.*

Mama George: What's wrong?

Mr. Big: . . . How old am I, Mama?

Mama George: How old?

Mr. Big: Do you know?

Mama George: How old are you?

Mr. Big: Don't you remember?

Mama George: I remember everything.

Mr. Big: Do you?

Mama George: Of course. So do you.

Mr. Big: No.

Mama George: The important things you remember.

Mr. Big: It's hard to tell.

Mama George: Why's that?

Mr. Big: Does the fact they're remembered make them important? I get the feeling they're trivial things I remember. They don't add up to much . . . except for Leah.

Mama George: What a thing for you to be sayin'.

Mr. Big: Yet I do say it.

Mama George: Where is your vision a "intersectin' worlds cartwheelin' through space?" *Pause.* Can you no longer perceive people "glowin' and blazin' like crystal shards caught in a rainbow?" *Pause.* Is your great and glorious construction a the universe based on nothin' more than the frail embrace of a child?

Mr. Big: . . . Would it be . . . any less valid were that to be so?

Mama George: Children grow up.

Mr. Big: Do they? . . . I remember—a little boy . . . not so unlike Leah when I found her . . . but this male child, an unattractive child, an ugly child who found no Mr. Big . . . so he created one.

Mama George: He became one.

Mr. Big: Mr. Big.

Mama George: She's grown up.

Mr. Big: No.

Mama George: Do you remember when we met?

Mr. Big: I ... I was erectin' canvas, two by fours, and papier-maché worlds, barkin' on a midway—but just behind the eyes, that frightened little boy peeked out.

Mama George: I could see him.

Mr. Big: Can you see him still?

Mama George: No.

Mr. Big: You lie.

During the following Mama manages to inject Mr. Big with some of his former energy and effervescence.

Mama George: Can you remember shootin' crap in Bismarck? . . .

Mr. Big smiles.

Mama George: The crowd the night we heard Wilfrid Laurier speak? . . . And destitute in Winnipeg? . . . Your speculation in the real estate? . . .

Mr. Big laughs softly.

Mama George: Do you remember the night we watched the shootin' stars, the night the sky was green with Northern Lights? . . . Do you remember? *She quotes Mr. Big from a former occasion.* "Had Lucifer not fallen from grace there'd be no such thing as choice!"

Mr. Big: "There is no Hell as men imagine it."

Mama George: "Hell is doing what other people tell you to!"

Mr. Big: *Semblance of his former self.* "Men are most like animals and least like gods when they relinquish choice! Heaven is freely choosing with respect for the choice of others."

Mama George: *Calls out, as if from the crowd.* "What's that mean?"

Mr. Big: "It means the one thing that keeps us from achievin' Holy Grace is government!"

Mama George: Go on!

Mr. Big: "For governments remove choice. It's only when individuals choose and suffer the consequences of their actions that humanity can progress!"

Mama George: Live by those words! ... I believed them.... Do you remember the night you brought Leah home?

Mr. Big: For you.

Mama George: I could never give you that most valuable thing.

Mr. Big: That didn't matter.

Mama George: It mattered to me—and to you.

Mr. Big: We had Leah.

Mama George: But that wasn't the same.

Mr. Big: You do love Leah?

Mama George: It's you I love most of all.

Pause. Mr. Big does not respond.

Mama George: She didn't go with you today.... *Pause.* Do you think I don't know why I find you sitting alone? ... Did you think I never knew? Did you think, with all the things we shared, I wouldn't know? ... Did you think she wouldn't tell me?

Mr. Big: Tell you what?

Mama George: You picked her off the street, you gave her everything, and in return she ...

Mr. Big: She what?

Mama George: Paid.

Mr. Big: It was not like that!

Mama George: I know how it was.

Mr. Big: She never told you that!

Mama George: She was afraid.

Mr. Big: It was not like that!

Mama George: She was tired of runnin'!

Mr. Big: She did not say that!

Mama George: I know what she said!

Mr. Big: She did not seduce me to assure . . .

Mama George: How does a child seduce?

Mr. Big: Nor did I seduce or force her!

Mama George: With what devices could a child resist?

Mr. Big: She never said those things to you!

Mama George: And it was me she came to. . . . Do you know what I did? . . . I reassured her.

Mr. Big: She didn't need it.

Mama George: Oh but she did. See how I love you.

Mr. Big: You've done none a this outta love.

Mama George: I have.

Mr. Big: Then it's a despicable thing.

Mama George: Despicable things are done in its name—could you argue with that?

Mr. Big: And grand things as well!

Mama George: She's leavin' you, Mr. Big.

Mr. Big: Where would she go?

Mama George: You need me now.

Mr. Big: Who would she go to?

Mama George: Who'd have her now? Who would she have?

Mr. Big: I see you plain.

Mama George: She didn't go with you today.

Mr. Big: You want to tarnish, to destroy, to vandalize.

Mama George: She won't tomorrow either.

Mr. Big: You know nothing!

Mama George: I know who she loves. Do you?

Mr. Big begins to laugh.

Mr. Big: Yes! I know who she loves! She loves me!

Mama George: No.

Mr. Big: It's me who she loves!

Mama George: You've gone blind starin' at stars. . . . It's Johnny she loves.

Mr. Big: Johnny? . . .

Pause.

Mama George: We are old, Mr. Big.

Mr. Big: Don't.

Mama George: We're old.

Mr. Big: No more . . . I . . . beg you . . . leave me alone . . . go.

Mama George exits.

He shuts his eyes. After a moment he gets up, goes behind the bar to get a glass. He stops. He brings out the gun which is beneath the bar. He looks at it. He cocks it, places it on the bar. He gets a glass and pours himself a drink. Johnny enters as Mr. Big's back is towards him so that Mr. Big is not aware of his entrance. Johnny moves to the bar. When Mr. Big turns around Johnny is there. A pause. Mr. Big gives Johnny his own drink and he pours himself another. He notices the bruise on Johnny's face. He tilts Johnny's face up to look at it, reaches under the bar, brings out a cloth, dips it in the liquor, puts it to Johnny's face. Johnny holds the cloth against his face.

Johnny: *Low.* Bastard . . . sayin' things . . . I shoulda . . . I—bastard! *He hits the bar with his fist.* The Brit, he's sayin' things, makin' offers, who the hell does he think he is! He's sayin' things! To me! I won't have that dirty son of a whore . . .

He goes to take a drink. He stops. Looks at it. Pause. He puts it down. He looks at Mr. Big.

Johnny: I want you to tell me . . . what was it that killed William?

Mr. Big: *Searching, not his usual self. . . .* A . . . coming together . . . of random . . . incident . . . timber spongy from some rot within, pressure from above, then, from below, Earth sighed, a tiny tremor, not even one you'd notice . . .

Johnny: Why?

Mr. Big: Perhaps she's angry at the violation, the intrusion.

Johnny: Whyn't he move, jump clear, he must've, *must've* felt it comin', shiftin'.

Mr. Big: Perhaps.

Johnny: Whyn't he move!?

Mr. Big: He chose not to.

Pause.

Johnny: . . . He had a head that mornin' . . . from the drink.

Mr. Big: I expect he did.

Johnny: And?

Mr. Big: And what?

Johnny picks up the glass of booze and throws it. It breaks. Johnny stands there. After a moment he looks at Mr. Big.

Leah enters drawn by the sound of the breaking glass. She sees the two men. She stops. They look at her. She looks at them, then she stoops to clear up the glass. Johnny rushes over.

Johnny: No . . . don't. . . . I'll do it. It's all right, I'll do it.

The two of them pick up the glass. Mr. Big watches them without expression. Once they reach for the same piece, and look at each other, then back to the picking up of glass. When they're finished, Leah goes to get up and leave. Johnny grabs her hand and draws her up as he gets up. They become aware of Mr. Big's gaze. A pause with Johnny maintaining his grip on Leah's hand. She does not protest.

Mr. Big: What is it?

Johnny: *Releases his breath which he did not realize he was holding.* I wanna ask you somethin'.

Mr. Big: Yes.

After a moment Johnny looks down.

Mr. Big: ... I'm waiting.

Johnny: I—

Leah: *Low.* Don't.

Mr. Big: What is it?

Johnny: It's somethin' important.

Leah: *Low.* No.

Johnny: Maybe Leah shouldn't be here.

Mr. Big: Does this matter of import touch upon Leah?

He will not look directly at her through this section. He is garnering what appears to be the very last of his strength. Although there is no loss of control, it is taking everything to maintain his facade.

Johnny: Yes it does.

Mr. Big: Then it's imperative she's present.

Johnny: I don't think ...

Mr. Big: Leah stays.

Johnny looks at Leah and she looks at him. It seems she acquiesces to Mr. Big's statement.

Johnny: If that's what she wants.

Mr. Big: And in her rightful position.

Johnny: What?

Mr. Big: By my side, where she's been since eleven.

Leah looks at Johnny, he releases her hand, she joins Mr. Big. Johnny looks at the broken glass he holds in his hand; he places it on the bar.

He sees the gun.

Mr. Big: Well now . . . shall I sit or shall I stand for this question?

Johnny: Don't matter a lot.

Mr. Big: But it does. There's a world a difference. . . . Do you intend deliverin' the question sittin' or standin'?

Johnny: Standin'.

Mr. Big: No doubt 'tis somewhat abrasive then, mmm? And simple as well.

Johnny: Don't know about that.

Mr. Big: As in requirin' a yes or no answer. It's been my experience . . .

Johnny: It's a serious question.

Pause. Mr. Big is still, silent. His largesse of style and manner are gone. He looks directly at Leah for the first time.

Mr. Big: A serious question. *Mr. Big looks at Johnny, then he looks at neither but seems caught in an inward vision.* . . . Touchin' upon Leah . . . did I ever tell you . . . how I found Leah?

Johnny: I heard.

Mr. Big: *To Leah.* You told him, did you?

Leah: No.

Mr. Big: *Low.* Incandescence.

Johnny: What?

Mr. Big: Radiance.

Johnny: What's wrong?

Mr. Big: Stars . . . flarin' up . . . a brilliance consumin' all in its orb, then shrinkin' to a black pinhole in space . . . 'bout the size of a fist in the void . . . 'bout the size a my heart, but black, charry black, and cold. . . . You wanted to ask me. . . . The first time I saw Leah . . . I thought I'd slipped through a wrinkle in time and was seein' myself. . . . It was rainin', and she was walkin' a purposeful walk, and her eye was fixed on a destination so distant no mortal eye could discern it, and both of her arms were wrapped round herself, embracin' herself, maintainin' herself ... and I sat in my car and I wept for her ... and for all of us here.

Johnny makes a move as if to speak. Outside the hotel there is the glint of sun on metal, gun, motorcycle, appears, disappears. Perhaps it's the glitter of the odd star in the cosmos.

Mr. Big: Let me ... continue. Your question must wait, for I too have something of import to say that touches on Leah.

Leah: Mr. Big?

Mr. Big: I must, Leah. I'm hearin' it said that my ... fantastical comprehension a cosmic design does not spring from revelation or wisdom, intuition or insight. ... It is, rather, mere invention—and lies —which serve ...

Johnny places his hand near the gun.

Mr. Big: ... to legitimize ... an on-going affair ... with a child.

Johnny places his hand over the grip of the gun but he does not fully grasp it or pick it up.

Mr. Big: ... If—if all mankind could read the skies as I can, do you know what they'd do?

Johnny: What?

Mr. Big: They'd never lift their eyes from off the path in front of them! They fear dimension. They live in cracks between the baseboard and the wall in one corner of a mansion whose beauty and proportion is as boundless as the heavenly firmament! Is it strange their thoughts turn dark and ugly? Look at her! She's the product of my vision, not the inspiration of it! Could falsehood and contrivance bring forth such perfection? I ask you. Look at her ... of course I love her. Who would not love her? ... She is proof that my grasp of all worlds, real and imagined, is sound—and that soundness is proof that she's sound. I swear to you Johnny, Leah is without flaw or injury. She is founded on truth. *He appears spent.* And my love ... for her ... which I do not deny ... is as ... my love ... for you ... whom she loves ...

He does not look at Leah.

Johnny: Leah?

Glitter and glint from refracted images outside hotel. Gompers runs down the street.

Gompers: Johnny? Johnny!

Johnny: *Whose attention is on Leah.* What do you want?

Mr. Big is so still, so quiet that Gompers seems not to know he's there.

Gompers: Where the hell've you been?

Johnny: Here. I been here. *He glances at Gompers.* Are you loaded?

Gompers: Hell yes, I been waitin' for you; but didja take a look on the street?

Johnny: *Attention on Leah.* Yeah?

Gompers: On the street!

Johnny: What?

Gompers: The Brit's got her blocked off at the west end.

Johnny moves to look into the street.

Gompers: What the hell's he up to?

Johnny: I dunno.

Leah and Mr. Big look at each other.

Gompers: What're we gonna do?

Johnny: Gimme a minute.

Gompers: What're we gonna do!

Widow Popovitch scurries down the street towards the hotel.

Johnny: Where'd you leave the car?

Gompers: Right where we loaded.

Widow: Vere's Mama? I haf—do you know vat is happening out dere?

Johnny: Take the alley east, cut across the double lot that ain't fenced and go for the hills.

Widow: Mama!

Gompers: Jesus Johnny, what if—

Widow: Mama dey haf guns pointed down da street.

Johnny: Go!

Widow: Dey're coming d'other vay too.

Johnny: *Yells after Gompers.* You let the Brit stop you I'll kill you!

Widow: Look at dem Johnny.

Johnny: Jesus Christ, there's a keg out front.

Widow: Dey haf da guns at one end . . .

Johnny: Are cars blockin' the street?

Widow: No cars, jost da guns on dose motorcycles.

Johnny: I can bust through that easy. Where's the keys?

Mama joins the widow looking out on the street. Leah tries to keep Johnny from leaving.

Johnny: There's a keg in the car out front.

Leah shakes her head trying to hold him from going.

Johnny: Where's the keys? *He finds the keys. He pushes her aside.* I bust through them motorcycles, we're clear!

Leah: Johnny!

Johnny: I'll ditch the keg in Bossy's Creek, and I'll be right back. I'll be right back. Meet me at the corner lot. The corner lot, Leah!

He runs out the door, ducking and dodging, slowly making his way to the car without being seen. Mama and the widow follow him out. Their voices are heard off-stage.

Widow: Careful, Johnny.

Mama George: He's got to move that car.

Sound of car door slam. Image of the Whiskey Six flashing. Leah turns to listen. The engine revs up and the car pulls out. Amongst the off-stage voices we can hear . . .

Mama George: Look!

Widow: Look! He's headin' for them!

Sound of shots.

Widow: They're shootin'!

Mama George: He's gonna . . .

Sound of crash as the car hits the motorcycles.

Mama George: He's through!

Widow: Vight trew dem!

Sound of car receding in distance.

Mama George: He's gone!

Widow: Broke trew.

The car fades away. Silence. Leah looks at Mr. Big.

Leah: Did. . . . Did you think you could just tell a story and every-thing would be right? *Pause.* If he ever finds out . . . what will I do? . . . And if he believes you . . . how can I live like that?

Mr. Big: Pretend.

Leah: I'm tired of pretending. . . . Why didn't you leave me, Mr. Big? Why didn't you leave me that day in the rain? . . . But—you can still make it right. Yes you can. *She picks up the gun.* Here. Take it. . . . Hold it, Mr. Big.

He takes the gun.

Leah: Now—make it right.

Mr. Big: I can't.

Leah: Pretend. . . . Look. . . . I'm turning. . . . I'm runnin'. *She turns and starts to run towards the door.* I'm runnin' to him! *She is almost at the door.* Now!

Mr. Big fires at Leah hitting her in the back. The impact arches her back and he fires a second time. She collapses knocking over a chair. Lights fade. Plaintive note from the piano reminiscent of Act One opening. Will, Dolly, Cec, Old Sump, Mama, the Widow, Gompers seen in shifting light with the piano music growing, the figures swaying. Leah is seen amidst them as they begin to dance as at the beginning. Mr. Big joins them. The odd change of partner. Fluid. Not overly sad. Not sad at all. Bill the Brit watches. Johnny enters, moves past them, through them, obviously not of them. He picks up the chair, restoring it to its former position.

Dolly: *Voice-over.* And round.

Will: *Voice-over.* And whirl.

Cec: *Voice-over.* 'Cause to keep goin'.

Widow: *Voice-over.* Favourite.

Mama George: *Voice-over.* Love.

Mr. Big: *Voice-over.* Visage a heaven.

Dolly: *Voice-over.* Just so.

Will: *Voice-over.* You're pretty.

Mama George: *Voice-over.* He believes it.

Dolly: *Voice-over.* Lasts forever.

Mr. Big: *Voice-over.* Collidin' conjectures.

Cec: *Voice-over.* Good times him and me.

Sump: *Voice-over.* T'at's what we called it.

Leah: *Voice-over.* Was it?

Mr. Big: *Voice-over.* Invincible, Leah.

The voice-overs become murmurs, the wind in the foothills; the figures' movement becomes more static, light dimmer.

Johnny has taken off his jacket, slung it over his shoulder. He looks quite a bit older. He speaks to the audience.

Johnny: I was caught in his kaleidoscope worlds cartwheelin' through space. I believed in his crystal-shard people radiatin' light like a rainbow. She was livin' proof a transcendence.

The gossamer depiction of the Crowsnest Pass seen at the beginning slowly obscures Blairmore.

Johnny: Mr. Big once asked me—what do you suppose an oyster thinks of a pearl? ... What *does* an oyster think of a pearl? I didn't know. He didn't tell me.

He takes a few steps whistling. Stops.

Johnny: It may all have been lies, but that still doesn't mean it weren't true.

Whistle of the train. He looks. The headlight of the train grows. It appears he plans on catching it. The sound of the train increasing. Light of train grows as train approaches. Johnny starts to exit to catch it.

Blackout

Further Reading

About the Plays and Playwrights

Pamela Boyd

Bessai, Diane, "Western Theatre in Toronto," *NeWest Review*, April, 1986, pp. 17-18.

Crew, Robert, "Drama of bringing up baby . . . ," Toronto *Star*, March 3, 1986, p. D 1.

Devins, Susan, "Play dips into diaper pail," Toronto *Star*, Feb. 28, 1986, p. D 16.

Lacey, Liam, "Play turns motherhood Inside Out," *The Globe and Mail*, March 3, 1986, p. C 10.

Joanna M. Glass

Barnes, Clive, "'Play' that will live in memory," *New York Post*, April 27, 1984.

Bessai, Diane, "Biocritical Essay," *The Joanna M. Glass Papers*, Jean F. Tener and Appollonia Steele, eds., Calgary: University of Calgary, 1986, pp.

Clews, Hetty, "Kindred points: the twin worlds of Joanna M. Glass," *Atlantis*, (Autumn 1978), pp. 123-131.

Godfrey, Stephen, "A searing display of misery . . .," *The Globe and Mail*, Feb. 17, 1986, p. A 11.

Hum m, "Shows on Broadway: Play Memory," *Variety*, May 2, 1984, p. 162 and 164.

Klein, Alvin "A Compelling Drama of Despair at McCarter," *The New York Times, New Jersey Weekly Supplement*, Oct. 16, 1983, p. 15.

Parr, John, "Reflections of Joanna Glass," *Journal of Canadian Fiction*, 20 (1977) pp. 164-171.

Wendy Lill

Flynn, J., "Fascination of the Abomination," *NeWest Review*, April, 1986, p. 19.

Johnson, Chris, "*The Fighting Days* and the Problem of Goodness," *Arts Manitoba*, Summer, 1984, pp. 37-38.

Matheson, Sue, "Heather's Tale," *Alberta Report*, Mar. 24, 1986, p. 49.

Mitchell, Nick, "A Feeling for Our History: An Interview with Wendy Lill," *Prairie Fire*, Winter, 1985, pp. 16-19.

Sharon Pollock

Bessai, Diane, "Sharon Pollock's Women: A Study in Dramatic Process," *A Mazing Space: Writing Canadian Women Writing*, Shirley Neuman and Smaro Kamboureli, eds., Edmonton: Longspoon-NeWest, 1987, pp 126-136.

Brennan, Brian, "Whiskey Six is Pollock's best play yet," *Calgary Herald*, Feb. 11, 1983, p. F 1.

Conlogue, Ray, "A theatrical gem reflects the last, best west," *The Globe and Mail*, Mar. 7, 1983, p. 15.

Nunn, Robert C., "Sharon Pollock's Plays," *Theatre History in Canada*, 5.1 (Spring 1984) pp. 72-83.

Page, Malcolm, "Sharon Pollock: Committed Playwright," *Canadian Drama*, 5.2 (Fall 1979) pp. 104-111.

Russell, David, "The Direction of *Whiskey Six*," M.F.A., University of Alberta, 1987.

Wallace, Robert, "Sharon Pollock," *The Work: Conversations with English-Canadian Playwrights*, Robert Wallace and Cynthia Zimmerman, eds., Toronto: Coach House, 1982, pp. 115-126.

Further Reading

By the Authors

Glass, Joanna:

Artichoke, New York: Dramatists Play Service, 1979.
Canadian Gothic, in *Prairie Performance*, Edmonton: NeWest, 1980.
Canadian Gothic and *American Modern*, New York: Dramatists Play
  Service, 1977.
Play Memory, New York: Samuel French, 1984.
To Grandmother's House We Go, New York: Dramatists Play Service,
  1981.

Lill, Wendy:

The Fighting Days, Vancouver: Talonbooks, 1985.

Pollock, Sharon:

Blood Relations, in *Blood Relations and Other Plays*, Edmonton,
  NeWest Press, 1981.
Generations, in *Blood Relations and Other Plays*.
The Komagata Maru Incident, Toronto: Playwrights Canada, 1978.
One Tiger to a Hill, in *Blood Relations and Other Plays*.
Walsh, Vancouver: Talonbooks, 1983 (revised).

Prairie Play Series
Diane Bessai, General Editor

Published by NeWest Press:

Blood Relations and Other Plays, by Sharon Pollock.

Blood Relations
One Tiger to a Hill
Generations

Showing West: Three Prairie Docu-Dramas, edited by Diane Bessai and Don Kerr.

The West Show, Theatre Passe Muraille
Far as the Eye Can See, Rudy Wiebe and Theatre Passe Muraille
Medicare! Rex Deverell

Eight Plays for Young People, edited by Joyce Doolittle.

Tikta' liktak, Brian Paisley
Cornelius Dragon, Jan Truss
More of a Family, Alf Silver
The Other Side of the Pole, Marney Heatley, Stephen Heatley, and Edward Connell
Dr. Barnardo's Pioneers, Rick McNair
The Day Jake Made Her Rain, W.O. Mitchell
Melody Meets the Bag Lady, Rex Deverell
Vandal, William Horrocks

Five from the Fringe, edited by Nancy Bell.

Life After Hockey, Kenneth Brown
The Betrayal, Laurier Gareau
One Beautiful Evening, Small Change Theatre
The Land Called Morning, John Selkirk
Cut! Lyle Victor Albert